The Artisan Bread Machine

The Artisan Bread Machine

250 recipes for breads, rolls, flatbreads and pizzas

Judith Fertig

Robert
ROSE

For complete cataloguing information, see page 303.

Disclaimer
The recipes in this book have been carefully tested by our kitchen and our tasters. To the best of our knowledge, they are safe and nutritious for ordinary use and users. For those people with food or other allergies, or who have special food requirements or health issues, please read the suggested contents of each recipe carefully and determine whether or not they may create a problem for you. All recipes are used at the risk of the consumer. Consumers should always consult their bread machine manufacturer's manual for recommended procedures and cooking times.

We cannot be responsible for any hazards, loss or damage that may occur as a result of any recipe use.

For those with special needs, allergies, requirements or health problems, in the event of any doubt, please contact your medical adviser prior to the use of any recipe.

Design and Production: Daniella Zanchetta/PageWave Graphics Inc.
Editors: Sue Sumeraj and Jennifer MacKenzie
Recipe Testers: Jennifer MacKenzie, Kate Gammal, Teresa Makarewicz and Kendra Pickett
Proofreader: Sheila Wawanash
Indexer: Gillian Watts
Photographer: Colin Erricson
Associate Photographer: Matt Johannsson
Food Stylist: Kathryn Robertson
Prop Stylist: Charlene Erricson

Cover image: Braided Challah (page 38)

We acknowledge the financial support of the Government of Canada through the Book Publishing Industry Development Program (BPIDP) for our publishing activities.

Published by Robert Rose Inc.
120 Eglinton Avenue East, Suite 800, Toronto, Ontario, Canada M4P 1E2
Tel: (416) 322-6552 Fax: (416) 322-6936
www.robertrose.ca

Printed and bound in Canada

1 2 3 4 5 6 7 8 9 SP 19 18 17 16 15 14 13 12 11

Contents

Acknowledgments

GENERAL THANKS JUST won't do, for without the tireless efforts of many talented people, *The Artisan Bread Machine* would not have been possible. First, I wish to thank publisher Bob Dees, who went the extra mile and more, as well as everyone at Robert Rose Inc. I'm indebted to my agent, Lisa Ekus, for her support and sound advice. Sue Sumeraj tamed the copy in her usual excellent way, and Jennifer MacKenzie made sure the recipes worked, despite multiple bread machines, four graduating loaf sizes and diverse ingredients — in two different countries. Testers Kate Gammal, Teresa Makarewicz and Kendra Pickett lent their expertise when it was needed most.

My thanks to Daniella Zanchetta of PageWave Graphics for the design and production. Photographer Colin Erricson and associate photographer Matt Johannsson worked with food stylist Kathryn Robertson and prop stylist Charlene Erricson to make the breads pop off the pages.

I'm grateful to all the bread machine manufacturers who provided machines for recipe development and testing, especially Black & Decker, Breadman, Cuisinart, Oster, Panasonic, Sunbeam and Zojirushi.

Finally, the testers and I thank our many friends and neighbors who never complained about freshly baked breads (sometimes with a little piece missing) appearing on their doorsteps, even when it happened multiple times.

Introduction

WHEN THE FIRST automatic bread machine was released in Japan in 1986 by Matsushita Electric Industrial (now Panasonic), it slowly began to revolutionize the way bread was made in kitchens all over the world. By the late 1980s, Sanyo and Zojirushi were also producing bread machines. By the early 1990s, the automatic bread machine had started making new converts of traditional bread bakers in the United Kingdom and North America, where it had at first been viewed as a flash-in-the-bread-pan novelty.

The reason? The bread machine has become a trusted baking assistant, allowing us to enjoy homemade bread without hovering over a bowl of dough. We're free to get the rest of dinner prepared or that report finished or the laundry done while our trusty assistant is at work. You program the bread machine, and it does the rest — mixing, kneading and baking — all in a controlled environment, thanks to its built-in microchip. You don't have to worry about the temperature of the ingredients, your kitchen or the oven. The bread machine does it all for you — and it does a superior job of mixing and kneading. In addition, bread machines can make jams and preserves, bake quick breads and loaf-shaped cakes, and even mix and bake meatloaf.

But there are some things a bread machine can't do. For one thing, it has a limited range of baking temperatures, which is why many bread bakers make their dough on the Dough cycle, then form and bake the loaves by hand.

Baking temperatures range considerably among the most widely used bread machines. They also vary depending on which cycle you use. The Sweet Bread and Fruit & Nut cycles generally use the lowest temperatures, while the Basic/White cycle on older or more basic machines and the French or Italian cycle on new models use the highest temperature.

Looking at the chart below, you can see why the baking cycle takes longer in some machines than others. The temperatures in this range are fine for Classic Butter Crust Bread (page 22), Wildflower Honey and White Whole Wheat (page 54), Bacon, Green Onion and Blue Cheese Bread (page 110) or Lemon Poppy Seed Bread (page 116). But they're not what you need for a crusty Ciabatta loaf (page 147), which

Bread Machine Baking Temperatures

Bread Machine	Baking Temperature
Bread Machines from the 1990s	254°F (123°C) to 300°F (150°C)
Breadman Ultimate	250°F (121°C) to 375°F (190°C) in Bake Only mode
Cuisinart CBK-100 and CBK-200	192°F (89°C) to 208°F (98°C)
Oster	266°F (130°C) maximum temp
Panasonic SD-YD 250	400°F (200°C) maximum temp
Sunbeam 5891	266°F (130°C) maximum temp
Zojirushi BB-CEC20	254°F (121°C) to 290°F (143°C)

needs to bake at 450°F (230°C). If you want a really crusty artisan loaf with a honeycomb crumb, it needs to bake at a higher temperature than the bread machine offers.

A second limitation of the bread machine is that its bread pan dictates the shape of the bread it bakes; it will not make a long, slender baguette or a boule (a round loaf). If you want to bake that type of bread, you'll need to use the Dough or Artisan Dough cycle, form the loaf by hand and bake it in the oven.

As you flip through this book, you will see an "Oven-Baked" option for many recipes. Take Italian Scali Bread (page 148), for example. You can make the dough and bake the braided loaf in the bread machine, and it will have a wonderfully chewy texture and a golden top. But if you make it on the Dough or Artisan Dough cycle and bake it in the oven at the higher temperature, it will rise higher and will have a lighter texture and a burnished color all over. It's your choice.

And that's the beauty of today's bread machines. You have a wide range of options, both in terms of the features you can choose when you're shopping for a machine and in how you opt to use those features.

If you think of your bread machine as a not-quite-silent assistant under your supervision, you can make a surprising range of soul-satisfying artisan breads. Nothing says "you're home" like the aroma of bread baking — but who says it always has to be in your oven?

Using Your Bread Machine

IF YOU REMEMBER the late 1980s, when a wide variety of word processing software was available, then you probably remember working with WordPerfect or Q&A, like I did. Today, most word processing software is based on the Microsoft Word model.

A similar thing happened with bread machines. When bread machines really started to become popular in North America in the early 1990s, there were wide differences in how they worked. That diversity necessitated a book by bread expert Lora Brody and her mother, Millie Apter, who in 1993 co-wrote *Bread Machine Baking: Perfect Every Time — 75 Foolproof Bread and Dessert Recipes Custom-Created for the 12 Most Popular Bread Machines*. Beth Hensperger's encyclopedic *The Bread Lover's Bread Machine Cookbook : A Master Baker's 300 Favorite Recipes for Perfect-Every-Time Bread — from Every Kind of Machine*, published in 2000, also addressed this issue.

But by 2010, bread machine makers had merged (Oster with Sunbeam, and Breadman with Black & Decker, for example), some companies had gone out of business (DAK now sells electronics, but not bread machines), and three makers — Zojirushi, Cuisinart and Breadman — dominated the market. Today's bread machines are more alike than they are different.

When I tested the recipes in this book, though, I did notice some subtle differences between machines:

- Machines with two kneading paddles (like the Zojirushi) mix the dough very thoroughly, to the point that you must add any ingredients you want to remain separate and discrete — such as cubes of cheese or chopped nuts — at the very end of the kneading cycle or they get subsumed into the dough.

- Machines with one small kneading paddle and a tall, vertical bread pan (like the late-1990s Oster) do not mix as thoroughly.

- Machines with squarish bread pans and one kneading paddle (like the Cuisinart CBK-200 or the Breadman Ultimate) mix well. But you may have to scrape down the corners and sides of the bread pan with a spatula to incorporate all the flour, especially with the smaller loaves. If you don't bother to scrape, your loaf will turn out fine; it just might have a little flour dust in the corners.

- Some machines, like the Cuisinart and the Breadman, take longer to cool down than others, which could be an issue if you're waiting to start a new loaf.

The bottom line? As with any tool for any purpose, you have to work with what you have and try to maximize its performance. And that means getting to know your bread machine and how it works. The best way to do that is to read the instruction manual. If you have an old model or have bought a machine at a garage sale and the manual is nowhere to be found, try googling the bread machine maker and model number; many manuals are available online, usually in a downloadable PDF format.

The next step is to make a few loaves of bread using recipes from the manual. These recipes were specifically developed to work with your machine, so using them will tell you whether your machine works as it should. When I was testing recipes, one of the bread machines I used was a newly refurbished model (one that has a replaced microchip), which you can often purchase from online retailers. After two flops, I tried making two recipes from the manual, and those flopped too. That's when I knew the refurbished model had to go. When I tried the same recipes in a brand-new model of the same machine, they worked perfectly.

Walk-Away Bread vs. Hands-On Bread

Some people want to put the ingredients in the bread machine, walk away and come back later to a freshly baked loaf. If you're a walk-away baker, the first three chapters of this book are for you, as are many of the recipes in the Sweet Breads and Gluten-Free Breads chapters.

But some breads, such as swirl loaves, braids, flatbreads, pizzas, rolls and festive breads, require a little more participation from the baker. When you're following one of these hands-on recipes, the bread machine will still make the dough, and you can walk away while it does. But you'll need to come back and form the dough, then either return it to the machine to complete the baking cycle or bake it in the oven.

The introduction to each chapter has specific information on the cycles and ingredients specific to each type of bread.

Using the Delay Timer

If you want to put your ingredients in the bread machine, then time it to bake so that a warm loaf is ready when you get home or wake up, you'll need to learn how to use the delay timer.

First, you need to make sure the recipe you choose is suited to the delay timer. It must only contain ingredients that can be left out at room temperature for hours — so recipes that include raw eggs or fresh dairy products are out. The recipes in this book that will work with the delay timer have a "Delay Timer" tag in the upper left-hand corner.

Second, you need to know how long the cycle will take. For instance, let's say you're making a whole-grain bread that will take 3 hours and 45 minutes on the Whole Wheat cycle, and you're going to serve it with your dinner at 6:30 p.m. You want the bread machine to finish the cycle at 6:00, giving the loaf time to cool before dinner. Therefore, the cycle needs to start at 2:15 p.m. If it's 11:45 a.m. now, you want the cycle to start in two and a half hours.

How you proceed next depends on how your delay timer works. For some, you will set the start time, pressing the button until the start time reads 2 hours and 30 minutes. For others, you will set the total time (delay time plus cycle time) — in this case, 6 hours and 15 minutes.

Size Matters

The walk-away recipes in this book provide ingredient amounts for 1-lb (500 g), 1½-lb (750 g), 2-lb (1 kg) and 3-lb (1.5 kg) loaves of bread. Many newer machines can bake a range of sizes, but you must program the machine to bake the loaf size you want. You also need to know the largest loaf size your bread pan can accommodate. If you put ingredients for a 3-lb (1.5 kg) loaf into a machine with a 2-lb (1 kg) capacity and start a cycle, you're going to have a big mess, with rising dough spilling over the bread pan into the cavity of the bread machine — which is difficult to clean.

The capacity of a bread pan indicates the volume it can hold — specifically, a dough that has doubled in bulk or size. If you're not sure about the capacity of your bread pan, consult your bread machine manual or do a home test by pouring water into the bread pan:

- A bread pan that holds less than 10 cups (2.5 L) of water has a 1-lb (500 g) capacity.
- A bread pan that holds 10 cups (2.5 L) of water has a 1½-lb (750 g) capacity.
- A bread pan that holds 12 cups (3 L) of water has a 2-lb (1 kg) capacity.
- A bread pan that holds 14 cups (3.5 L) of water has a 3-lb (1.5 kg) capacity.

Larger-capacity bread machines can bake smaller loaves — the bread just gets done a little earlier. Insert an instant-read thermometer into the loaf in the bread pan so you can see when it's done, then remove it before the cycle has officially ended.

Although smaller-capacity bread machines can't bake larger loaves, they can often accommodate a larger dough on the Dough cycle. You just take the dough out at the end of the Dough cycle, then let it finish rising to its full height. If you're not sure, keep an eye on the dough as it goes through the Dough cycle and remove it if it gets too high in the bread pan.

- A machine with a 1-lb (500 g) capacity can process up to 2½ cups (625 mL) of flour, which makes a loaf of bread that will yield about 8 slices.
- A machine with a 1½-lb (750 g) capacity can process up to 3 cups (750 mL) of flour, which makes a loaf of bread that will yield about 12 slices.
- A machine with a 2-lb (1 kg) capacity can process up to 4½ cups (1.125 L) of flour, which makes a loaf of bread that will yield about 16 slices.
- A machine with a 2½-lb (1.25 kg) capacity can process up to 6 cups (1.5 mL) of flour, which makes a loaf of bread that will yield about 20 slices.
- A machine with a 3-lb (1.5 kg) capacity can process up to 7 cups (1.75 L) of flour, which makes a loaf of bread that will yield about 24 slices.

In this book, most of the hands-on recipes that use the Dough cycle make 1 to 2 lbs (500 g to 1 kg) of dough, so they can easily be prepared in most bread machines.

Stirring Things Up

Ingredient	What It Does for Bread
Flour	Provides carbohydrates to activate the yeast, as well as gluten, which forms muscular bands that trap the carbon dioxide released by the yeast, thereby causing the bread to rise
Egg	Adds color, richness and a soft texture
Milk, fresh or powdered	Contributes to a browner crust and a moist texture; adds flavor
Butter	Adds richness and flavor; adds a shiny crust when brushed on after baking
Buttermilk	Helps the yeast work quickly and vigorously
Sour cream	Adds richness; creates a mellow color and a crisper crust
Honey	Adds sweetness and moisture; helps activate the yeast
Sugar	Adds sweetness without moisture; aids in browning; helps activate the yeast
Fruit/vegetable purée	Adds color and flavor; softens the texture
Salt	Brings the flavors together; helps control the yeast
Yeast	Works with the carbohydrates in the flour and any sweeteners to produce carbon dioxide, which gets between the gluten fibers to help the dough rise

Dough Enhancers or Improvers

Dough enhancers or improvers are powdered mixtures that help every part of the dough work better. You can make your own Artisan Dough Enhancer (page 278) or buy packaged improvers. Here are some of the ingredients that do the work:

Ingredient	What It Is	What It Does
Soy lecithin	A fatty substance derived from soybeans	Helps bread stay fresh longer
Ascorbic acid	Vitamin C	Helps yeast work efficiently
Vital wheat gluten (or gluten flour)	A concentrated protein derived from wheat flour (not the same as wheat gluten, which is a combination of flour and vital wheat gluten)	Improves the rise and texture of bread
Non-diastatic malt	A powder derived from barley	Contributes to a softer, more tender crumb
Ground ginger	A spice made by drying and grinding fresh ginger	Helps boost the activity of yeast

Timing It Right

Many bread machine manuals explain, in great detail, how each cycle works and how long each stage of the cycle takes — how much time the machine spends mixing, kneading, rising, kneading, rising and baking. Armed with this knowledge, you can set your kitchen timer for the start of the second knead if you want to knead in ingredients that should stay whole in the dough; for the start of the final rise if you want to take the dough out and braid it before baking; or for the end of the final rise if you want to brush the loaf with egg wash before baking.

If you don't have a manual, or your manual doesn't outline detailed times, you'll learn how long the cycle will take when you select that cycle: the total time will pop up on the display window. Monitor a whole cycle and write down the time the machine takes to complete each stage, creating your own mini-manual. After making a few bread machine recipes, you'll get a good feel for how your machine mixes, kneads and bakes.

Bread Machine Ingredients

It's amazing how many more products are available for today's home baker than when I had my first bread machine in the early 1990s. When I was doing the testing for this book, I used a lot of King Arthur products — from flours and dough improvers to baking papers and pans — and I found all to be exceptional; check them out at www.kingarthurflour.com. I'm also lucky enough to live in an area where I can grind my own grain into flour at the grocery store. If you don't have that option, you can use a grain mill for freshly milled flour — it's well worth it. And I can now find more ethnic flours at Indian markets (atta) and Italian delis (doppio zero).

I used several kinds of bread machine yeast, including SAF (my personal favorite) and grocery store brands. You can get by with a smidgen less SAF yeast than you need with other brands, but as my goal was to make this book easy for bakers, I did not specify one yeast or another.

Each ingredient in bread contributes something to the flavor, texture and color. As you become confident enough to use these recipes as blueprints and customize them to suit your own tastes, you need to know how all the ingredients work together.

Temperature Matters

According to food scientist Shirley Corriher in *BakeWise*, manufactured yeast is most active between 86°F and 95°F (30°C and 35°C), while wild yeasts (like those in true sourdough starters) prefer lower temperatures. Your bread machine will provide the proper rising temperature for the type of bread you select. But you can help by heating liquids to the ideal temperature before adding them to the bread pan. Simply warm them in the microwave or in a saucepan on the stove.

Some machines, such as the Zojirushi and the Black & Decker, have a Preheat setting built in to heat liquids to the right temperature so you don't have to heat them before adding them to the pan. But you, the adder of the ingredients, have to know that you can inadvertently kill yeast by adding liquids that are too hot. Yeast cells die when they're exposed to temperatures hotter than 138°F to 140°F (59°C to 60°C). So make sure to use your instant-read thermometer to take the temperature of any cooked whole-grain cereal or scalded milk before you add it to the bread pan.

Steps in a Bread Machine Recipe

Now that you have the equipment and ingredients, what will you do with them? Each recipe involves various steps. Here are some details about how to perform each step.

Measuring

The recipes for each size require the precise measurements as specified. Some of the amounts may seem unusual and won't add up by straight math. For example, a 3-lb (1.5 kg) loaf is not a straight doubling of the 1½-lb (750 g) loaf ingredients, and in some larger loaves, less yeast is required than in the smaller loaves. This is a result of the way the flour and other dry ingredients absorb liquid, the way the yeast reacts with the other ingredients, and the overall nature of the dough. The balance of the wet and dry ingredients and yeast is much more important in bread machine breads than in handmade breads because of the closed environment of the machine. Because you can't let the dough rise a little longer or a little less, or increase or decrease the baking time once the cycle is set, it's important to follow the recipes as accurately as possible.

How you measure the flour makes an enormous difference to the final product. If you just stick a measuring cup in a bag or container of flour and scoop, the flour packs into the measuring cup more. One cup (250 mL) of scooped flour will weigh around 5¼ oz (about 157 g). If you spoon flour from the bag or container into the measuring cup, then use a flat edge to sweep away excess flour so that it is level with the top of the cup, the flour gently settles in. One cup (250 mL) of spooned flour will weigh around 4½ oz (about 140 g). Multiply that by the number of cups

you need in a recipe, and it's clear that the measuring method makes a big difference. More flour means denser, heavier baked goods. And that's not what you want.

All of the recipes in *The Artisan Bread Machine* have been tested with the spooned method of measuring dry ingredients, using dry, nesting-style measuring cups for amounts ¼ cup (60 mL) or larger and measuring spoons for amounts less than ¼ cup (60 mL).

You'll need to measure the other ingredients — especially any yeast or liquid — accurately too. Measure yeast with a measuring spoon, then level it with your finger. Fill liquid measuring cups right to the applicable line, holding the cup up at eye level to make sure the liquid is level with the line — a little bit under or over can make a difference to the bread.

If you're measuring in imperial, the less even amounts called for in some recipes (e.g., 2½ tbsp) can be tricky to measure accurately if you don't have a ½-tbsp measuring spoon. Just keep in mind that 1 tbsp = 3 tsp; therefore, ½ tbsp = 1½ tsp. Another helpful hint is that you don't have to measure an amount such as 7 tbsp by individual tablespoons if you know some measuring math. Here are some basic conversions:

4 tbsp = ¼ cup
5 tbsp + 1 tsp = ⅓ cup
8 tbsp = ½ cup
10 tbsp + 2 tsp = ⅔ cup
12 tbsp = ¾ cup
16 tbsp = 1 cup

So, for 7 tbsp, you can measure ¼ cup plus 3 tbsp.

If you're measuring in metric, the volumes are much more logical for the less even numbers, but do make sure to measure *all* ingredients in metric. If you mix imperial and metric measures, the balance of ingredients will be off and could ruin your bread.

Scalding

For some sweet and festive breads, pastries or rolls, you must scald the milk first. Milk contains an enzyme called protease, which can retard the action of the yeast, especially in a heavier dough that also contains sugar and eggs; scalding reduces the effects of this enzyme. To scald milk, you simply heat it in a saucepan until small bubbles form around the edges — do not bring it to a full boil, which produces a skin on the surface of the milk. Let the scalded milk cool to lukewarm, between 86°F and 95°F (30°C and 35°C), testing it with an instant-read thermometer. If you add hot milk to yeast, the heat will kill the yeast. Make sure to use your instant-read thermometer to take the temperature of any scalded milk mixture before you add it to the bread pan.

Adding the Ingredients to the Machine

Most bread machine manuals tell you to put the liquids in first, then the dry ingredients, then the yeast. I've found that adding the salt, sugar and milk powder with the liquids helps them dissolve better and helps the yeast work faster. For certain loaves, such as Blue Ribbon Bread Machine Bread (page 24), I've also discovered that you can add water, sugar and yeast to the bread pan and let them bubble up for several minutes, then add the dry ingredients; this produces a high, airy, tender loaf that kids love.

Starting the Machine

Once the basic ingredients are in the bread pan, you have choices to make. Many machines offer at least five different cycles, along with crust choices (light, medium, dark) and sometimes a choice of loaf size.

Choose the cycle, the loaf size and your crust preference. Use the Basic/White cycle and Light Crust as your default settings for recipes you're not sure about.

If you don't wish to be attentive to the bread machine, you can leave the kneading paddle(s) in the machine for the entire cycle, then remove them from the bottom of the bread after baking and cooling. (Just remember to do so! It's especially easy with one-paddle machines to forget that the paddle is still in the loaf — until you cut into it.) But if you prefer to remove them before the baking stage, you can press Pause or simply lift the lid, remove the dough, remove the kneading paddle(s), return the dough to the bread pan and let the cycle continue. Some machines have an alert signal that beeps before the final rise to let you know it's time to remove the paddle(s). Whether you leave the paddle(s) in or remove them before the baking stage, the loaf will have a small hole or two in the bottom from the stem(s) of the kneading paddle(s).

Kneading In

If you're baking the loaf in the machine, add any knead-in ingredients to the fruit and nut dispenser, if you have one, or at the "add ingredient" or "mix in" signal, and bake the recipe on the specified cycle. If you have a dispenser, consult your manual for instructions on how to use it. If you use the Fruit & Nut cycle, your loaf may not turn out as brown, as it bakes on a lower temperature.

If you're a hands-on baker and you want to ensure that the ingredients don't get broken up (as they might when the machine does the kneading), pause the bread machine at the start of the second knead. Remove the dough from the bread pan and transfer it to a floured surface. Press or roll out the dough into an oval and sprinkle half the knead-in ingredients on the top half of the oval. Fold the bottom half over the top, rotate the dough a quarter turn and knead it with your knuckles or the heel of your hand.

Ready, Set, Bake!

The cycles on your bread machine allow you to do everything from mixing and kneading a dough to baking bread, making sourdough starter, mixing and baking quick breads and cakes, and even making preserves. Each recipe in this book specifies a cycle or two that will work best for that recipe. Here are the cycles that are relevant to the recipes in this book:

- **Basic/White.** For bread recipes that use predominantly all-purpose flour or bread flour. This cycle mixes and kneads vigorously to activate the gluten in the flours.

- **Whole Wheat.** For bread recipes that use predominantly whole-grain flours. This cycle allows the flours a longer time to soak up liquid, for a more tender crumb.

- **French or Italian.** For bread recipes that use little or no dairy products and sugar. The breads have a longer time to develop on this cycle and bake to a crisper crust. This cycle works well for slow-rise breads if your machine doesn't have a designated slow-rise cycle.

- **Fruit & Nut.** For bread recipes with fruits, nuts, chocolate chips or coconut. This cycle allows these ingredients to be added after kneading, and the bread bakes at a slightly lower temperature so the added ingredients do not burn.

- **Gluten-Free.** For bread recipes that use gluten-free ingredients, which don't require kneading.

- **Sweet.** For bread recipes that have a higher proportion of sugar, butter or oil and protein. This cycle usually bakes at a lower temperature to prevent over-browning.

- **Sourdough.** On some machines, this cycle mixes and bakes sourdough bread. On others, it mixes sourdough starter, which you use to bake bread on the Basic cycle. Read your manual to find out which task this cycle performs on your machine. If you don't have the manual, check how long the cycle takes. A time of less than $2\frac{1}{2}$ hours indicates that the cycle makes a starter.

- **Rapid or Express.** For bread recipes that have more yeast, for a quicker rising time, or that use gluten-free ingredients, which don't require kneading.

- **Dough.** Any bread machine recipe can be made on the Dough cycle, which mixes and kneads the dough through the first rise. At the end of the cycle, you simply remove the dough from the bread pan and form it into a loaf, flatbread, rolls, etc. In most recipes, you let the formed dough rise again for a short period, then bake in the oven.

- **Artisan Dough.** For artisan bread recipes that will be baked in the oven. The doughs have a longer time to develop on this cycle, which enhances the development of their texture and taste.

- **Bake Only.** For doughs that have already been formed, this cycle does just what it says — bakes only.

- **Jam.** For making homemade jams and preserves that use natural pectin (in apples) or powdered pectin as a setting agent. You add all the ingredients to the bread pan, and the machine does the rest.

Repeat with the remaining ingredients. Remove the kneading paddle(s) from the bread pan. Return the dough to the bread pan and continue the cycle.

Topping

Either at the start of the final rise or right before baking begins, the crust of some loaves gets brushed with water, milk, melted butter or an egg or egg white wash and/or sprinkled with a topping such as sesame seeds. For simplicity's sake, you can simply brush the top of the loaf while it's in the bread pan and add any topping. If you want to cover the loaf more evenly, you can remove it from the bread pan, transfer it to a floured surface, brush the top and sides of the loaf, sprinkle it with topping, remove the kneading paddle(s) from the bread pan, return the loaf to the bread pan and continue the cycle. If you're a walk-away baker, you can skip the topping step entirely.

Forming

To form loaves, rolls, flatbreads and more by hand, after the Dough cycle you'll remove the dough from the bread pan to a floured or oiled surface, depending on the recipe. Flour a rolling pin, or flour or oil your hands, before working with the dough. Work the dough as little as possible and sprinkle it with flour as necessary. You want to use enough flour that you are able to work the dough, with the help of a dough scraper, without it sticking to your hands, the rolling pin or the flat surface. But you don't want to add so much flour that you'll get a heavy loaf. Use a pastry brush to brush off any excess flour.

Filling

Some swirl loaves and rolls will get a filling. You simply brush or spoon the filling over the rolled-out dough, usually leaving a $1/2$- or 1-inch (1 or 2.5 cm) perimeter, then roll the dough up and form it.

Making Braided Loaves

Bread machines that bake regular or squarish horizontal loaves (like the Zojirushi, Cuisinart and Breadman Ultimate) can also accommodate braids. First, check the kneading and baking cycle chart in your manual so you know what time to come back to your dough. At the start of the final rise,

- *If your machine has a Pause button:* Press Pause, remove the dough from the bread pan and transfer it to a floured surface. Form the dough into the desired shape. Remove the kneading paddle(s) from the bread pan. Return the formed dough to the bread pan and press the Start button to continue the cycle.

- *If your machine does not have a Pause button:* Open the lid, remove the dough from the bread pan and transfer it to a floured surface. Form the dough into the desired shape. Remove the kneading paddle(s) from the bread pan. Return the formed dough to the bread pan and close the lid. (Make sure to form the loaf immediately and quickly, as a bread machine without a Pause button continues its rising cycle even without the dough in the bread pan. It's okay to take about 5 minutes to form the loaf, but don't delay more than that.)

If your machine makes domed, cylindrical loaves, prepare the dough using the Dough cycle. Form the loaf by hand, then bake it in the oven. You will find instructions for this oven-baked method in many recipes throughout the book.

Letting the Dough Rise

Some doughs that are made on the Dough cycle and then formed need a little more time for development before they are baked in the oven. Cover the dough with clean, lint-free towels or plastic wrap and let it rise in a draft-free place at a warm room temperature, between 72°F and 86°F (22°C and 30°C). The warmer the room, the faster the bread will rise. Some doughs, such as slow-rise doughs, will not rise appreciably at room temperature but will finish rising when they hit the heat of the oven.

Baking

For recipes that will be baked in the oven rather than the bread machine, such as baguettes, boules, flatbreads, rolls and most festive breads, you'll preheat the oven to the correct temperature while the shaped dough is rising, then bake for the amount of time specified in the recipe.

Cooling

For breads baked in the machine, when the machine signals that the cycle is finished, remove the bread pan from the machine and transfer it to a wire rack to let the bread cool for 5 minutes. Turn the bread out of the pan, removing the kneading paddles if necessary, then turn the loaf upright and let it cool on the rack. For breads baked in the oven, remove the loaf or rolls to a wire rack to cool as directed in the recipe. It is best to let bread cool for 30 minutes before slicing it. If you cut into a loaf too soon, it tends to get squished and the texture will be gummy.

Glazing or Icing

Let rolls cool for at least 10 minutes and let bread cool for at least 1 hour before glazing or icing.

At the end of it all, you come to the very best part of any recipe — enjoy!

Storing Bread

Bread machine breads tend to be best within a day or two of baking, but if you want to store them for longer, the freezer is best. Place completely cooled loaves or slices in freezer bags (cutting large loaves as necessary to fit bags) or wrap with plastic wrap, then place in an airtight container. Label and date the packages and freeze for up to 3 months.

For breads with a glaze or icing, freeze before decorating. Let frozen breads thaw, wrapped, at room temperature, then prepare the glaze or icing and decorate the thawed bread.

Oops! Did You Forget Something?

If the phone rings or the baby cries while you're making a bread machine recipe, and you forget something, here's what to do:

- *If you forgot to add instant or bread machine yeast or salt:* While the dough is mixing (not kneading) in the bread machine, you can still add the yeast or salt.

- *If you forgot to add "mix-in" ingredients at the signal:* If your bread has not started baking yet, you can quickly remove the dough from the bread pan, transfer it to a floured surface and knead in the ingredients, one-quarter at a time, by hand. Return the dough to the bread pan and close the lid to continue the cycle. (If your bread machine has a Pause button, so much the better. Press Pause, remove the dough and knead in the ingredients, then push Start to resume the cycle when you're ready.)

- *If you forgot to add the topping:* If the loaf is in its final rise or just starting to bake, you can quickly lift the lid, brush on any wash, sprinkle on any topping, then close the lid. But the worst-case scenario is that you have great-tasting bread without a topping.

- *If you forgot to remove the loaf from the bread machine as soon as it was done:* Don't worry about it — the bread will simply be a little more done and a little crustier than if you had removed it when the cycle ended.

Finally, a solution to a common problem: A kneading paddle will sometimes get stuck inside a baked loaf when you turn it out from the bread pan. Check the interior of the pan to see whether a paddle is missing in action. Before you forget, turn the loaf upside down and use a paring knife, tongs and an oven mitt to remove the likely-still-hot paddle while the loaf is warm.

Cleaning Tips for Bread Machine Users

Most bread machines, even the older models, have nonstick surfaces that make cleaning easier. But prevention can be worth a pound of cure.

- To keep your kitchen cleaner, spoon and measure the flour over your sink or a large baking tray so the mess is corralled.
- To keep your bread machine tidier, fill the bread pan away from the machine. Then snap the pan in place in the machine.

- To remove bits of ingredients or browned flour from the bottom of your bread machine, remove the bread pan, unplug the machine and wait for it to cool. Then use the wand attachment of a vacuum cleaner to gently suction out the debris without disturbing the heating element or clamps.

- To wash the bread pan and kneading paddle(s), follow your manual's directions. Most instruct you to use a mild detergent and a soft cloth. If the kneading paddle is stuck in the bottom of the pan, place the pan in the sink and fill it with warm water. Let it soak for 30 minutes, then gently twist the paddle to remove it. Washing the bread pan in the dishwasher can result in discoloration, pitting and/or rust.

- To clean the window of the bread machine, inside and out, use a damp cloth.

- To store your bread machine while it's not in use, place the clean bread pan and paddle inside the machine and store it in a cool, dry, covered area, such as a kitchen cabinet.

Classic White Breads

WHEN WE IMAGINE the wonderful, homey aroma of bread baking in the oven, it's white bread we're thinking about. The classic loaf of white bread, whether used for breakfast toast or sandwiches, is the basic bread we all want to get right. Luckily, your trusty baking assistant — your bread machine — does a great job of mixing, kneading, rising and baking that loaf, and all at the right temperatures in a controlled environment.

Try several recipes in this chapter, then come up with your own signature house bread. With all the flours that are available now, you can find or create the perfect loaf for your family.

It's amazing, really, how many white breads there are. This chapter is a mere sampling of the ones I've tried and liked and that seemed to do the best in the bread machine. If you want bakery-style bread, choose Classic Butter Crust Bread (page 22). If you're looking for a high-rising, airy, very tender bread your kids will love, then it's Blue Ribbon Bread

Machine Bread (page 24) for you. Add a little egg and oil or butter, and you get Braided Challah (page 38) or Brioche (page 40) — a little richer but still airy and light.

I am not a fan of low-carb breads, but I have no problem with a delicious, higher-protein loaf, such as High-Protein White Bread (page 26), which helps you keep fuller, longer.

The breads in this chapter use a variety of flours, from the soft doppio zero (Italian-style flour) to high-protein bread flour. The cycle of choice for most of the breads is the Basic/White cycle with the Light Crust setting. Make a few loaves to see how your bread machine bakes the crust, then change the crust setting if you like.

Flour Power

There are more flours available today than ever before, some right from the grocery store shelf, others from ethnic markets or online catalogs. It also helps to know the protein content of a flour if you want to make a bread recipe from another country or successfully substitute one type of flour for another, such as T-55 for all-purpose, or strong flour for bread flour.

For more information on comparing North American and European flours, visit www.kingarthurflour.com/flour/european-flour-equivalents.html.

Ingredient	Protein Percentage	What It Does for the Bread
Doppio zero (Italian flour)	8% to 8.5%	Adds a very soft crumb and very tender texture
Whole-grain flours	8% to 14%	Add color, texture, fiber and nutrients
Plain flour (British)	8% to 10%	Adds a soft crumb and tender texture
Irish whole-meal flour	10%	Adds a soft crumb, fiber and texture
All-purpose flour (bleached and unbleached)	10% to 12%	Adds a soft crumb and tender texture
T-55 (French and Quebecois)	10% to 11.5%	Adds creamier color and toasty flavor
Type 550 (German)	10% to 11.5%	Adds a soft crumb and tender texture
White whole wheat	10% to 12%	Adds texture, fiber, nutrients, flavor
European-style (French)	11.5%	Adds a soft crumb that can honeycomb
European-style (artisan)	11.7%	Adds a soft crumb that can honeycomb
Bread flour (bleached and unbleached)	12% to 14%	Adds a more muscular, chewy texture
Strong flour (British)	12% to 14%	Adds a more muscular, chewy texture
Durum or semolina flour	14%	Adds a very muscular, chewy texture
Vital wheat gluten (gluten flour)	75% to 80%	Adds protein/gluten and a muscular texture

Classic Butter Crust Bread

Makes 1 loaf

Evoking memories of small-town bakeries, this classic white loaf does it all — breakfast toast, sandwiches, bread with a pot roast dinner. Leftovers make great croutons, French toast or bread pudding. Choosing the Light Crust setting will ensure that your bread comes out buttery and golden.

Tip

Ideally, the buttermilk should be between 86°F and 95°F (30°C and 35°C), the temperature range in which yeast is most active. Warm it in the microwave or in a saucepan on the stove, and check the temperature with an instant-read thermometer.

1 lb (500 g)

2 tbsp	granulated sugar	30 mL
1 tsp	salt	5 mL
¾ cup	lukewarm buttermilk (see tip, at left)	175 mL
2 tbsp	butter, softened	30 mL
2 cups	all-purpose flour	500 mL
1 tsp	instant or bread machine yeast	5 mL
Topping		
2 tbsp	butter, melted	30 mL

1½ lb (750 g)

3 tbsp	granulated sugar	45 mL
1½ tsp	salt	7 mL
1 cup	lukewarm buttermilk (see tip, at left)	250 mL
3 tbsp	butter, softened	45 mL
2½ cups	all-purpose flour	625 mL
1½ tsp	instant or bread machine yeast	7 mL
Topping		
2 tbsp	butter, melted	30 mL

2 lb (1 kg)

¼ cup	granulated sugar	60 mL
2 tsp	salt	10 mL
1½ cups	lukewarm buttermilk (see tip, at left)	375 mL
¼ cup	butter, softened	60 mL
4 cups	all-purpose flour	1 L
1½ tsp	instant or bread machine yeast	7 mL
Topping		
2 tbsp	butter, melted	30 mL

3 lb (1.5 kg)

7 tbsp	granulated sugar	105 mL
2¼ tsp	salt	11 mL
2 cups	lukewarm buttermilk (see tip, at left)	500 mL
½ cup	butter, softened	125 mL
5½ cups	all-purpose flour	1.375 L
1¼ tsp	instant or bread machine yeast	6 mL
Topping		
2 tbsp	butter, melted	30 mL

If your bread machine doesn't have a Pause button, simply raise the lid, cut the slash and brush with butter, then close the lid again.

Bread machine breads tend to be best within a day or two of baking, but if you want to store them for longer, wrap and freeze loaves or slices in labeled and dated freezer-proof packages for up to 3 months. Cut large loaves to fit freezer storage bags.

1. Add sugar, salt, buttermilk and butter to the bread pan. Spoon flour on top of liquid. Add yeast.

2. Select the Basic/White cycle and the Light Crust setting and press Start.

3. *Topping*: After the final rise and just before baking (see "Timing It Right," page 13), press Pause. Raise the lid, cut a ½-inch (1 cm) slash down the length or across the top of the loaf and brush with melted butter. Close the lid and press Start to continue the cycle.

Buttery Breakfast Bread
For a breakfast bread, use packed dark brown sugar in place of the granulated sugar.

Blue Ribbon Bread Machine Bread

Makes 1 loaf

If bread machine users gave out blue ribbons, this recipe would win. The method is a bit unusual — the yeast is mixed with sugar and warm water *before* the dry ingredients are added — but it works. You'll get a high-rising, tender, airy loaf with a homemade flavor and texture that kids love.

Tip

Warm the water in the microwave or in a saucepan on the stove, and check the temperature with an instant-read thermometer.

1 lb (500 g)

4 tsp	granulated sugar	20 mL
1 tsp	instant or bread machine yeast	5 mL
2/3 cup	warm water (110°F/43°C)	150 mL
2 1/2 tbsp	vegetable oil	37 mL
2 cups	bread flour	500 mL
1 1/2 tsp	salt	7 mL

1 1/2 lb (750 g)

2 tbsp	granulated sugar	30 mL
1 1/4 tsp	instant or bread machine yeast	6 mL
1 cup	warm water (110°F/43°C)	250 mL
1/4 cup	vegetable oil	60 mL
3 cups	bread flour	750 mL
1 1/2 tsp	salt	7 mL

2 lb (1 kg)

8 tsp	granulated sugar	40 mL
1 1/2 tsp	instant or bread machine yeast	7 mL
1 1/3 cups	warm water (110°F/43°C)	325 mL
1/3 cup	vegetable oil	75 mL
4 cups	bread flour	1 L
2 tsp	salt	10 mL

3 lb (1.5 kg)

1/4 cup	granulated sugar	60 mL
3/4 tsp	instant or bread machine yeast	3 mL
2 cups	warm water (110°F/43°C)	500 mL
1/2 cup	vegetable oil	125 mL
6 cups	bread flour	1.5 L
2 1/2 tsp	salt	12 mL

1. Add sugar, yeast and water to the bread pan. Let stand for 10 minutes or until yeast starts to bubble.

2. Add oil. Spoon flour on top of liquid. Add salt.

3. Select the Basic/White cycle and the Light Crust setting and press Start.

Tips

When making the smallest loaf allowed by your machine, check the dough a few minutes after kneading starts to make sure the ingredients are incorporated. You may need to help the machine along by using a rubber spatula to scrape the corners of the pan.

Bread machine breads tend to be best within a day or two of baking, but if you want to store them for longer, wrap and freeze loaves or slices in labeled and dated freezer-proof packages for up to 3 months. Cut large loaves to fit freezer storage bags.

Blue Ribbon Boule

Prepare the recipe through step 2, then select the Dough cycle and press Start. Line a baking sheet with parchment paper. When the cycle is finished, transfer dough to a floured surface and punch down gently. Form into a boule and place on prepared baking sheet. Cover with a clean towel and let rise in a warm, draft-free place for 30 minutes. Meanwhile, preheat oven to 425°F (220°C). Using a serrated knife, cut 3 to 5 deep diagonal slashes across top of loaf. Spray loaf with water. Bake until risen and dark brown on top and an instant-read thermometer inserted in the center registers 190°F (90°C). Remove from pan and let cool on a wire rack.

Dough Size	Baking Time
1 lb (500 g)	23 to 26 minutes
1½ lb (750 g)	26 to 30 minutes
2 lb (1 kg)	28 to 32 minutes
3 lb (1.5 kg)	35 to 37 minutes

High-Protein White Bread

Makes 1 loaf

Rather than engineering a low-carb bread with liquid lecithin and other odd ingredients, why not create a high-protein bread that keeps you feeling fuller, longer? Whether you use American or Canadian bread flour, you get about 16 grams of protein per cup (250 mL) of flour. When you add a bit of whey protein concentrate (a powdered milk–based product used in protein bars and drink mixes), an egg and some cottage cheese to the dough, you dramatically increase the protein content — to about 8.5 grams per slice! The dough is meant to be moist and soft — more like a thick batter — so the whey protein does not turn gummy in the bread. The result is a moist, mellow, substantial bread full of good things.

1 lb (500 g)

¼ tsp	salt	1 mL
1	small egg, beaten	1
¼ cup	lukewarm water (see tip, at right)	60 mL
3 tbsp	unsweetened applesauce or mashed ripe banana	45 mL
3 tbsp	low-fat cottage cheese	45 mL
1½ tbsp	vegetable oil	22 mL
4 tsp	liquid honey or agave syrup	20 mL
1¾ cups	bread flour	425 mL
3 tbsp	unflavored powdered whey protein concentrate	45 mL
1 tsp	instant or bread machine yeast	5 mL

1½ lb (750 g)

½ tsp	salt	2 mL
1	large egg, beaten	1
⅓ cup	lukewarm water (see tip, at right)	75 mL
¼ cup	unsweetened applesauce or mashed ripe banana	60 mL
¼ cup	low-fat cottage cheese	60 mL
2½ tbsp	vegetable oil	37 mL
2 tbsp	liquid honey or agave syrup	30 mL
2½ cups	bread flour	625 mL
¼ cup	unflavored powdered whey protein concentrate	60 mL
1¼ tsp	instant or bread machine yeast	6 mL

2 lb (1 kg)

1 tsp	salt	5 mL
2	small eggs, beaten	2
½ cup	lukewarm water (see tip, at right)	125 mL
⅓ cup	unsweetened applesauce or mashed ripe banana	75 mL
⅓ cup	low-fat cottage cheese	75 mL
¼ cup	vegetable oil	60 mL
3 tbsp	liquid honey or agave syrup	45 mL
3½ cups	bread flour	875 mL
⅓ cup	unflavored powdered whey protein concentrate	75 mL
1½ tsp	instant or bread machine yeast	7 mL

Tips

Ideally, the water should be between 86°F and 95°F (30°C and 35°C), the temperature range in which yeast is most active. Warm it in the microwave or in a saucepan on the stove, and check the temperature with an instant-read thermometer.

When you're making the 1-lb (500 g) loaf, if you can't find small eggs, beat 1 large egg until blended, then measure 2 tbsp + 1 tsp (35 mL) to equal the volume of 1 small egg, reserving any remaining egg for another use. For the 2-lb (1 kg) loaf, beat 2 large eggs until blended, then measure 1/4 cup + 2 tsp (70 mL) to equal the volume of 2 small eggs.

Whey protein concentrate contains 16 g protein per 1/4 cup (60 mL). You can find it in the specialty flour or organic section of well-stocked grocery stores and at health food stores.

3 lb (1.5 kg)

1 1/2 tsp	salt	7 mL
2	large eggs, beaten	2
2/3 cup	lukewarm water (see tip, at left)	150 mL
1/2 cup	unsweetened applesauce or mashed ripe banana	125 mL
1/2 cup	low-fat cottage cheese	125 mL
1/4 cup	vegetable oil	60 mL
1/4 cup	liquid honey or agave syrup	60 mL
4 2/3 cups	bread flour	1.15 L
1/2 cup	unflavored powdered whey protein concentrate	125 mL
1 1/2 tsp	instant or bread machine yeast	7 mL

1. Add salt, egg(s), water, applesauce, cottage cheese, oil and honey to the bread pan. Spoon flour on top of liquid. Add whey protein concentrate and yeast.

2. Select the Basic/White or Sweet cycle and the Light Crust setting and press Start.

Fast and Easy White Bread

Makes 1 loaf

Delay Timer

Sometimes, you've just gotta have it: white bread, right now. This recipe makes use of the Rapid or Express Cycle and uses a little more yeast to get the job done fast. If your machine doesn't have a Rapid or Express Cycle, you can make this bread on the Basic cycle; it will take longer and you will need to decrease the yeast as follows: use $1\frac{1}{2}$ tsp (7 mL) for a 1- or $1\frac{1}{2}$-lb (500 or 750 g) loaf; use $1\frac{3}{4}$ tsp (8 mL) for a 2- or 3-lb (1 or 1.5 kg) loaf.

Tip

Ideally, the water should be between 86°F and 95°F (30°C and 35°C), the temperature range in which yeast is most active. Warm it in the microwave or in a saucepan on the stove, and check the temperature with an instant-read thermometer.

1 lb (500 g)

4 tsp	instant skim milk powder	20 mL
2 tsp	granulated sugar	10 mL
$\frac{3}{4}$ tsp	salt	3 mL
$\frac{3}{4}$ cup	lukewarm water (see tip, at left)	175 mL
2 tsp	butter, softened	10 mL
2 cups	bread flour	500 mL
2 tsp	instant or bread machine yeast	10 mL

$1\frac{1}{2}$ lb (750 g)

2 tbsp	instant skim milk powder	30 mL
1 tbsp	granulated sugar	15 mL
1 tsp	salt	5 mL
$1\frac{1}{4}$ cups	lukewarm water (see tip, at left)	300 mL
1 tbsp	butter, softened	15 mL
3 cups	bread flour	750 mL
2 tsp	instant or bread machine yeast	10 mL

2 lb (1 kg)

$2\frac{1}{2}$ tbsp	instant skim milk powder	37 mL
$1\frac{1}{2}$ tbsp	granulated sugar	22 mL
$1\frac{1}{2}$ tsp	salt	7 mL
$1\frac{1}{3}$ cups + 2 tbsp	lukewarm water (see tip, at left)	355 mL
$1\frac{1}{2}$ tbsp	butter, softened	22 mL
$4\frac{1}{4}$ cups	bread flour	1.06 L
$2\frac{1}{4}$ tsp	instant or bread machine yeast	11 mL

3 lb (1.5 kg)

3 tbsp	instant skim milk powder	45 mL
2 tbsp	granulated sugar	30 mL
2 tsp	salt	10 mL
2 cups	lukewarm water (see tip, at left)	500 mL
2 tbsp	butter, softened	30 mL
5 cups	bread flour	1.25 L
$2\frac{1}{2}$ tsp	instant or bread machine yeast	12 mL

1. Add milk powder, sugar, salt, water and butter to the bread pan. Spoon flour on top of liquid. Add yeast.

2. Select the Rapid or Express cycle and press Start.

Tips

If your dough does not form a ball during the first few minutes of kneading, do one of two things: if the dough looks dry and crumbly, add 1 tbsp (15 mL) water at 1-minute intervals until the dough forms a ball; if the dough looks wet, add 1 tbsp (15 mL) bread flour at 1-minute intervals until the dough forms a ball.

Bread machine breads tend to be best within a day or two of baking, but if you want to store them for longer, wrap and freeze loaves or slices in labeled and dated freezer-proof packages for up to 3 months. Cut large loaves to fit freezer storage bags.

Fast and Easy Dinner Rolls

Prepare the recipe through step 2, then select the Dough cycle and press Start. Grease as many 12-cup muffin pans as you'll need for the dough size (see chart, below). When the cycle is finished, transfer dough to a floured surface and punch down gently. Flour your hands and pinch off portions of dough, dividing dough into the appropriate number of portions for the dough size. Roll each portion into a rough ball, dip in $\frac{1}{4}$ to $\frac{1}{2}$ cup (60 to 125 mL) melted butter and place one ball in each prepared muffin cup. Cover with a clean towel and let rise in a warm, draft-free place for 30 minutes. Meanwhile, preheat oven to 350°F (180°C). Bake for 15 to 20 minutes or until risen and lightly browned on top and an instant-read thermometer inserted in the center of a roll registers 190°F (90°C).

Dough Size	Number of Rolls
1 lb (500 g)	8
1$\frac{1}{2}$ lb (750 g)	12
2 lb (1 kg)	16
3 lb (1.5 kg)	24

Muffuletta

This classic, crusty bread from New Orleans has a fine crumb and a topping of sesame seeds. Although it's usually baked as a round loaf, you can also bake it entirely in the bread machine.

Tips

Ideally, the water should be between 86°F and 95°F (30°C and 35°C), the temperature range in which yeast is most active. Warm it in the microwave or in a saucepan on the stove, and check the temperature with an instant-read thermometer.

When making the smallest loaf allowed by your machine, check the dough a few minutes after kneading starts to make sure the ingredients are incorporated. You may need to help the machine along by using a rubber spatula to scrape the corners of the pan.

1 lb (500 g)

2 tsp	granulated sugar	10 mL
1 tsp	salt	5 mL
²/₃ cup	lukewarm water (see tip, at left)	150 mL
1½ tbsp	butter, softened	22 mL
2 cups	bread flour	500 mL
1 tsp	instant or bread machine yeast	5 mL
Topping		
1 tbsp	sesame seeds	15 mL

1½ lb (750 g)

1 tbsp	granulated sugar	15 mL
1½ tsp	salt	7 mL
1 cup	lukewarm water (see tip, at left)	250 mL
2 tbsp	butter, softened	30 mL
3 cups	bread flour	750 mL
1¼ tsp	instant or bread machine yeast	6 mL
Topping		
1 tbsp	sesame seeds	15 mL

2 lb (1 kg)

4 tsp	granulated sugar	20 mL
2 tsp	salt	10 mL
1⅓ cups	lukewarm water (see tip, at left)	325 mL
3 tbsp	butter, softened	45 mL
4 cups	bread flour	1 L
1½ tsp	instant or bread machine yeast	7 mL
Topping		
1 tbsp	sesame seeds	15 mL

3 lb (1.5 kg)

2 tbsp	granulated sugar	30 mL
2½ tsp	salt	12 mL
2 cups	lukewarm water (see tip, at left)	500 mL
⅓ cup	butter, softened	75 mL
6 cups	bread flour	1.5 L
¾ tsp	instant or bread machine yeast	3 mL
Topping		
1 tbsp	sesame seeds	15 mL

1. Add sugar, salt, water and butter to the bread pan. Spoon flour on top of liquid. Add yeast.

Tips

If your bread machine doesn't have a Pause button, simply raise the lid, brush with water and sprinkle with seeds, then close the lid again.

To make an authentic muffuletta sandwich, split the loaf and fill it with layers of thinly sliced Genoa salami, boiled ham and provolone. Top with a deli olive salad made with pimento-stuffed olives and capers in red wine vinaigrette. Muffuletta bread also tastes wonderful filled with softened goat cheese, pesto, roasted red peppers and chopped kalamata olives.

2. Select the Basic/White cycle and press Start.

3. *Topping*: After the final rise and just before baking (see "Timing It Right," page 13), press the Pause button. Raise the lid, brush the top of the loaf with water and sprinkle with sesame seeds, pressing the seeds into the dough. Close the lid and press Start to continue the cycle.

Oven-Baked Muffuletta

Prepare the recipe through step 1, then select the Dough cycle and press Start. Line a large baking sheet with parchment paper. When the cycle is finished, transfer dough to a floured surface and punch down gently. Form into a boule and place on prepared baking sheet. Brush dough with water and sprinkle with sesame seeds, pressing the seeds into the dough. Cover with a clean towel and let rise in a warm, draft-free place for 30 minutes. Meanwhile, preheat oven to 425°F (220°C). Bake until risen and golden brown and an instant-read thermometer inserted in the center registers 190°F (90°C). Remove from pan and let cool on a wire rack.

Dough Size	Baking Time
1 lb (500 g)	23 to 25 minutes
1½ lb (750 g)	26 to 28 minutes
2 lb (1 kg)	28 to 31 minutes
3 lb (1.5 kg)	33 to 35 minutes

English Muffin Bread

Baked as a loaf, this bread makes wonderful breakfast toast or sandwich bread. You can also make individual English Muffins (see page 209), which you bake on a griddle.

Tips

Ideally, the milk and buttermilk should be between 86°F and 95°F (30°C and 35°C), the temperature range in which yeast is most active. Warm them in the microwave or in a saucepan on the stove, and check the temperature with an instant-read thermometer.

When making the smallest loaf allowed by your machine, check the dough a few minutes after kneading starts to make sure the ingredients are incorporated. You may need to help the machine along by using a rubber spatula to scrape the corners of the pan.

1 lb (500 g)

1½ tsp	granulated sugar	7 mL
1 tsp	salt	5 mL
½ cup	lukewarm milk (see tip, at left)	125 mL
⅓ cup	lukewarm buttermilk	75 mL
2 cups	all-purpose flour	500 mL
1½ tsp	instant or bread machine yeast	7 mL
⅛ tsp	baking soda	0.5 mL
	Cornmeal	

1½ lb (750 g)

2 tsp	granulated sugar	10 mL
1 tsp	salt	5 mL
¾ cup	lukewarm milk (see tip, at left)	175 mL
½ cup	lukewarm buttermilk	125 mL
3 cups	all-purpose flour	750 mL
1¾ tsp	instant or bread machine yeast	8 mL
¼ tsp	baking soda	1 mL
	Cornmeal	

2 lb (1 kg)

1 tbsp	granulated sugar	15 mL
2 tsp	salt	10 mL
1⅓ cups	lukewarm milk (see tip, at left)	325 mL
⅓ cup	lukewarm buttermilk	75 mL
4 cups	all-purpose flour	1 L
1½ tsp	instant or bread machine yeast	7 mL
¼ tsp	baking soda	1 mL
	Cornmeal	

3 lb (750 g)

2 tbsp	granulated sugar	30 mL
1½ tsp	salt	7 mL
1 cup	lukewarm milk (see tip, at left)	250 mL
1 cup	lukewarm buttermilk	250 mL
5 cups	all-purpose flour	1.25 L
1¾ tsp	instant or bread machine yeast	8 mL
½ tsp	baking soda	2 mL
	Cornmeal	

1. Add sugar, salt, milk and buttermilk to the bread pan. Spoon flour on top of liquid. Add yeast and baking soda.

Tips

Bread machine breads tend to be best within a day or two of baking, but if you want to store them for longer, wrap and freeze loaves or slices in labeled and dated freezer-proof packages for up to 3 months. Cut large loaves to fit freezer storage bags.

If your bread machine doesn't have a Pause button, simply raise the lid, remove the dough and sprinkle it with cornmeal, remove the kneading paddle(s) from the pan, then return the dough to the pan and close the lid again.

2. Select the Basic/White cycle and the Light Crust setting and press Start.

3. At the start of the final rise (see "Timing It Right," page 13), press Pause. Remove dough from bread pan and transfer to a floured surface. Sprinkle bottom and sides of dough with cornmeal.

4. Remove kneading paddle(s) from bread pan. Return dough to pan and press Start to continue the cycle.

> ### Whole Wheat English Muffin Bread
> Replace half the all-purpose flour with white whole wheat flour or whole wheat flour.

Nonna's Italian Bread

Makes 1 loaf

In traditional Italian families throughout North America, the keeper of the culinary flame was Nonna, or Grandmother. Every few days, she would bake loaves of this easy, basic, crusty bread meant to mop up every last bit of her unique simmered-for-hours pasta sauce. Today, when you want to make panini, bruschetta or crostini, use this bread. You can make and bake it entirely in the bread machine, but for the traditional shape, use the Dough cycle, then form it by hand and bake it in the oven.

Tips

Ideally, the water should be between 86°F and 95°F (30°C and 35°C), the temperature range in which yeast is most active. Warm it in the microwave or in a saucepan on the stove, and check the temperature with an instant-read thermometer.

When you're making the 1-lb (500 g) loaf, if you can't find small eggs, beat 1 large egg until blended, then measure 2 tbsp + 1 tsp (35 mL) to equal the volume of 1 small egg, reserving any remaining egg for another use.

1 lb (500 g)

½ tsp	fine sea salt	2 mL
1	small egg, beaten	1
⅔ cup	lukewarm water (see tip, at left)	150 mL
2 tsp	olive oil	10 mL
2 cups	bread flour	500 mL
1 tsp	instant or bread machine yeast	5 mL
Topping		
2 tsp	milk	10 mL
2 tsp	sesame seeds	10 mL

1½ lb (750 g)

1 tsp	fine sea salt	5 mL
1	large egg, beaten	1
1 cup	lukewarm water (see tip, at left)	250 mL
1 tbsp	olive oil	15 mL
3 cups	bread flour	750 mL
1 tsp	instant or bread machine yeast	5 mL
Topping		
1 tbsp	milk	15 mL
1 tbsp	sesame seeds	15 mL

2 lb (1 kg)

1½ tsp	fine sea salt	7 mL
1	large egg, beaten	1
1⅓ cups	lukewarm water (see tip, at left)	325 mL
4 tsp	olive oil	20 mL
4 cups	bread flour	1 L
1¼ tsp	instant or bread machine yeast	6 mL
Topping		
1 tbsp	milk	15 mL
1 tbsp	sesame seeds	15 mL

3 lb (1.5 kg)

2 tsp	fine sea salt	10 mL
2	large eggs, beaten	2
1½ cups	lukewarm water (see tip, at left)	375 mL
3 tbsp	olive oil	45 mL
5¾ cups	bread flour	1.425 L
1 tsp	instant or bread machine yeast	5 mL
Topping		
1 tbsp	milk	15 mL
1 tbsp	sesame seeds	15 mL

Tips

If your dough does not form a ball during the first few minutes of kneading, do one of two things: if the dough looks dry and crumbly, add 1 tbsp (15 mL) water at 1-minute intervals until the dough forms a ball; if the dough looks wet, add 1 tbsp (15 mL) bread flour at 1-minute intervals until the dough forms a ball.

If your bread machine doesn't have a Pause button, simply raise the lid, brush with milk and sprinkle with seeds, then close the lid again.

Placing a pan of water in the bottom of the oven while the bread is baking creates steam that helps form a good crust.

1. Add salt, egg(s), water and oil to the bread pan. Spoon flour on top of liquid. Add yeast.

2. Select the Basic/White cycle and press Start.

3. *Topping:* At the start of the final rise (see "Timing It Right," page 13), press the Pause button. Raise the lid, brush the top of the loaf with milk and sprinkle with sesame seeds, pressing the seeds into the dough. Close the lid and press Start to continue the cycle.

Oven-Baked Nonna's Italian Bread

Prepare the recipe through step 1, then select the Dough cycle and press Start. Line a large baking sheet with parchment paper. When the cycle is finished, transfer dough to a floured surface and punch down gently. Form into an oblong loaf (see chart, below) and place on prepared baking sheet. Cover with a clean towel and let rise in a warm, draft-free place for 30 minutes. Meanwhile, preheat oven to 350°F (180°C) and place a broiler pan on the bottom rack. Using a serrated knife, cut 3 deep diagonal slashes across top of loaf. Brush loaf with milk and sprinkle with sesame seeds, pressing the seeds into the dough. Add 2 cups (500 mL) hot water to the broiler pan. Place baking sheet on the middle rack. Bake until bread is risen and browned on top and an instant-read thermometer inserted in the center registers 190°F (90°C). Remove from pan and let cool on a wire rack.

Dough Size	Loaf Size	Baking Time
1 lb (500 g)	10 inches (25 cm) long	26 to 28 minutes
1½ lb (750 g)	11 inches (28 cm) long	28 to 34 minutes
2 lb (1 kg)	12 inches (30 cm) long	30 to 35 minutes
3 lb (1.5 kg)	14 inches (35 cm) long	35 to 40 minutes

Doppio Zero Italian Bread

Doppio zero ("00") is an 8% protein Italian flour. Because it has less protein than North American all-purpose flour and bread flour, it is softer than these flours and creates a soft, feathery crumb when added to bread. Doppio zero flour is available at Italian grocery stores and online. Use this mellow, crusty bread with its honeycomb crumb to make Italian sandwiches or mop up every last bit of homemade pasta sauce.

Tips

When you're making the 1-lb (500 g) loaf, if you can't find small eggs, beat 1 large egg until blended, then measure 2 tbsp + 1 tsp (35 mL) to equal the volume of 1 small egg, reserving any remaining egg for another use.

Ideally, the water should be between 86°F and 95°F (30°C and 35°C), the temperature range in which yeast is most active. Warm it in the microwave or in a saucepan on the stove, and check the temperature with an instant-read thermometer.

1 lb (500 g)

1 tsp	fine sea salt	5 mL
1	small egg, beaten	1
2/3 cup	lukewarm water (see tip, at left)	150 mL
2 tsp	olive oil	10 mL
1 cup	bread flour	250 mL
3/4 cup + 2 tbsp	doppio zero flour	205 mL
1/4 cup	semolina flour	60 mL
3/4 tsp	instant or bread machine yeast	3 mL
Topping		
2 tsp	milk	10 mL
2 tsp	sesame seeds	10 mL

1½ lb (750 g)

1¼ tsp	fine sea salt	6 mL
1	large egg, beaten	1
1 cup	lukewarm water (see tip, at left)	250 mL
1 tbsp	olive oil	15 mL
1¾ cups	bread flour	425 mL
1 cup	doppio zero flour	250 mL
1/2 cup	semolina flour	125 mL
1 tsp	instant or bread machine yeast	5 mL
Topping		
1 tbsp	milk	15 mL
1 tbsp	sesame seeds	15 mL

2 lb (1 kg)

1½ tsp	fine sea salt	7 mL
1	large egg, beaten	1
1⅓ cups	lukewarm water (see tip, at left)	325 mL
4 tsp	olive oil	20 mL
2 cups	bread flour	500 mL
1½ cups	doppio zero flour	375 mL
2/3 cup	semolina flour	150 mL
1 tsp	instant or bread machine yeast	5 mL
Topping		
1 tbsp	milk	15 mL
1 tbsp	sesame seeds	15 mL

Tips

If your dough does not form a ball during the first few minutes of kneading, do one of two things: if the dough looks dry and crumbly, add 1 tbsp (15 mL) water at 1-minute intervals until the dough forms a ball; if the dough looks wet, add 1 tbsp (15 mL) bread flour at 1-minute intervals until the dough forms a ball.

This bread works best on the Medium crust setting when baked in the machine.

If your bread machine doesn't have a Pause button, simply raise the lid, brush with milk and sprinkle with seeds, then close the lid again.

This is a great bread to cut and serve with flavored olive oils for dipping.

Placing a pan of water in the bottom of the oven while the bread is baking creates steam that helps form a good crust.

3 lb (1.5 kg)

2 tsp	fine sea salt	10 mL
2	large eggs, beaten	2
1⅔ cups	lukewarm water (see tip, page 36)	400 mL
3 tbsp	olive oil	45 mL
3¼ cups	bread flour	800 mL
2¼ cups	doppio zero flour	550 mL
¾ cup	semolina flour	175 mL
¾ tsp	instant or bread machine yeast	3 mL

Topping

1 tbsp	milk	15 mL
1 tbsp	sesame seeds	15 mL

1. Add salt, egg(s), water and oil to the bread pan. Spoon bread flour, doppio zero flour and semolina flour on top of liquid. Add yeast.

2. Select the Basic/White cycle and press Start.

3. *Topping:* At the start of the final rise (see "Timing It Right," page 13), press the Pause button. Raise the lid, brush the top of the loaf with milk and sprinkle with sesame seeds, pressing the seeds into the dough. Close the lid and press Start to continue the cycle.

Oven-Baked Doppio Zero Italian Bread

Prepare the recipe through step 1, then select the Dough cycle and press Start. Line a large baking sheet with parchment paper. When the cycle is finished, transfer dough to a floured surface and punch down gently. Form into an oblong loaf (see chart, below) and place on prepared baking sheet. Cover with a clean towel and let rise in a warm, draft-free place for 30 minutes. Meanwhile, preheat oven to 350°F (180°C) and place a broiler pan on the bottom rack. Brush loaf with milk and sprinkle with sesame seeds, pressing the seeds into the dough. Add 2 cups (500 mL) hot water to the broiler pan. Place baking sheet on the middle rack. Bake until bread is risen and browned on top and an instant-read thermometer inserted in the center registers 190°F (90°C). Remove from pan and let cool on a wire rack.

Dough Size	Loaf Size	Baking Time
1 lb (500 g)	10 inches (25 cm) long	26 to 28 minutes
1½ lb (750 g)	11 inches (28 cm) long	28 to 34 minutes
2 lb (1 kg)	12 inches (30 cm) long	30 to 35 minutes
3 lb (1.5 kg)	14 inches (35 cm) long	35 to 40 minutes

Braided Challah

Makes 1 loaf

In September, Rosh Hashanah, the Day of Judgment, begins the New Year in the Jewish calendar. The 10-day observance, revolving around the themes of judgment, repentance and renewal, ends with a fast day on Yom Kippur, the Day of Atonement. As families gather to feast on Rosh Hashanah, or after the Yom Kippur fast is broken, they share foods made with honey (to signify sweetness in the coming year) and foods that are round (to signify a year with no endings).

Tips

Ideally, the water should be between 86°F and 95°F (30°C and 35°C), the temperature range in which yeast is most active. Warm it in the microwave or in a saucepan on the stove, and check the temperature with an instant-read thermometer.

Egg wash gives a loaf a golden or burnished color and helps toppings stick to the crust.

When you're making the 1-lb (500 g) loaf, if you can't find small eggs, beat 1 large egg until blended, then measure 2 tbsp + 1 tsp (35 mL) to equal the volume of 1 small egg, reserving any remaining egg for another use.

1 lb (500 g)

½ tsp	salt	2 mL
1	small egg, beaten	1
⅔ cup	lukewarm water (see tip, at left)	150 mL
⅓ cup	liquid honey	75 mL
1 tbsp	vegetable oil	15 mL
2 cups	bread flour	500 mL
1¼ tsp	instant or bread machine yeast	6 mL

Topping

1	small egg, beaten	1
	Sesame seeds or poppy seeds (optional)	

1½ lb (750 g)

1 tsp	salt	5 mL
1	large egg, beaten	1
¾ cup	lukewarm water (see tip, at left)	175 mL
⅓ cup	liquid honey	75 mL
1½ tbsp	vegetable oil	22 mL
2¾ cups	bread flour	675 mL
1¼ tsp	instant or bread machine yeast	6 mL

Topping

1	large egg, beaten	1
	Sesame seeds or poppy seeds (optional)	

2 lb (1 kg)

1½ tsp	salt	7 mL
1	large egg, beaten	1
1	large egg yolk, beaten	1
1 cup	lukewarm water (see tip, at left)	250 mL
½ cup	liquid honey	125 mL
2½ tbsp	vegetable oil	37 mL
4⅔ cups	bread flour	1.15 L
1¼ tsp	instant or bread machine yeast	6 mL

Topping

1	large egg, beaten	1
	Sesame seeds or poppy seeds (optional)	

3 lb (1.5 kg)

2 tsp	salt	10 mL
3	large eggs, beaten	3
1⅓ cups	lukewarm water (see tip, at left)	325 mL
¾ cup	liquid honey	175 mL
¼ cup	vegetable oil	60 mL
5¼ cups	bread flour	1.3 L
1 tsp	instant or bread machine yeast	5 mL

Tips

If your instruction manual doesn't outline the timing of the knead and rise cycles and you miss the start of the final rise, you can omit the braiding step and let the loaf rise and bake in the machine. Add the topping before the bake cycle, if possible, or omit it.

If your bread machine doesn't have a Pause button, simply raise the lid, remove the dough, form and top it, then remove the kneading paddle(s) from the pan, place the braid in the pan and close the lid again. Work quickly, as the rising cycle will continue even without the bread in the pan.

Topping

1	large egg, beaten	1
	Sesame seeds or poppy seeds (optional)	

1. Add salt, egg(s), water, honey and oil to the bread pan. Spoon flour on top of liquid. Add yeast.

2. Select the Basic/White or Sweet cycle and the Light Crust setting and press Start.

3. At the start of the final rise (see page 13), press Pause. Remove dough from bread pan, transfer to a floured surface and punch down gently. Divide dough into thirds. Roll each third into a 10-inch (25 cm) long rope. Lay the three ropes out parallel to each other on a floured surface so that they are very close but not touching. Braid ropes together snugly. Tuck ends under to form an oblong loaf.

4. *Topping:* Brush braid with beaten egg and sprinkle with sesame seeds, if desired, pressing the seeds into the dough.

5. Remove kneading paddle(s) from bread pan. Place braid in pan and press Start to continue the cycle.

Oven-Baked Braided Challah

Prepare the recipe through step 1, then select the Dough cycle and press Start. Line a large baking sheet with parchment paper. When the cycle is finished, transfer dough to a floured surface and punch down gently. Divide dough into thirds. Roll each third into a 16-inch (40 cm) long rope. Braid ropes together, tucking ends under. Place on prepared baking sheet. Cover with a clean towel and let rise in a warm, draft-free place for 1 to 1½ hours or until doubled in bulk. Meanwhile, preheat oven to 350°F (180°C). Brush braid with beaten egg and sprinkle with sesame seeds, if desired, pressing the seeds into the dough. Bake until risen and golden and an instant-read thermometer inserted in the center registers 190°F (90°C). Remove from pan and let cool on a wire rack.

Oven-Baked Round Challah

Prepare the recipe through step 1, then select the Dough cycle and press Start. Line a large baking sheet with parchment paper. When the cycle is finished, transfer dough to a floured surface and form into a round loaf. Place on prepared baking sheet. Cover with a clean towel and let rise in a warm, draft-free place for 1 to 1½ hours or until doubled in bulk. Meanwhile, preheat oven to 350°F (180°C). Brush loaf with beaten egg and sprinkle with sesame seeds, if desired, pressing the seeds into the dough. Bake until risen and golden and an instant-read thermometer inserted in the center registers 190°F (90°C). Remove from pan and let cool on a wire rack.

Dough Size	Baking Time (for Braided or Round Loaf)
1 lb (500 g)	30 to 34 minutes
1½ lb (750 g)	34 to 36 minutes
2 lb (1 kg)	35 to 40 minutes
3 lb (1.5 kg)	38 to 42 minutes

Brioche

French brioche, a rich, eggy bread with a characteristic topknot of dough usually baked in a fluted mold (see page 238), can also be made as a loaf in the bread machine. Brioche is fabulous toasted for breakfast, makes wonderful French toast and can be the basis of desserts such as dark chocolate hazelnut bread pudding or sour cherry bread pudding. Because brioche is so rich, it needs a somewhat bitter or tangy flavor, such as sharp fruit preserves, as a counterpoint. In the larger loaves, the dough might seem thick and batter-like, but it all works out in the end.

Tip

Ideally, the buttermilk and water should be between 86°F and 95°F (30°C and 35°C), the temperature range in which yeast is most active. Warm them in the microwave or in a saucepan on the stove, and check the temperature with an instant-read thermometer.

1 lb (500 g)

4 tsp	granulated sugar	20 mL
1 tsp	salt	5 mL
2	large eggs, beaten	2
1/3 cup	unsalted butter, softened	75 mL
1/4 cup	lukewarm buttermilk (see tip, at left)	60 mL
2 tbsp	lukewarm water	30 mL
2 cups	bread flour	500 mL
3/4 tsp	instant or bread machine yeast	3 mL

1 1/2 lb (750 g)

2 tbsp	granulated sugar	30 mL
1 1/2 tsp	salt	7 mL
2	large eggs, beaten	2
1/2 cup	unsalted butter, softened	125 mL
1/3 cup	lukewarm buttermilk (see tip, at left)	75 mL
3 tbsp	lukewarm water	45 mL
3 cups	bread flour	750 mL
1 tsp	instant or bread machine yeast	5 mL

2 lb (1 kg)

3 tbsp	granulated sugar	45 mL
2 tsp	salt	10 mL
3	large eggs, beaten	3
2/3 cup	unsalted butter, softened	150 mL
1/2 cup	lukewarm buttermilk (see tip, at left)	125 mL
1/4 cup	lukewarm water	60 mL
4 cups	bread flour	1 L
1 1/2 tsp	instant or bread machine yeast	7 mL

3 lb (1.5 kg)

1/4 cup	granulated sugar	60 mL
1 1/2 tsp	salt	7 mL
4	large eggs, beaten	4
1/2 cup	unsalted butter, softened	125 mL
2/3 cup	lukewarm buttermilk (see tip, at left)	150 mL
1/3 cup	lukewarm water	75 mL
4 1/2 cups	bread flour	1.125 L
1 1/2 tsp	instant or bread machine yeast	7 mL

1. Add sugar, salt, eggs, butter, buttermilk and water to the bread pan. Spoon flour on top of liquid. Add yeast.

2. Select the Basic/White or Sweet cycle and the Light Crust setting and press Start.

Tips

When making the smallest loaf allowed by your machine, check the dough a few minutes after kneading starts to make sure the ingredients are incorporated. You may need to help the machine along by using a rubber spatula to scrape the corners of the pan.

If your dough does not form a ball during the first few minutes of kneading, do one of two things: if the dough looks dry and crumbly, add 1 tbsp (15 mL) water at 1-minute intervals until the dough forms a ball; if the dough looks wet, add 1 tbsp (15 mL) bread flour at 1-minute intervals until the dough forms a ball.

Rich, eggy breads like this one make great French toast and airy bread puddings.

Rosemary Brioche

Add dried rosemary with the yeast as follows:

Loaf Size	Amount of Rosemary
1 lb (500 g)	1 tsp (5 mL)
1½ lb (750 g)	1½ tsp (7 mL)
2 lb (1 kg)	2 tsp (10 mL)
3 lb (1.5 kg)	2½ tsp (12 mL)

Pullman Loaf

Also known by the French term *pain de mie*, this bread is meant for sandwiches: it's dense, uniformly shaped and yeasty good. You can make it completely in the bread machine if your bread machine has a 2-lb (1 kg) capacity (see page 43). But to achieve the uniform shape and lighter crust of a classic Pullman loaf, you need to use the Dough cycle and form it by hand, as described at right. You then bake it in a Pullman loaf pan — a 12- by 4-inch (30 by 10 cm) metal pan with a lid that slides on. I've also used a ceramic pâté pan of the same dimensions, and that worked great too.

Oven-Baked Pullman Loaf

¼ cup	instant skim milk powder	60 mL
2 tsp	salt	10 mL
1½ cups	lukewarm water (see tip, at right)	375 mL
6 tbsp	unsalted butter, softened	90 mL
2 tsp	liquid honey	10 mL
4 cups	bread flour	1 L
2 tsp	instant or bread machine yeast	10 mL

1. Add milk powder, salt, water, butter and honey to the bread pan. Spoon flour on top of liquid. Add yeast.

2. Select the Dough cycle and press Start.

3. Oil the inside of loaf pan and lid. When the cycle is finished, transfer dough to a floured surface and punch down gently. Roll out or pat into a 10- by 8-inch (50 by 40 cm) rectangle. Fold into thirds, like folding a business letter. Rotate a quarter turn, then use your hands to press and roll dough into a 12- by 4-inch (30 by 10 cm) cylinder. Place in prepared loaf pan, cover with a clean towel and let rise in a warm, draft-free place for 30 to 45 minutes or until almost to the top of the pan. Meanwhile, preheat oven to 425°F (220°C).

4. Remove towel and place lid on pan. Bake for 20 minutes. Remove lid and bake for 20 to 23 minutes or risen and browned and an instant-read thermometer inserted in the center registers 190°F (90°C). Remove from pan and let cool on a wire rack.

Equipment

- Bread machine with a 2-lb (1 kg) capacity

Tips

Ideally, the water should be between 86°F and 95°F (30°C and 35°C), the temperature range in which yeast is most active. Warm it in the microwave or in a saucepan on the stove, and check the temperature with an instant-read thermometer.

Bread machine breads tend to be best within a day or two of baking, but if you want to store them for longer, wrap and freeze loaves or slices in labeled and dated freezer-proof packages for up to 3 months. Cut large loaves to fit freezer storage bags.

Bread Machine Pullman Loaf

¼ cup	instant skim milk powder	60 mL
2 tsp	salt	10 mL
1½ cups	lukewarm water (see tip, at left)	375 mL
6 tbsp	unsalted butter, softened	90 mL
2 tsp	liquid honey	10 mL
4 cups	bread flour	1 L
1 tsp	instant or bread machine yeast	5 mL

1. Add milk powder, salt, water, butter and honey to the bread pan. Spoon flour on top of liquid. Add yeast.

2. Select the Basic/White cycle and the Light Crust setting and press Start.

> ### Black Pepper Pullman Loaf
> Add 4 tsp (20 mL) coarsely ground black pepper with the flour.

Acadian Buckwheat Bread

Makes 1 loaf

Acadians — French settlers in Nova Scotia, Prince Edward Island, New Brunswick, Maine and, later, Louisiana — brought with them a love of buckwheat, which grows well in colder climates. Because buckwheat has no gluten, you only use a little in this recipe to add robust flavor, color and texture. Acadians love this bread with maple syrup or molasses, but it's also delicious with ham and cheese (think of the filling in a buckwheat crêpe).

Tip

When you're making the 1-lb (500 g) loaf, if you can't find small eggs, beat 1 large egg until blended, then measure 2 tbsp + 1 tsp (35 mL) to equal the volume of 1 small egg, reserving any remaining egg for another use.

1 lb (500 g)

1 tsp	salt	5 mL
1	small egg, beaten	1
¾ cup	lukewarm water (see tip, page 43)	175 mL
3 tbsp	liquid honey or pure maple syrup	45 mL
2 tsp	vegetable oil	10 mL
1¾ cups	bread flour	425 mL
1 cup	buckwheat flour	250 mL
1¼ tsp	instant or bread machine yeast	6 mL

1½ lb (750 g)

1¼ tsp	salt	6 mL
1	large egg, beaten	1
1 cup	lukewarm water (see tip, page 43)	250 mL
3 tbsp	liquid honey or pure maple syrup	45 mL
1 tbsp	vegetable oil	15 mL
2¼ cups	bread flour	550 mL
1⅓ cups	buckwheat flour	325 mL
1½ tsp	instant or bread machine yeast	7 mL

2 lb (1 kg)

1½ tsp	salt	7 mL
1	large egg, beaten	1
1 cup	lukewarm water (see tip, page 43)	250 mL
⅓ cup	liquid honey or pure maple syrup	75 mL
5 tsp	vegetable oil	25 mL
2½ cups	bread flour	625 mL
1½ cups	buckwheat flour	375 mL
1¾ tsp	instant or bread machine yeast	8 mL

3 lb (1 kg)

2 tsp	salt	10 mL
2	large eggs, beaten	2
1¼ cups	lukewarm water (see tip, page 43)	300 mL
½ cup	liquid honey or pure maple syrup	125 mL
2 tbsp	vegetable oil	30 mL
4 cups	bread flour	1 L
1⅔ cups	buckwheat flour	400 mL
1¾ tsp	instant or bread machine yeast	8 mL

Tips

You can find buckwheat flour in bulk at better grocery and health food stores. It's available in both a light and a dark version. The light flour is more refined, while the dark flour contains the whole grain, making it a more nutritious choice and better suited to this recipe.

When making the smallest loaf allowed by your machine, check the dough a few minutes after kneading starts to make sure the ingredients are incorporated. You may need to help the machine along by using a rubber spatula to scrape the corners of the pan.

If your dough does not form a ball during the first few minutes of kneading, do one of two things: if the dough looks dry and crumbly, add 1 tbsp (15 mL) water at 1-minute intervals until the dough forms a ball; if the dough looks wet, add 1 tbsp (15 mL) bread flour at 1-minute intervals until the dough forms a ball.

1. Add salt, egg(s), water, honey and oil to the bread pan. Spoon bread flour and buckwheat flour on top of liquid. Add yeast.

2. Select the Basic/White cycle and press Start.

> ### Molasses Buckwheat Bread
> Replace the honey with light (fancy) molasses for a stronger flavor.

Buttermilk Honey Oatmeal Bread

Makes 1 loaf

This easy bread has the yeasty, homemade flavor that is the essence of home-baked bread. With just enough rolled oats to add a little texture and fiber, it's a good transition loaf from white to whole-grain bread. You can either use regular buttermilk or reconstitute powdered buttermilk to equal the amount needed in this recipe.

Tips

Ideally, the buttermilk and water should be between 86°F and 95°F (30°C and 35°C), the temperature range in which yeast is most active. Warm them in the microwave or in a saucepan on the stove, and check the temperature with an instant-read thermometer.

Medium-flavored honeys, such as clover or wildflower, are best for artisan bread machine doughs.

1 lb (500 g)

¾ tsp	salt	3 mL
½ cup	lukewarm buttermilk (see tip, at left)	125 mL
½ cup	lukewarm water	125 mL
1½ tbsp	vegetable oil	22 mL
1½ tbsp	liquid honey	22 mL
2½ cups	bread flour	625 mL
¼ cup	large-flake (old-fashioned) rolled oats	60 mL
¾ tsp	instant or bread machine yeast	3 mL

1½ lb (750 g)

1 tsp	salt	5 mL
⅔ cup	lukewarm buttermilk (see tip, at left)	150 mL
½ cup	lukewarm water	125 mL
2 tbsp	vegetable oil	30 mL
2 tbsp	liquid honey	30 mL
3 cups	bread flour	750 mL
⅓ cup	large-flake (old-fashioned) rolled oats	75 mL
¾ tsp	instant or bread machine yeast	3 mL

2 lb (1 kg)

1½ tsp	salt	7 mL
1 cup	lukewarm buttermilk (see tip, at left)	250 mL
½ cup	lukewarm water	125 mL
3 tbsp	vegetable oil	45 mL
3 tbsp	liquid honey	45 mL
3¾ cups	bread flour	925 mL
½ cup	large-flake (old-fashioned) rolled oats	125 mL
¾ tsp	instant or bread machine yeast	3 mL

3 lb (1.5 kg)

2 tsp	salt	10 mL
1 cup	lukewarm buttermilk (see tip, at left)	250 mL
⅔ cup	lukewarm water	150 mL
¼ cup	vegetable oil	60 mL
¼ cup	liquid honey	60 mL
4½ cups	bread flour	1.125 L
¾ cup	large-flake (old-fashioned) rolled oats	175 mL
¾ tsp	instant or bread machine yeast	3 mL

Tips

When making the smallest loaf allowed by your machine, check the dough a few minutes after kneading starts to make sure the ingredients are incorporated. You may need to help the machine along by using a rubber spatula to scrape the corners of the pan.

If your dough does not form a ball during the first few minutes of kneading, do one of two things: if the dough looks dry and crumbly, add 1 tbsp (15 mL) water at 1-minute intervals until the dough forms a ball; if the dough looks wet, add 1 tbsp (15 mL) bread flour at 1-minute intervals until the dough forms a ball.

1. Add salt, buttermilk, water, oil and honey to the bread pan. Spoon flour and oats on top of liquid. Add yeast.

2. Select the Basic/White cycle and press Start.

Honey Oatmeal Seed Bread

Add unsalted roasted sunflower seeds, toasted green pumpkin seeds (pepitas) or millet, or a combination, as follows:

Loaf Size	Amount of Seeds
1 lb (500 g)	⅓ cup (75 mL)
1½ lb (750 g)	½ cup (125 mL)
2 lb (1 kg)	⅔ cup (150 mL)
3 lb (1.5 kg)	¾ cup (175 mL)

Place seeds in the dispenser or add at the "add ingredient" or "mix in" signal.

Sour Cream Bread

Rich, golden and fine-textured from the sour cream, this bread has a pleasant tang and a soft crumb. It pairs well with meatloaf or barbecued beef for a savory sandwich. Try using the Light Crust setting so the loaf will bake to a pale gold.

Tips

Full-fat sour cream works best in this recipe, adding richness, moisture and golden color.

For the best results, let the sour cream warm to room temperature before adding it to the bread pan. Cold ingredients will decrease the activity of the yeast.

1 lb (500 g)

1½ tbsp	granulated sugar	22 mL
1 tsp	salt	5 mL
¾ cup	sour cream	175 mL
2 tbsp	water	30 mL
2 cups	bread flour	500 mL
1¼ tsp	instant or bread machine yeast	6 mL
¼ tsp	baking soda	1 mL

1½ lb (750 g)

2 tbsp	granulated sugar	30 mL
1½ tsp	salt	7 mL
1 cup + 2 tbsp	sour cream	280 mL
3 tbsp	water	45 mL
3 cups	bread flour	750 mL
1¼ tsp	instant or bread machine yeast	6 mL
½ tsp	baking soda	2 mL

2 lb (1 kg)

3 tbsp	granulated sugar	45 mL
1½ tsp	salt	7 mL
1½ cups	sour cream	375 mL
¼ cup	water	60 mL
4 cups	bread flour	1 L
1¾ tsp	instant or bread machine yeast	8 mL
½ tsp	baking soda	2 mL

3 lb (1.5 kg)

⅓ cup	granulated sugar	75 mL
2 tsp	salt	10 mL
2 cups	sour cream	500 mL
6 tbsp	water	90 mL
5½ cups	bread flour	1.375 L
1¼ tsp	instant or bread machine yeast	6 mL
¾ tsp	baking soda	3 mL

1. Add sugar, salt, sour cream and water to the bread pan. Spoon flour on top of liquid. Add yeast and baking soda.

2. Select the Basic/White cycle and press Start.

Tips

When making the smallest loaf allowed by your machine, check the dough a few minutes after kneading starts to make sure the ingredients are incorporated. You may need to help the machine along by using a rubber spatula to scrape the corners of the pan.

If your dough does not form a ball during the first few minutes of kneading, do one of two things: if the dough looks dry and crumbly, add 1 tbsp (15 mL) water at 1-minute intervals until the dough forms a ball; if the dough looks wet, add 1 tbsp (15 mL) bread flour at 1-minute intervals until the dough forms a ball.

Herbed Sour Cream Bread

Add dried basil, dried rosemary or dried thyme, or a combination, with the yeast as follows:

Loaf Size	Amount of Herbs
1 lb (500 g)	1 tsp (5 mL)
1½ lb (750 g)	1½ tsp (7 mL)
2 lb (1 kg)	2 tsp (10 mL)
3 lb (1.5 kg)	1 tbsp (15 mL)

Whole-Grain Breads

T RADITIONAL EUROPEAN BREADS, such as German vollkornbrot (dark wheat with cooked wheat berries) and pumpernickel bread (coarse wheat and rye), are compact, heavy and dense. That style of bread is not suited to the bread machine. However, it makes delicious whole-grain breads that rise high and have a light, airy texture.

Whole-grain flours have less gluten than bread flour because the outer bran and inner germ of the whole grain displace some of the gluten-bearing middle part of the kernel (the endosperm) in the flour. To make up for the reduced amount of gluten, you have two choices: you can use a combination of high-gluten bread and whole-grain flours; or, for 100% whole-grain bread, you can pair the whole-grain flour with a dough improver or enhancer and vital wheat gluten. You'll see both methods in use in the recipes in this chapter.

High-Gluten Whole-Grain Flours

Atta (Indian whole wheat flour, used for roti, naan and chapati)

Whole wheat flour

White whole wheat flour (milled from an albino strain of hard winter wheat)

Graham flour (coarsely ground whole wheat)

Semolina flour (coarsely ground and granular wheat usually used for pasta)

Durum wheat flour (available packaged, but you can also buy hard spring wheat berries and grind your own flour)

Sprouted whole-grain hard winter wheat flour

No-Gluten or Low-Gluten Whole-Grain Flours

Amaranth flour

Buckwheat flour

Chickpea (garbanzo bean) flour

Corn flour

Millet flour

Oat flour

Quinoa flour

Rice flour (glutinous or brown)

Rye flour

Soy flour

Spelt flour

Tapioca flour

Teff flour

Not the Same Old Grind

Freshly ground whole wheat flour is a revelation — it has a much richer flavor than its pale, all-purpose cousin or even packaged whole wheat flour. Home bakers who want the freshest flours possible might want to invest in an electric grain mill that can grind wheat and rye berries, barley, soybeans and quinoa into coarse, medium or fine flours. Available through mail order sources, online or at health food stores, electric grain mills are easy to use; the process is much like grinding your own coffee at the grocery store.

An electric grain mill will convert:

- 3 cups (750 mL) whole-grain berries or kernels to 7 cups (1.75 L) finely ground flour;
- 3 cups (750 mL) small dried beans or tiny grains to 7 to $7\frac{1}{4}$ cups (1.75 to 1.8 L) finely ground flour.

Using an electric mill, it will take you about 8 minutes to grind enough flour to make three loaves of whole wheat bread. Freeze any leftover flour, as the oil in the wheat germ can cause it to spoil quickly.

100% Whole Wheat Bread

Makes 1 loaf

Delay Timer

Now that whole wheat berries are available in the bulk aisle and electric grain mills are so quiet and efficient, city folk can bake bread as delicious as that made on the farm, as Jane Pigue of Greenwood, Missouri, learned. "I wanted the goodness of whole grains, but I wanted a light loaf with a tender crumb and a high rise," she says. Her bread is so delicious you won't believe it's good for you. The dough stays batter-like, moist and sticky, and rises as it bakes.

Tip

Ideally, the water should be between 86°F and 95°F (30°C and 35°C), the temperature range in which yeast is most active. Warm it in the microwave or in a saucepan on the stove, and check the temperature with an instant-read thermometer.

1 lb (500 g)

1 tsp	salt	5 mL
2/3 cup	lukewarm water (see tip, at left)	150 mL
2 tbsp	liquid honey or agave syrup	30 mL
1 tbsp	vegetable oil	15 mL
2 cups	finely ground whole wheat flour	500 mL
1 tsp	Artisan Dough Enhancer (page 278) or packaged dough enhancer	5 mL
1 tsp	vital wheat gluten	5 mL
1 1/4 tsp	instant or bread machine yeast	6 mL

1 1/2 lb (750 g)

1 1/2 tsp	salt	7 mL
1 cup	lukewarm water (see tip, at left)	250 mL
3 tbsp	liquid honey or agave syrup	45 mL
1 1/2 tbsp	vegetable oil	22 mL
2 2/3 cups	finely ground whole wheat flour	650 mL
2 tsp	Artisan Dough Enhancer (page 278) or packaged dough enhancer	10 mL
1 tsp	vital wheat gluten	5 mL
1 1/2 tsp	instant or bread machine yeast	7 mL

2 lb (1 kg)

2 tsp	salt	10 mL
1 1/2 cups	lukewarm water (see tip, at left)	375 mL
1/4 cup	liquid honey or agave syrup	60 mL
2 1/2 tbsp	vegetable oil	37 mL
3 2/3 cups	finely ground whole wheat flour	900 mL
1 tbsp	Artisan Dough Enhancer (page 278) or packaged dough enhancer	15 mL
2 tsp	vital wheat gluten	10 mL
1 1/2 tsp	instant or bread machine yeast	7 mL

Tips

Three cups (750 mL) whole wheat berries (available in bulk at health food stores) will finely grind to make 7 cups (1.75 L) whole wheat flour. Use some for this recipe and freeze the rest in an airtight container for up to 12 months.

When making the smallest loaf allowed by your machine, check the dough a few minutes after kneading starts to make sure the ingredients are incorporated. You may need to help the machine along by using a rubber spatula to scrape the corners of the pan.

If your dough does not form a ball during the first few minutes of kneading, do one of two things: if the dough looks dry and crumbly, add 1 tbsp (15 mL) water at 1-minute intervals until the dough forms a ball; if the dough looks wet, add 1 tbsp (15 mL) whole wheat flour at 1-minute intervals until the dough forms a ball.

3 lb (1.5 kg)

2¼ tsp	salt	11 mL
2 cups + 2 tbsp	lukewarm water (see tip, page 52)	530 mL
6 tbsp	liquid honey or agave syrup	90 mL
⅓ cup	vegetable oil	75 mL
5½ cups	finely ground whole wheat flour	1.375 L
1 tbsp	Artisan Dough Enhancer (page 278) or packaged dough enhancer	15 mL
1 tbsp	vital wheat gluten	15 mL
1¾ tsp	instant or bread machine yeast	8 mL

1. Add salt, water, honey and oil to the bread pan. Spoon flour on top of liquid. Add dough enhancer, wheat gluten and yeast.

2. Select the Whole Wheat cycle and press Start.

Wildflower Honey and White Whole Wheat Bread

Made in summer, when bees visit wildflowers in bloom, wildflower honey has a true honey flavor without being too sweet. White whole wheat flour is milled from an albino variety of hard winter wheat that has a milder flavor and a lighter color, so it doesn't have to be mixed with all-purpose or bread flour to produce a delicious loaf. Together, these ingredients help yield a nutty-tasting wheat bread with a moist, tender crumb and a touch of sweetness — a great way to introduce your family to whole-grain breads. The dough starts out a little moist but rounds out as the flour absorbs the liquid, and it rises as it bakes. The dough enhancer and vital wheat gluten help produce a high-rising, light-textured 100% whole wheat loaf.

1 lb (500 g)		
1 tsp	salt	5 mL
2/3 cup	lukewarm water (see tip, page 52)	150 mL
1/3 cup	liquid wildflower or other amber honey	75 mL
2 tbsp	vegetable oil	30 mL
2 cups	white whole wheat flour	500 mL
1 1/2 tsp	Artisan Dough Enhancer (page 278) or packaged dough enhancer	7 mL
1 1/2 tsp	vital wheat gluten	7 mL
1 1/2 tsp	instant or bread machine yeast	7 mL

1 1/2 lb (750 g)		
1 1/2 tsp	salt	7 mL
1 cup	lukewarm water (see tip, page 52)	250 mL
1/2 cup	liquid wildflower or other amber honey	125 mL
3 tbsp	vegetable oil	45 mL
3 cups	white whole wheat flour	750 mL
2 tsp	Artisan Dough Enhancer (page 278) or packaged dough enhancer	10 mL
2 tsp	vital wheat gluten	10 mL
1 1/2 tsp	instant or bread machine yeast	7 mL

2 lb (1 kg)		
2 tsp	salt	10 mL
1 cup + 2 tbsp	lukewarm water (see tip, page 52)	280 mL
1/2 cup + 1 tbsp	liquid wildflower or other amber honey	140 mL
1/4 cup	vegetable oil	60 mL
3 2/3 cups	white whole wheat flour	900 mL
1 tbsp	Artisan Dough Enhancer (page 278) or packaged dough enhancer	15 mL
2 tsp	vital wheat gluten	10 mL
1 3/4 tsp	instant or bread machine yeast	8 mL

Tips

Medium-flavored honeys, such as wildflower and clover, balance out the heartiness of the whole wheat and add moisture to the bread.

You can use regular whole wheat flour in place of the white whole wheat.

If your dough does not form a ball during the first few minutes of kneading, do one of two things: if the dough looks dry and crumbly, add 1 tbsp (15 mL) water at 1-minute intervals until the dough forms a ball; if the dough looks wet, add 1 tbsp (15 mL) white whole wheat flour at 1-minute intervals until the dough forms a ball.

3 lb (1.5 kg)

2¼ tsp	salt	11 mL
1½ cups	lukewarm water (see tip, page 52)	375 mL
⅔ cup	liquid wildflower or other amber honey	150 mL
6 tbsp	vegetable oil	90 mL
5 cups	white whole wheat flour	1.25 L
1½ tbsp	Artisan Dough Enhancer (page 278) or packaged dough enhancer	22 mL
1½ tbsp	vital wheat gluten	22 mL
2¼ tsp	instant or bread machine yeast	11 mL

1. Add salt, water, honey and oil to the bread pan. Spoon flour on top of liquid. Add dough enhancer, wheat gluten and yeast.

2. Select the Whole Wheat cycle and press Start.

English Granary-Style Bread

When I was a college student in England for a semester, and then lived there again in the 1980s, I enjoyed making toast or sandwiches from an English Granary, or Hovis, loaf. I also discovered the English love of malty flavors — even their corn flakes taste maltier than ours. The proprietary English Granary loaf is made from a blend of bread flour and malted whole-grain flour. The topping is usually rolled oats or wheat flakes and stone-ground wheat. I've approximated the texture and flavor with ingredients available in North America, including malted milk powder and malt syrup, which you can find in the grocery aisles devoted to hot beverages and health food.

Tip

Ideally, the milk should be between 86°F and 95°F (30°C and 35°C), the temperature range in which yeast is most active. Warm it in the microwave or in a saucepan on the stove, and check the temperature with an instant-read thermometer.

1 lb (500 g)

1 tsp	salt	5 mL
1	large egg yolk, beaten	1
⅔ cup	lukewarm milk (see tip, at left)	150 mL
2 tbsp	malt syrup	30 mL
1½ tbsp	vegetable oil	22 mL
1¼ cups	bread flour	300 mL
¾ cup	Irish whole-meal or whole wheat flour	175 mL
¼ cup	malted milk powder	60 mL
2 tbsp	wheat flakes or large-flake (old-fashioned) rolled oats	30 mL
1½ tsp	instant or bread machine yeast	7 mL

Topping

1	large egg white, beaten	1
2 tsp	large-flake (old-fashioned) rolled oats	10 mL
2 tsp	whole wheat flour, preferably stone-ground	10 mL

1½ lb (750 g)

1½ tsp	salt	7 mL
1	large egg, beaten	1
¾ cup	lukewarm milk (see tip, at left)	175 mL
3 tbsp	malt syrup	45 mL
2 tbsp	vegetable oil	30 mL
1⅓ cups	bread flour	325 mL
1 cup + 2 tbsp	Irish whole-meal or whole wheat flour	280 mL
⅓ cup	malted milk powder	75 mL
3 tbsp	wheat flakes or large-flake (old-fashioned) rolled oats	45 mL
2 tsp	instant or bread machine yeast	10 mL

Topping

1	large egg white, beaten	1
1 tbsp	large-flake (old-fashioned) rolled oats	15 mL
1 tbsp	whole wheat flour, preferably stone-ground	15 mL

2 lb (1 kg)

2 tsp	salt	10 mL
1	large egg, beaten	1
1 cup	lukewarm milk (see tip, at left)	250 mL
¼ cup	malt syrup	60 mL
2½ tbsp	vegetable oil	37 mL
2 cups	bread flour	500 mL

Tips

If your bread machine doesn't have a Pause button, simply raise the lid, brush with egg white and sprinkle with oats and flour, then close the lid again.

Egg white wash adds a clear shine to the loaf and helps toppings stick to the crust.

This dark and malty-flavored bread tastes wonderful paired with aged Cheddar and crisp apple wedges.

1 1/3 cups	Irish whole-meal or whole wheat flour	325 mL
1/2 cup	malted milk powder	125 mL
1/4 cup	wheat flakes or large-flake (old-fashioned) rolled oats	60 mL
2 tsp	instant or bread machine yeast	10 mL

Topping

1	large egg white, beaten	1
1 tbsp	large-flake (old-fashioned) rolled oats	15 mL
1 tbsp	whole wheat flour, preferably stone-ground	15 mL

3 lb (1.5 kg)

2 1/2 tsp	salt	12 mL
2	large eggs, beaten	2
1 1/3 cups	lukewarm milk (see tip, page 56)	325 mL
6 tbsp	malt syrup	90 mL
3 tbsp	vegetable oil	45 mL
3 cups	bread flour	750 mL
1 1/2 cups	Irish whole-meal or whole wheat flour	375 mL
1/2 cup	malted milk powder	125 mL
1/3 cup	wheat flakes or large-flake (old-fashioned) rolled oats	75 mL
2 1/4 tsp	instant or bread machine yeast	11 mL

Topping

1	large egg white, beaten	1
1 tbsp	large-flake (old-fashioned) rolled oats	15 mL
1 tbsp	whole wheat flour, preferably stone-ground	15 mL

1. Add salt, egg(s), milk, malt syrup and oil to the bread pan. Spoon bread flour, whole-meal flour, malted milk powder and wheat flakes on top of liquid. Add yeast.

2. Select the Whole Wheat cycle and press Start.

3. *Topping:* At the start of the final rise (see "Timing It Right," page 13), press Pause. Raise the lid, brush the top of the loaf with egg white and sprinkle with oats and flour. Close the lid and press Start to continue the cycle.

Cracked Wheat Bread

Makes 1 loaf

Cracked wheat adds great texture and a toasty flavor to this whole-grain bread. Use it as a sandwich bread when you want a contrast to smooth fillings such as cheese, sliced meats or spreads.

Tips

Cracked wheat, as dry cereal or in bulk, is available at larger grocery stores and at health food stores. If you can't find it, try your favorite cracked grain cereal blend, such as Red River, Hodgson Mill or Bob's Red Mill.

Ideally, the buttermilk should be between 86°F and 95°F (30°C and 35°C), the temperature range in which yeast is most active. Warm it in the microwave or in a saucepan on the stove, and check the temperature with an instant-read thermometer.

1 lb (500 g)

¼ cup	cracked wheat	60 mL
¼ cup	water	60 mL
⅔ cup	lukewarm buttermilk (see tip, at left)	150 mL
1 tsp	salt	5 mL
1½ tbsp	liquid honey	22 mL
1 tbsp	vegetable oil	15 mL
1 cup	Irish whole-meal or whole wheat flour	250 mL
⅔ cup	bread flour	150 mL
1½ tsp	vital wheat gluten	7 mL
¾ tsp	instant or bread machine yeast	3 mL

1½ lb (750 g)

⅓ cup	cracked wheat	75 mL
⅓ cup	water	75 mL
¾ cup	lukewarm buttermilk (see tip, at left)	175 mL
1½ tsp	salt	7 mL
2 tbsp	liquid honey	30 mL
1½ tbsp	vegetable oil	22 mL
1 cup	Irish whole-meal or whole wheat flour	250 mL
1 cup	bread flour	250 mL
1 tsp	vital wheat gluten	5 mL
1 tsp	instant or bread machine yeast	5 mL

2 lb (1 kg)

½ cup	cracked wheat	125 mL
½ cup	water	125 mL
1¼ cups	lukewarm buttermilk (see tip, at left)	300 mL
2 tsp	salt	10 mL
2½ tbsp	liquid honey	37 mL
2 tbsp	vegetable oil	30 mL
1⅔ cups	Irish whole-meal or whole wheat flour	400 mL
1½ cups	bread flour	375 mL
1 tsp	vital wheat gluten	5 mL
1 tsp	instant or bread machine yeast	5 mL

If your dough does not form a ball during the first few minutes of kneading, do one of two things: if the dough looks dry and crumbly, add 1 tbsp (15 mL) water at 1-minute intervals until the dough forms a ball; if the dough looks wet, add 1 tbsp (15 mL) whole-meal flour at 1-minute intervals until the dough forms a ball.

Bread machine breads tend to be best within a day or two of baking, but if you want to store them for longer, wrap and freeze loaves or slices in labeled and dated freezer-proof packages for up to 3 months. Cut large loaves to fit freezer storage bags.

3 lb (1.5 g)

⅔ cup	cracked wheat	150 mL
1¼ cups	water	300 mL
1⅓ cups	lukewarm buttermilk (see tip, page 58)	325 mL
2¾ tsp	salt	13 mL
3 tbsp	liquid honey	45 mL
3 tbsp	vegetable oil	45 mL
2½ cups	Irish whole-meal or whole wheat flour	625 mL
2¼ cups	bread flour	550 mL
1 tsp	vital wheat gluten	5 mL
¾ tsp	instant or bread machine yeast	3 mL

1. In a saucepan, combine cracked wheat and water. Bring to a boil over medium-high heat. Remove from heat and let stand for about 10 minutes or until wheat is slightly softened. Transfer to the bread pan and stir in buttermilk. If necessary, let cool to lukewarm (between 86°F and 95°F/30°C and 35°C).

2. Add salt, honey and oil to the bread pan. Spoon whole-meal flour and bread flour on top of liquid. Add wheat gluten and yeast.

3. Select the Whole Wheat cycle and press Start.

Honey Wheat Berry Bread

This recipe is great in the winter months, when you don't mind heating up the kitchen to make something substantial and soul-satisfying. Wheat berries — whole kernels of wheat — are available where bulk foods and natural foods are sold. Use hard red winter wheat berries for the best results. This recipe produces a hearty loaf with an enhanced texture from the softened wheat berries.

Tip

Ideally, the buttermilk should be between 86°F and 95°F (30°C and 35°C), the temperature range in which yeast is most active. Warm it in the microwave or in a saucepan on the stove, and check the temperature with an instant-read thermometer.

1 lb (500 g)

1 tsp	salt	5 mL
2/3 cup	lukewarm buttermilk (see tip, at left)	150 mL
3 tbsp	liquid wildflower or other medium-colored honey	45 mL
1 tbsp	vegetable oil	15 mL
1 1/3 cups	bread flour	325 mL
1/2 cup	whole wheat flour	125 mL
1/3 cup	cooked wheat berries	75 mL
1 1/4 tsp	instant or bread machine yeast	6 mL

1 1/2 lb (750 g)

1 1/2 tsp	salt	7 mL
1 cup	lukewarm buttermilk (see tip, at left)	250 mL
1/4 cup	liquid wildflower or other medium-colored honey	60 mL
2 tbsp	vegetable oil	30 mL
2 cups	bread flour	500 mL
1 cup	whole wheat flour	250 mL
1/2 cup	cooked wheat berries	125 mL
1 1/2 tsp	instant or bread machine yeast	7 mL

2 lb (1 kg)

2 tsp	salt	10 mL
1 1/3 cups	lukewarm buttermilk (see tip, at left)	325 mL
5 tbsp	wildflower or other medium-colored honey	75 mL
2 tbsp	vegetable oil	30 mL
2 1/2 cups	bread flour	625 mL
1 1/4 cups	whole wheat flour	300 mL
2/3 cup	cooked wheat berries	150 mL
1 1/4 tsp	instant or bread machine yeast	6 mL

3 lb (1.5 kg)

2 1/4 tsp	salt	11 mL
1 3/4 cups	lukewarm buttermilk (see tip, at left)	425 mL
6 tbsp	wildflower or other medium-colored honey	90 mL
3 tbsp	vegetable oil	45 mL
3 1/2 cups	bread flour	875 mL
1 3/4 cups	whole wheat flour	425 mL
3/4 cup	cooked wheat berries	175 mL
3/4 tsp	instant or bread machine yeast	3 mL

Tips

If your dough does not form a ball during the first few minutes of kneading, do one of two things: if the dough looks dry and crumbly, add 1 tbsp (15 mL) water at 1-minute intervals until the dough forms a ball; if the dough looks wet, add 1 tbsp (15 mL) bread flour at 1-minute intervals until the dough forms a ball.

To cook wheat berries, use about half the volume of dry wheat berries to make the volume of cooked for your recipe. Rinse berries in a sieve and drain. Place in a saucepan with four times the volume of cold water. Bring to a boil over high heat; cover, reduce heat to low and simmer for 45 to 60 minutes or until wheat berries are tender. Drain and let cool.

1. Add salt, buttermilk, honey and oil to the bread pan. Spoon bread flour and whole wheat flour on top of liquid. Add wheat berries and yeast.

2. Select the Basic/White or Whole Wheat cycle and press Start.

Honey Rye Berry Bread
Replace the wheat berries with rye berries.

Anadama Bread

This traditional dense, hearty bread from Gloucester, Massachusetts, has the old New England flavors of molasses and cornmeal. It gets texture as well from coarsely ground whole wheat flour. Today, this medium-brown, fiber-rich bread is valued as a toasting or sandwich bread.

Tip

If your dough does not form a ball during the first few minutes of kneading, do one of two things: if the dough looks dry and crumbly, add 1 tbsp (15 mL) water at 1-minute intervals until the dough forms a ball; if the dough looks wet, add 1 tbsp (15 mL) all-purpose flour at 1-minute intervals until the dough forms a ball.

1 lb (500 g)

3 tbsp	stone-ground yellow cornmeal	45 mL
½ tsp	salt	5 mL
¼ cup	fancy (light) molasses	60 mL
1 tbsp	vegetable oil	15 mL
¾ cup	boiling water	175 mL
1 cup	all-purpose flour	250 mL
1 cup	stone-ground or coarsely ground whole wheat flour	250 mL
1¼ tsp	instant or bread machine yeast	6 mL

1½ lb (750 g)

¼ cup	stone-ground yellow cornmeal	60 mL
1 tsp	salt	5 mL
6 tbsp	fancy (light) molasses	90 mL
1½ tbsp	vegetable oil	22 mL
1 cup	boiling water	250 mL
1½ cups	all-purpose flour	375 mL
1⅓ cups	stone-ground or coarsely ground whole wheat flour	325 mL
2 tsp	instant or bread machine yeast	10 mL

2 lb (1 kg)

⅓ cup	stone-ground yellow cornmeal	75 mL
1½ tsp	salt	7 mL
½ cup	light (fancy) molasses	125 mL
2 tbsp	vegetable oil	30 mL
1⅓ cups	boiling water	325 mL
2 cups	all-purpose flour	500 mL
1⅔ cups	stone-ground or coarsely ground whole wheat flour	400 mL
2 tsp	instant or bread machine yeast	10 mL

3 lb (1.5 kg)

½ cup	stone-ground yellow cornmeal	125 mL
2 tsp	salt	10 mL
⅔ cup	light (fancy) molasses	150 mL
2½ tbsp	vegetable oil	37 mL
1⅔ cups	boiling water	400 mL
2⅔ cups	all-purpose flour	650 mL
2 cups	stone-ground or coarsely ground whole wheat flour	500 mL
1¾ tsp	instant or bread machine yeast	8 mL

Tips

When making the smallest loaf allowed by your machine, check the dough a few minutes after kneading starts to make sure the ingredients are incorporated. You may need to help the machine along by using a rubber spatula to scrape the corners of the pan.

Enjoy this bread with an aged Cheddar cheese.

Bread machine breads tend to be best within a day or two of baking, but if you want to store them for longer, wrap and freeze loaves or slices in labeled and dated freezer-proof packages for up to 3 months. Cut large loaves to fit freezer storage bags.

1. Add cornmeal, salt, molasses and oil to the bread pan. Pour in boiling water, stir and let stand for 15 to 25 minutes or until cornmeal is softened and mixture has cooled to lukewarm (between 86°F and 95°F/30°C and 35°C).

2. Spoon all-purpose flour and whole wheat flour on top of liquid. Add yeast.

3. Select the Whole Wheat cycle and press Start.

Maple Anadama Bread
Substitute pure maple syrup for the molasses.

Mennonite Oatmeal Whole Wheat Bread

Makes 1 loaf

Home cooks of the conservative Mennonite culture are not averse to using an automatic bread machine to make their work easier. This delicious bread has full flavor and a surprisingly soft crumb, perfect for sandwiches.

If you like a little more texture, you can replace up to half of the quick-cooking rolled oats with large-flake (old-fashioned) rolled oats.

Tip

Ideally, the milk and water should be between 86°F and 95°F (30°C and 35°C), the temperature range in which yeast is most active. Warm them in the microwave or in a saucepan on the stove, and check the temperature with an instant-read thermometer.

1 lb (500 g)

2 tbsp	packed light or dark brown sugar	30 mL
1 tsp	salt	5 mL
½ cup	lukewarm milk (see tip, at left)	125 mL
¼ cup	lukewarm water	60 mL
2 tbsp	vegetable oil	30 mL
1½ cups	bread flour	375 mL
⅓ cup	whole wheat flour	75 mL
⅓ cup	quick-cooking rolled oats	75 mL
1½ tsp	instant or bread machine yeast	7 mL

1½ lb (750 g)

3 tbsp	packed light or dark brown sugar	45 mL
1½ tsp	salt	7 mL
½ cup	lukewarm milk (see tip, at left)	125 mL
½ cup	lukewarm water	125 mL
3 tbsp	vegetable oil	45 mL
2 cups	bread flour	500 mL
½ cup	whole wheat flour	125 mL
½ cup	quick-cooking rolled oats	125 mL
1½ tsp	instant or bread machine yeast	7 mL

2 lb (1 kg)

¼ cup	packed light or dark brown sugar	60 mL
2 tsp	salt	10 mL
¾ cup	lukewarm milk (see tip, at left)	175 mL
½ cup	lukewarm water	125 mL
¼ cup	vegetable oil	60 mL
2½ cups	bread flour	625 mL
⅔ cup	whole wheat flour	150 mL
⅔ cup	quick-cooking rolled oats	150 mL
1¾ tsp	instant or bread machine yeast	8 mL

continued after photos…

Braided Challah (page 38)

Nonna's Italian Bread (page 34)

100% Whole Wheat Cheddar Bread (page 72)

Great Plains Granola Bread
(page 68)

Tips

If your dough does not form a ball during the first few minutes of kneading, do one of two things: if the dough looks dry and crumbly, add 1 tbsp (15 mL) water at 1-minute intervals until the dough forms a ball; if the dough looks wet, add 1 tbsp (15 mL) whole wheat flour at 1-minute intervals until the dough forms a ball.

Bread machine breads tend to be best within a day or two of baking, but if you want to store them for longer, wrap and freeze loaves or slices in labeled and dated freezer-proof packages for up to 3 months. Cut large loaves to fit freezer storage bags.

3 lb (1.5 kg)

6 tbsp	packed light or dark brown sugar	90 mL
2½ tsp	salt	12 mL
1 cup	lukewarm milk (see tip, page 64)	250 mL
⅔ cup	lukewarm water	150 mL
6 tbsp	vegetable oil	90 mL
3 cups	bread flour	750 mL
1 cup	whole wheat flour	250 mL
1 cup	quick-cooking rolled oats	250 mL
1¾ tsp	instant or bread machine yeast	8 mL

1. Add sugar, salt, milk, water and oil to the bread pan. Spoon bread flour, whole wheat flour and oats on top of liquid. Add yeast.

2. Select the Whole Wheat cycle and press Start.

Flavored Mennonite Oatmeal Whole Wheat Bread

Substitute flavored instant oatmeal for the quick-cooking oats.

Oatmeal Honey Bread

This tender, mellow bread is a great choice for a ploughman's lunch — thick slices of bread, a little mayo, good sliced cheese and fresh garden tomatoes, with some imported cracked green olives and pepperoncini on the side.

Tip

Ideally, the water and milk should be between 86°F and 95°F (30°C and 35°C), the temperature range in which yeast is most active. Warm them in the microwave or in a saucepan on the stove, and check the temperature with an instant-read thermometer.

1 lb (500 g)

1 tbsp	instant skim milk powder	15 mL
1/4 tsp	salt	1 mL
1/2 cup	lukewarm water (see tip, at left)	125 mL
1/4 cup	lukewarm milk	60 mL
2 tbsp	liquid honey	30 mL
1 tbsp	vegetable oil	15 mL
1 3/4 cups	bread flour	425 mL
2/3 cup	large-flake (old-fashioned) or quick-cooking rolled oats	150 mL
1 tsp	instant or bread machine yeast	5 mL

1 1/2 lb (750 g)

1 1/2 tbsp	instant skim milk powder	22 mL
1/2 tsp	salt	2 mL
3/4 cup	lukewarm water (see tip, at left)	175 mL
1/4 cup	lukewarm milk	60 mL
3 tbsp	liquid honey	45 mL
1 1/2 tbsp	vegetable oil	22 mL
2 cups	bread flour	500 mL
1 cup	large-flake (old-fashioned) or quick-cooking rolled oats	250 mL
1 1/2 tsp	instant or bread machine yeast	7 mL

2 lb (1 kg)

2 tbsp	instant skim milk powder	30 mL
1 tsp	salt	5 mL
1 cup	lukewarm water (see tip, at left)	250 mL
1/2 cup	lukewarm milk	125 mL
1/4 cup	liquid honey	60 mL
2 tbsp	vegetable oil	30 mL
3 1/2 cups	bread flour	875 mL
1 1/3 cups	large-flake (old-fashioned) or quick-cooking rolled oats	325 mL
1 1/2 tsp	instant or bread machine yeast	7 mL

Tips

When making the smallest loaf allowed by your machine, check the dough a few minutes after kneading starts to make sure the ingredients are incorporated. You may need to help the machine along by using a rubber spatula to scrape the corners of the pan.

If your dough does not form a ball during the first few minutes of kneading, do one of two things: if the dough looks dry and crumbly, add 1 tbsp (15 mL) water at 1-minute intervals until the dough forms a ball; if the dough looks wet, add 1 tbsp (15 mL) bread flour at 1-minute intervals until the dough forms a ball.

3 lb (1.5 kg)

3 tbsp	instant skim milk powder	45 mL
1½ tsp	salt	7 mL
1¼ cups	lukewarm water (see tip, page 66)	300 mL
⅔ cup	lukewarm milk	150 mL
6 tbsp	liquid honey	90 mL
3 tbsp	vegetable oil	45 mL
4½ cups	bread flour	1.125 L
1⅔ cups	large-flake (old-fashioned) or quick-cooking rolled oats	400 mL
1 tsp	instant or bread machine yeast	5 mL

1. Add milk powder, salt, water, milk, honey and oil to the bread pan. Spoon flour and oats on top of liquid. Add yeast.

2. Select the Basic/White cycle and the Light Crust setting and press Start.

Great Plains Granola Bread

In the 1970s, Peavey flour mills in Minneapolis, Minnesota, milled a granola flour that made a wonderful, nutty-tasting bread. Today, you can make a terrific granola bread yourself by grinding granola in the food processor. This whole-grain loaf has wonderful texture.

Tips

You can vary the flavor of this bread by using different varieties of prepared granola.

You can use regular whole wheat flour in place of the white whole wheat flour.

If your machine has a dispenser, check the manual for the correct operating instructions.

1 lb (500 g)

2/3 cup	prepared granola	150 mL
2 tbsp	large-flake (old-fashioned) rolled oats	30 mL
2 tbsp	dried sour cherries or cranberries	30 mL
1/4 tsp	salt	2 mL
1 1/2 tbsp	vegetable oil	22 mL
4 tsp	liquid honey	20 mL
1 cup	boiling water	250 mL
2 cups	white whole wheat flour	500 mL
1 1/2 tsp	instant or bread machine yeast	7 mL
2/3 cup	raisins (optional)	150 mL
1/3 cup	sliced almonds, finely chopped nuts or unsweetened flaked coconut (optional)	75 mL

1 1/2 lb (750 g)

3/4 cup	prepared granola	175 mL
3 tbsp	large-flake (old-fashioned) rolled oats	45 mL
3 tbsp	dried sour cherries or cranberries	45 mL
1/2 tsp	salt	2 mL
2 tbsp	vegetable oil	30 mL
5 tsp	liquid honey	25 mL
1 1/4 cups	boiling water	300 mL
2 1/2 cups	white whole wheat flour	625 mL
1 1/2 tsp	instant or bread machine yeast	7 mL
3/4 cup	raisins (optional)	175 mL
1/3 cup	sliced almonds, finely chopped nuts or unsweetened flaked coconut (optional)	75 mL

2 lb (1.5 kg)

1 cup	prepared granola	250 mL
1/3 cup	large-flake (old-fashioned) rolled oats	75 mL
1/3 cup	dried sour cherries or cranberries	75 mL
1 tsp	salt	5 mL
3 tbsp	vegetable oil	45 mL
3 tbsp	liquid honey	45 mL
1 2/3 cups	boiling water	400 mL
3 cups	white whole wheat flour	750 mL
2 tsp	instant or bread machine yeast	10 mL
1 cup	raisins (optional)	250 mL
1/2 cup	sliced almonds, finely chopped nuts or unsweetened flaked coconut (optional)	125 mL

Tips

Use the Light Crust setting for a medium brown crust; some prepared granolas have a higher sugar content than others and can cause the bread to brown at darker crust settings.

If your dough does not form a ball during the first few minutes of kneading, do one of two things: if the dough looks dry and crumbly, add 1 tbsp (15 mL) water at 1-minute intervals until the dough forms a ball; if the dough looks wet, add 1 tbsp (15 mL) white whole wheat flour at 1-minute intervals until the dough forms a ball.

3 lb (1.5 kg)

1¼ cups	prepared granola	300 mL
½ cup	large-flake (old-fashioned) rolled oats	125 mL
½ cup	dried sour cherries or cranberries	125 mL
1½ tsp	salt	7 mL
¼ cup	vegetable oil	60 mL
3 tbsp	liquid honey	45 mL
1¾ cups	boiling water	425 mL
3¼ cups	white whole wheat flour	800 mL
2¼ tsp	instant or bread machine yeast	11 mL
1⅓ cups	raisins (optional)	325 mL
⅔ cup	sliced almonds, finely chopped nuts or unsweetened flaked coconut (optional)	150 mL

1. In food processor, pulse granola until it resembles coarse crumbs.

2. Add granola, oats, dried cherries, salt, oil and honey to the bread pan. Pour in boiling water, stir and let cool for 15 to 25 minutes or until mixture has cooled to lukewarm (between 86°F and 95°F/30°C and 35°C).

3. Spoon flour on top of liquid. Add yeast. Place raisins and almonds (if using) in the dispenser (or add at the "add ingredient" or "mix in" signal).

4. Select the Whole Wheat cycle and the Light Crust setting and press Start.

Seeds Galore Durum Wheat Bread

Durum flour, milled from hard white spring wheat, has a higher protein content than bread flour. When I found hard white spring wheat berries in bulk at my local grocery, ready to mill right there at the store, I decided to come up with a bread to celebrate my find — one with crunchy, flavorful seeds all the way through instead of just on the crust.

Tips

Ideally, the water should be between 86°F and 95°F (30°C and 35°C), the temperature range in which yeast is most active. Warm it in the microwave or in a saucepan on the stove, and check the temperature with an instant-read thermometer.

If durum wheat is not available in your area, use half additional bread flour and half semolina flour in its place.

1 lb (500 g)

4 tsp	instant skim milk powder	20 mL
¾ tsp	salt	3 mL
¾ cup + 1 tbsp	lukewarm water (see tip, at left)	190 mL
2 tsp	vegetable oil	10 mL
1⅓ cups	bread flour	325 mL
⅔ cup	freshly ground durum wheat flour	150 mL
2 tsp	sesame seeds or millet	10 mL
2 tsp	poppy or nigella seeds	10 mL
2 tsp	fennel or dill seeds	10 mL
1 tsp	instant or bread machine yeast	5 mL

1½ lb (750 g)

2 tbsp	instant skim milk powder	30 mL
1¼ tsp	salt	6 mL
1¼ cups	lukewarm water (see tip, at left)	300 mL
1 tbsp	vegetable oil	15 mL
2 cups	bread flour	500 mL
1 cup	freshly ground durum wheat flour	250 mL
1 tbsp	sesame seeds or millet	15 mL
1 tbsp	poppy or nigella seeds	15 mL
1 tbsp	fennel or dill seeds	15 mL
1¼ tsp	instant or bread machine yeast	6 mL

2 lb (1 kg)

2½ tbsp	instant skim milk powder	37 mL
1½ tsp	salt	7 mL
1½ cups	lukewarm water (see tip, at left)	375 mL
1½ tbsp	vegetable oil	22 mL
2½ cups	bread flour	625 mL
1⅓ cups	freshly ground durum wheat flour	325 mL
1½ tbsp	sesame seeds or millet	22 mL
1½ tbsp	poppy or nigella seeds	22 mL
1½ tbsp	fennel or dill seeds	22 mL
1½ tsp	instant or bread machine yeast	7 mL

Tips

If your dough does not form a ball during the first few minutes of kneading, do one of two things: if the dough looks dry and crumbly, add 1 tbsp (15 mL) water at 1-minute intervals until the dough forms a ball; if the dough looks wet, add 1 tbsp (15 mL) bread flour at 1-minute intervals until the dough forms a ball.

Try adding this mixture of seeds to other whole-grain breads for extra color and crunch.

3 lb (1.5 kg)

3 tbsp	instant skim milk powder	45 mL
2¹/₂ tsp	salt	12 mL
2¹/₃ cups	lukewarm water (see tip, page 70)	575 mL
3 tbsp	vegetable oil	45 mL
4 cups	bread flour	1 L
2 cups	freshly ground durum wheat flour	500 mL
2¹/₂ tbsp	sesame seeds or millet	37 mL
2¹/₂ tbsp	poppy or nigella seeds	37 mL
1¹/₂ tbsp	fennel or dill seeds	22 mL
2 tsp	instant or bread machine yeast	10 mL

1. Add milk powder, salt, water and oil to the bread pan. Spoon bread flour and durum wheat flour on top of liquid. Add sesame seeds, poppy seeds, fennel seeds and yeast.

2. Select the Basic/White cycle and press Start.

100% Whole Wheat Cheddar Bread

For a healthy meal bursting with flavor, set a big pot of homemade soup on the stove to slowly simmer while you get this bread going in the machine. The leftover bread is delicious lightly toasted.

Tips

Ideally, the water should be between 86°F and 95°F (30°C and 35°C), the temperature range in which yeast is most active. Warm it in the microwave or in a saucepan on the stove, and check the temperature with an instant-read thermometer.

Choose a whole wheat flour that is finely ground rather than a coarse flour to prevent a heavy loaf.

When you're baking the bread in the machine, shredded cheese works much better than cubes because it gets distributed more evenly through the bread. If you want cubes of cheese studded throughout the loaf, make the oven-baked version.

1 lb (500 g)

¾ tsp	salt	3 mL
⅔ cup	lukewarm water (see tip, at left)	150 mL
2 tbsp	liquid honey or agave syrup	30 mL
1 tbsp	vegetable oil	15 mL
2 cups	whole wheat flour (see tip, at left)	500 mL
1 tsp	Artisan Dough Enhancer (page 278) or packaged dough enhancer	5 mL
1 tsp	vital wheat gluten	5 mL
3 oz	aged (old) Cheddar cheese, shredded (see tip, at left)	90 g
1½ tsp	instant or bread machine yeast	7 mL

1½ lb (750 g)

1 tsp	salt	5 mL
1 cup	lukewarm water (see tip, at left)	250 mL
3 tbsp	liquid honey or agave syrup	45 mL
1½ tbsp	vegetable oil	22 mL
2⅔ cups	whole wheat flour (see tip, at left)	650 mL
2 tsp	Artisan Dough Enhancer (page 278) or packaged dough enhancer	10 mL
1 tsp	vital wheat gluten	5 mL
4 oz	aged (old) Cheddar cheese, shredded (see tip, at left)	125 g
2 tsp	instant or bread machine yeast	10 mL

2 lb (1 kg)

1½ tsp	salt	7 mL
1½ cups	lukewarm water (see tip, at left)	375 mL
¼ cup	liquid honey or agave syrup	60 mL
2½ tbsp	vegetable oil	37 mL
3⅔ cups	whole wheat flour (see tip, at left)	900 mL
1 tbsp	Artisan Dough Enhancer (page 278) or packaged dough enhancer	15 mL
2 tsp	vital wheat gluten	10 mL
5 oz	aged (old) Cheddar cheese, shredded (see tip, at left)	150 g
1½ tsp	instant or bread machine yeast	7 mL

3 lb (1.5 kg)

2¼ tsp	salt	11 mL
1¾ cups	lukewarm water (see tip, at left)	425 mL

Tips

If your dough does not form a ball during the first few minutes of kneading, do one of two things: if the dough looks dry and crumbly, add 1 tbsp (15 mL) water at 1-minute intervals until the dough forms a ball; if the dough looks wet, add 1 tbsp (15 mL) whole wheat flour at 1-minute intervals until the dough forms a ball.

Bread machine breads tend to be best within a day or two of baking, but if you want to store them for longer, wrap and freeze loaves or slices in labeled and dated freezer-proof packages for up to 3 months. Cut large loaves to fit freezer storage bags.

⅓ cup	liquid honey or agave syrup	75 mL
⅓ cup	vegetable oil	75 mL
4 cups	whole wheat flour (see tip, page 72)	1 L
1 tbsp	Artisan Dough Enhancer (page 278) or packaged dough enhancer	15 mL
1 tbsp	vital wheat gluten	15 mL
6 oz	aged (old) Cheddar cheese, shredded (see tip, page 72)	175 g
1¾ tsp	instant or bread machine yeast	8 mL

1. Add salt, water, honey and oil to the bread pan. Spoon whole wheat flour, dough enhancer and wheat gluten on top of liquid. Add cheese and yeast.

2. Select the Whole Wheat cycle and press Start.

Oven-Baked Whole Wheat Cheddar Bread

Instead of shredding the cheese, cut it into ½-inch (1 cm) cubes. Prepare the recipe through step 1, but do not add the cheese. Select the Dough cycle and press Start. Grease a metal loaf pan (see chart, below). When the cycle is finished, transfer dough to a floured surface and punch down gently. Press dough into an oval and sprinkle half the cheese on the top half of the oval. Fold the bottom half over the top, rotate the dough a quarter turn and press with the heel of your hand or your knuckles to flatten it into an oval again. Repeat with the remaining cheese. Form dough into a log to fit the loaf pan, pinching any seams together. Place seam side down in prepared pan. (If you've made 3 lbs/1.5 kg of dough, divide the dough in half and knead half the cheese into each half of the dough as described above, then form into two logs and place one in each pan.) Cover with a clean towel and let rise in a warm, draft-free place for 30 minutes. Meanwhile, preheat oven to 350°F (180°C). Using a serrated knife, cut 3 deep diagonal slashes across top of loaf. Bake until risen and browned and an instant-read thermometer inserted in the center registers 190°F (90°C). Remove from pan and let cool on a wire rack.

Dough Size	Loaf Pan Size	Baking Time
1 lb (500 g)	8- by 4-inch (20 by 10 cm)	28 to 32 minutes
1½ lb (750 g)	8- by 4-inch (20 by 10 cm)	32 to 35 minutes
2 lb (1 kg)	9- by 5-inch (23 by 12.5 cm)	35 to 38 minutes
3 lb (1.5 kg)	Two 8- by 4-inch (20 by 10 cm)	32 to 35 minutes

Whole Wheat, Dill and Onion Bread

This 100% whole wheat bread makes the most delicious grilled cheese sandwiches. The dough looks wet at first but rounds out as the flour slowly absorbs the liquid. The dough enhancer and vital wheat gluten help produce a high-rising loaf with a soft texture and a moist crumb.

Tip

Ideally, the water should be between 86°F and 95°F (30°C and 35°C), the temperature range in which yeast is most active. Warm it in the microwave or in a saucepan on the stove, and check the temperature with an instant-read thermometer.

1 lb (500 g)

¼ cup	grated onion	60 mL
¾ tsp	salt	3 mL
½ cup	lukewarm water (see tip, at left)	125 mL
2 tbsp	liquid honey	30 mL
1 tbsp	vegetable oil	15 mL
2 cups	finely ground whole wheat flour	500 mL
1 tbsp	dried dillweed	15 mL
1 tsp	Artisan Dough Enhancer (page 278) or packaged dough enhancer	5 mL
1 tsp	vital wheat gluten	5 mL
1¼ tsp	instant or bread machine yeast	6 mL

1½ lb (750 g)

⅓ cup	grated onion	75 mL
1 tsp	salt	5 mL
¾ cup	lukewarm water (see tip, at left)	175 mL
3 tbsp	liquid honey	45 mL
1½ tbsp	vegetable oil	22 mL
2⅔ cups	finely ground whole wheat flour	650 mL
1½ tbsp	dried dillweed	22 mL
2 tsp	Artisan Dough Enhancer (page 278) or packaged dough enhancer	10 mL
1 tsp	vital wheat gluten	5 mL
1½ tsp	instant or bread machine yeast	7 mL

2 lb (1 kg)

½ cup	grated onion	125 mL
1½ tsp	salt	7 mL
1 cup + 2 tbsp	lukewarm water (see tip, at left)	280 mL
¼ cup	liquid honey	60 mL
2½ tbsp	vegetable oil	37 mL
3¾ cups	finely ground whole wheat flour	925 mL
2 tbsp	dried dillweed	30 mL
1 tbsp	Artisan Dough Enhancer (page 278) or packaged dough enhancer	15 mL
2 tsp	vital wheat gluten	10 mL
1½ tsp	instant or bread machine yeast	7 mL

Tips

Three cups (750 mL) whole wheat berries (available in bulk at health food stores) will finely grind to make 7 cups (1.75 L) whole wheat flour. Use some for this recipe and freeze the rest in an airtight container for up to 12 months.

If your dough does not form a ball during the first few minutes of kneading, do one of two things: if the dough looks dry and crumbly, add 1 tbsp (15 mL) water at 1-minute intervals until the dough forms a ball; if the dough looks wet, add 1 tbsp (15 mL) whole wheat flour at 1-minute intervals until the dough forms a ball.

When making the smallest loaf allowed by your machine, check the dough a few minutes after kneading starts to make sure the ingredients are incorporated. You may need to help the machine along by using a rubber spatula to scrape the corners of the pan.

3 lb (1.5 kg)

²∕₃ cup	grated onion	150 mL
2¼ tsp	salt	11 mL
1²∕₃ cups	lukewarm water (see tip, page 74)	400 mL
⅓ cup	liquid honey	75 mL
⅓ cup	vegetable oil	75 mL
5½ cups	finely ground whole wheat flour	1.375 L
2½ tbsp	dried dillweed	37 mL
1 tbsp	Artisan Dough Enhancer (page 278) or packaged dough enhancer	15 mL
1 tbsp	vital wheat gluten	15 mL
1¾ tsp	instant or bread machine yeast	8 mL

1. Add onion, salt, water, honey and oil to the bread pan. Spoon flour on top of liquid. Add dill, dough enhancer, wheat gluten and yeast.

2. Select the Whole Wheat cycle and press Start.

Northern Prairie Barley Sunflower Bread

Makes 1 loaf

Delay Timer

On the northern prairies of the United States and in Canada, barley is harvested as sunflowers grow tall in the gardens, turning their heads to face the sun and finally giving up their seeds in late August or early September. Then the two come together in this hearty, cream-colored, bold-flavored bread. Use it to make toasted cheese sandwiches to accompany a satisfying soup or stew.

Tip

Packaged barley flour is usually ground from pearl barley (kernels that have been steamed and polished). If you buy hulled barley or barley kernels in bulk, you can mill your own flour that also contains the bran. Three cups (750 mL) hulled barley will mill to 7 to 7¼ cups (1.75 to 1.8 L) finely ground flour. While you're at it, you may as well grind your own wheat flour. Three cups (750 mL) whole wheat berries will mill to 7 cups (1.75 L) finely ground flour.

1 lb (500 g)

¾ tsp	salt	3 mL
¾ cup + 3 tbsp	lukewarm water (see tip, page 74)	220 mL
2 tsp	vegetable oil	10 mL
1⅔ cups	bread flour	400 mL
⅔ cup	barley flour	150 mL
1½ tsp	instant or bread machine yeast	7 mL
⅓ cup	salted roasted sunflower seeds	75 mL

1½ lb (750 g)

1 tsp	salt	5 mL
1⅓ cups	lukewarm water (see tip, page 74)	325 mL
1 tbsp	vegetable oil	15 mL
2½ cups	bread flour	625 mL
1 cup	barley flour	250 mL
1½ tsp	instant or bread machine yeast	7 mL
½ cup	salted roasted sunflower seeds	125 mL

2 lb (1 kg)

1½ tsp	salt	7 mL
1½ cups	lukewarm water (see tip, page 74)	375 mL
4 tsp	vegetable oil	20 mL
2⅔ cups	bread flour	650 mL
1⅓ cups	barley flour	325 mL
2 tsp	instant or bread machine yeast	10 mL
⅔ cup	salted roasted sunflower seeds	150 mL

3 lb (1.5 kg)

2 tsp	salt	10 mL
1¾ cups	lukewarm water (see tip, page 74)	425 mL
2 tbsp	vegetable oil	30 mL
3 cups	bread flour	750 mL
1½ cups	barley flour	375 mL
2 tsp	instant or bread machine yeast	10 mL
1 cup	salted roasted sunflower seeds	250 mL

Tips

In place of barley flour, you can use millet flour, for a mellow, creamy-colored bread.

If your machine has a dispenser, check the manual for the correct operating instructions.

If your dough does not form a ball during the first few minutes of kneading, do one of two things: if the dough looks dry and crumbly, add 1 tbsp (15 mL) water at 1-minute intervals until the dough forms a ball; if the dough looks wet, add 1 tbsp (15 mL) bread flour at 1-minute intervals until the dough forms a ball.

1. Add salt, water and oil to the bread pan. Spoon bread flour and barley flour on top of liquid. Add yeast. Place sunflower seeds in the dispenser (or add at the "add ingredient" or "mix in" signal).

2. Select the Whole Wheat cycle and press Start.

Barley Pumpkin Seed Bread
Replace the sunflower seeds with toasted green pumpkin seeds (pepitas).

Northern Lakes Wild Rice Bread

This dense, hearty loaf, studded with wild rice, is delicious sliced thin and eaten with cheese or sliced meat. You can make the loaf entirely in the bread machine, or you can use the Dough cycle, then form it into a round loaf and bake it in the oven.

Tip

Ideally, the water should be between 86°F and 95°F (30°C and 35°C), the temperature range in which yeast is most active. Warm it in the microwave or in a saucepan on the stove, and check the temperature with an instant-read thermometer.

1 lb (500 g)

1 tsp	salt	5 mL
½ tsp	freshly ground white pepper	2 mL
⅔ cup	lukewarm water (see tip, at left)	150 mL
2 tbsp	wildflower, clover or other pale amber honey	30 mL
1⅓ cups	bread flour	325 mL
½ cup	stone-ground dark rye flour	125 mL
⅔ cup	cooked wild rice	150 mL
1 tsp	Artisan Dough Enhancer (page 278) or packaged dough enhancer	5 mL
1¼ tsp	instant or bread machine yeast	6 mL

1½ lb (750 g)

1 tsp	salt	5 mL
¾ tsp	freshly ground white pepper	3 mL
1 cup	lukewarm water (see tip, at left)	250 mL
3 tbsp	wildflower, clover or other pale amber honey	45 mL
2 cups	bread flour	500 mL
1 cup	stone-ground dark rye flour	250 mL
1 cup	cooked wild rice	250 mL
2 tsp	Artisan Dough Enhancer (page 278) or packaged dough enhancer	10 mL
1¼ tsp	instant or bread machine yeast	6 mL

2 lb (1 kg)

2 tsp	salt	10 mL
1 tsp	freshly ground white pepper	5 mL
1⅓ cups	lukewarm water (see tip, at left)	325 mL
¼ cup	wildflower, clover or other pale amber honey	60 mL
2½ cups	bread flour	625 mL
1⅓ cups	stone-ground dark rye flour	325 mL
1⅓ cups	cooked wild rice	325 mL
1 tbsp	Artisan Dough Enhancer (page 278) or packaged dough enhancer	15 mL
1¼ tsp	instant or bread machine yeast	6 mL

Tips

Make sure the wild rice is well drained before you add it to the bread pan.

Cook and freeze wild rice ahead of time to have on hand for recipes like this one. Cooked wild rice will keep in the freezer for up to 1 year.

If your dough does not form a ball during the first few minutes of kneading, do one of two things: if the dough looks dry and crumbly, add 1 tbsp (15 mL) water at 1-minute intervals until the dough forms a ball; if the dough looks wet, add 1 tbsp (15 mL) bread flour at 1-minute intervals until the dough forms a ball.

3 lb (1.5 kg)

2½ tsp	salt	12 mL
1½ tsp	freshly ground white pepper	7 mL
1½ cups	lukewarm water (see tip, page 78)	375 mL
⅓ cup	wildflower, clover or other pale amber honey	75 mL
3 cups	bread flour	750 mL
1½ cups	stone-ground rye flour	375 mL
1½ cups	cooked wild rice	375 mL
4 tsp	Artisan Dough Enhancer (page 278) or packaged dough enhancer	20 mL
1¼ tsp	instant or bread machine yeast	6 mL

1. Add salt, pepper, water and honey to the bread pan. Spoon bread flour, rye flour and wild rice on top of liquid. Add dough enhancer and yeast.

2. Select the Basic/White cycle and press Start.

Oven-Baked Wild Rice Boule

Prepare the recipe through step 1, then select the Dough cycle and press Start. Line a baking sheet with parchment paper. When the cycle is finished, transfer dough to a floured surface and punch down gently. Form into a boule and place on prepared baking sheet. Cover with a clean towel and let rise in a warm, draft-free place for 30 minutes. Meanwhile, preheat oven to 425°F (220°C). Using a serrated knife, cut 3 to 5 deep diagonal slashes across top of loaf. Spray loaf with water. Bake until risen and dark brown on top and an instant-read thermometer inserted in the center registers 190°F (90°C). Remove from pan and let cool on a wire rack.

Dough Size	Baking Time
1 lb (500 g)	25 to 27 minutes
1½ lb (750 g)	28 to 30 minutes
2 lb (1 kg)	30 to 35 minutes
3 lb (1.5 kg)	33 to 38 minutes

Sorghum, Amaranth, Millet and Quinoa Bread

Ancient cereal grains are now more available than ever to contemporary bread bakers. You can find sorghum, spelt, amaranth, millet and quinoa flours at health food stores, packaged by Bob's Red Mill, or online in flours such as Ancient Grains Blend from King Arthur. These grains are all either low in gluten or gluten-free, so you need to add vital wheat gluten so the dough will rise.

Tip

Ideally, the water should be between 86°F and 95°F (30°C and 35°C), the temperature range in which yeast is most active. Warm it in the microwave or in a saucepan on the stove, and check the temperature with an instant-read thermometer.

1 lb (500 g)

2 tbsp	instant skim milk powder	30 mL
1 tsp	salt	5 mL
¾ cup	lukewarm water (see tip, at left)	175 mL
1 tbsp	vegetable oil	15 mL
1 tbsp	liquid honey	15 mL
1½ cups	bread flour	375 mL
2 tbsp	sorghum or spelt flour	30 mL
2 tbsp	amaranth flour	30 mL
2 tbsp	millet flour	30 mL
2 tbsp	quinoa flour	30 mL
2 tsp	vital wheat gluten	10 mL
1¼ tsp	instant or bread machine yeast	6 mL

1½ lb (750 g)

¼ cup	instant skim milk powder	60 mL
1¼ tsp	salt	6 mL
1 cup + 1 tbsp	lukewarm water (see tip, at left)	265 mL
4 tsp	vegetable oil	20 mL
1½ tbsp	liquid honey	22 mL
2¼ cups	bread flour	550 mL
3 tbsp	sorghum or spelt flour	45 mL
3 tbsp	amaranth flour	45 mL
3 tbsp	millet flour	45 mL
3 tbsp	quinoa flour	45 mL
1 tbsp	vital wheat gluten	15 mL
1½ tsp	instant or bread machine yeast	7 mL

Tips

Try other alternative grain flours, such as Ethiopian teff or Egyptian Kamut, in place of the amaranth, millet or quinoa.

When making the smallest loaf allowed by your machine, check the dough a few minutes after kneading starts to make sure the ingredients are incorporated. You may need to help the machine along by using a rubber spatula to scrape the corners of the pan.

If your dough does not form a ball during the first few minutes of kneading, do one of two things: if the dough looks dry and crumbly, add 1 tbsp (15 mL) water at 1-minute intervals until the dough forms a ball; if the dough looks wet, add 1 tbsp (15 mL) bread flour at 1-minute intervals until the dough forms a ball.

2 lb (1 kg)

⅓ cup	instant skim milk powder	75 mL
1½ tsp	salt	7 mL
1½ cups	lukewarm water (see tip, page 80)	375 mL
2 tbsp	vegetable oil	30 mL
2 tbsp	liquid honey	30 mL
2¾ cups	bread flour	675 mL
¼ cup	sorghum or spelt flour	60 mL
¼ cup	amaranth flour	60 mL
¼ cup	millet flour	60 mL
¼ cup	quinoa flour	60 mL
4 tsp	vital wheat gluten	20 mL
1¾ tsp	instant or bread machine yeast	8 mL

3 lb (1.5 kg)

½ cup	instant skim milk powder	125 mL
2 tsp	salt	10 mL
1¾ cups	lukewarm water (see tip, page 80)	425 mL
¼ cup	vegetable oil	60 mL
¼ cup	liquid honey	60 mL
3¾ cups	bread flour	925 mL
⅓ cup	sorghum or spelt flour	75 mL
⅓ cup	amaranth flour	75 mL
⅓ cup	millet flour	75 mL
¼ cup	quinoa flour	60 mL
1½ tbsp	vital wheat gluten	22 mL
1½ tsp	instant or bread machine yeast	7 mL

1. Add milk powder, salt, water, oil and honey to the bread pan. Spoon bread flour, sorghum flour, amaranth flour, millet flour and quinoa flour on top of liquid. Add wheat gluten and yeast.

2. Select the Basic/White cycle and press Start.

Sauerkraut Rye Bread

With grilled bratwurst and a little horseradish, or with shaved ham and homemade mayonnaise, there's no better sandwich bread than this one. It also stands up to Tilsit and Limburger cheeses. If you bake it as a boule, pull out the center section with your hands to make a concave bowl that you can fill with a retro-style creamy vegetable dip. The boule is also delicious split in half and piled with your favorite sandwich fillings; cut it into wedges for a casual supper or tailgate party.

Tips

To ensure that you don't get too much juice, remove the sauerkraut from its container with a fork, but do not press dry. Place it in a bowl and snip it with kitchen shears, then add it to the bread pan along with any juice from the bowl.

Ideally, the buttermilk and water should be between 86°F and 95°F (30°C and 35°C), the temperature range in which yeast is most active. Warm them in the microwave or in a saucepan on the stove, and check the temperature with an instant-read thermometer.

1 lb (500 g)

¾ tsp	salt	3 mL
½ cup	drained sauerkraut, finely snipped (see tip, at left)	125 mL
⅓ cup	lukewarm buttermilk (see tip, at left)	75 mL
2 tbsp	lukewarm water	30 mL
2 tbsp	vegetable oil	30 mL
4 tsp	light (fancy) molasses	20 mL
4 tsp	Dijon mustard	20 mL
1⅓ cups	bread flour	325 mL
1 cup	pumpernickel rye flour or coarse stone-ground dark rye flour	250 mL
4 tsp	caraway seeds	20 mL
4 tsp	unsweetened cocoa powder	20 mL
2 tsp	vital wheat gluten	10 mL
1½ tsp	instant or bread machine yeast	7 mL

1½ lb (750 g)

1 tsp	salt	5 mL
⅔ cup	drained sauerkraut, finely snipped (see tip, at left)	150 mL
½ cup	lukewarm buttermilk (see tip, at left)	125 mL
2½ tbsp	vegetable oil	37 mL
5 tsp	light (fancy) molasses	25 mL
5 tsp	Dijon mustard	25 mL
1½ cups	bread flour	375 mL
1¼ cups	pumpernickel rye flour or coarse stone-ground dark rye flour	300 mL
2 tbsp	caraway seeds	30 mL
2 tbsp	unsweetened cocoa powder	30 mL
2 tsp	vital wheat gluten	10 mL
1½ tsp	instant or bread machine yeast	7 mL

2 lb (1 kg)

1 tsp	salt	5 mL
1 cup	drained sauerkraut, finely snipped (see tip, at left)	250 mL
⅓ cup	lukewarm buttermilk (see tip, at left)	75 mL
2 tbsp	lukewarm water	30 mL
3 tbsp	vegetable oil	45 mL
1½ tbsp	light (fancy) molasses	22 mL
1½ tbsp	Dijon mustard	22 mL
1¾ cups	bread flour	425 mL
1½ cups	pumpernickel rye flour or coarse stone-ground dark rye flour	375 mL
2 tbsp	caraway seeds	30 mL
2½ tbsp	unsweetened cocoa powder	37 mL

If your dough does not form a ball during the first few minutes of kneading, do one of two things: if the dough looks dry and crumbly, add 1 tbsp (15 mL) water at 1-minute intervals until the dough forms a ball; if the dough looks wet, add 1 tbsp (15 mL) bread flour at 1-minute intervals until the dough forms a ball.

Bread machine breads tend to be best within a day or two of baking, but if you want to store them for longer, wrap and freeze loaves or slices in labeled and dated freezer-proof packages for up to 3 months. Cut large loaves to fit freezer storage bags.

Placing a pan of water in the bottom of the oven while the bread is baking creates steam that helps form a good crust.

1 tbsp	vital wheat gluten	15 mL
2 tsp	instant or bread machine yeast	10 mL

3 lb (1.5 kg)

1¼ tsp	salt	6 mL
1⅓ cups	drained sauerkraut, finely snipped (see tip, page 82)	325 mL
½ cup	lukewarm buttermilk (see tip, page 82)	125 mL
3 tbsp	vegetable oil	45 mL
2 tbsp	light (fancy) molasses	30 mL
2 tbsp	Dijon mustard	30 mL
2⅓ cups	bread flour	575 mL
1⅔ cups	pumpernickel rye flour or coarse stone-ground dark rye flour	400 mL
3 tbsp	caraway seeds	45 mL
3 tbsp	unsweetened cocoa powder	45 mL
2 tsp	vital wheat gluten	10 mL
2 tsp	instant or bread machine yeast	10 mL

1. Add salt, sauerkraut, buttermilk, water (if called for), oil, molasses and mustard to the bread pan. Spoon bread flour and rye flour on top of liquid. Add caraway seeds, cocoa powder, wheat gluten and yeast.

2. Select the Whole Wheat cycle and press Start.

Oven-Baked Sauerkraut Rye Boule

Prepare the recipe through step 2, then select the Dough cycle and press Start. Line a baking sheet with parchment paper. When the cycle is finished, transfer dough to a floured surface and punch down gently. Form into a boule and place on prepared baking sheet. Cover with a clean towel and let rise in a warm, draft-free place for 30 minutes. Meanwhile, preheat oven to 350°F (180°C) and place a broiler pan on the bottom rack. Using a serrated knife, cut 3 to 5 deep diagonal slashes across top of loaf. Add 2 cups (500 mL) hot water to the broiler pan. Place baking sheet on the middle rack. Bake until risen and browned on top and an instant-read thermometer inserted in the center registers 190°F (90°C). Remove from pan and let cool on a wire rack.

Dough Size	Baking Time
1 lb (500 g)	30 to 35 minutes
1½ lb (750 g)	35 to 40 minutes
2 lb (1 kg)	45 to 50 minutes
3 lb (1.5 kg)	50 to 55 minutes

Flavored Breads

YOU CAN MAKE signature breads in your bread machine just by adding or changing a few ingredients. When you use buttermilk, apple juice, cider, beer or a vegetable or fruit purée among the liquid ingredients, you change the flavor and perhaps the color of the bread. When you add cheese, vegetables, fruits, bacon or ham, nuts, seeds, herbs, spices or dried seasoning mixes, you incorporate even more flavor.

For most flavored breads, you'll use the Basic/White cycle. Some machines feature a dispenser that will add these ingredients for you at the appropriate time and knead them into the dough. If your machine doesn't have a dispenser, just add the ingredients at the "add ingredient" or "mix in" signal.

The recipes in this chapter offer a blueprint for your creativity. Feel free to replace the flavoring ingredients I've chosen with an equal amount of your favorite ingredients. Aim for a bread with a pleasing overall flavor, not one that is overpowered by the flavorings.

Flavor Up

Flavoring	How to Use
Bacon or ham	Place in the dispenser or add at the "add ingredient" or "mix in" signal
Cheese	Add after the flour
Chocolate chips	Place in the dispenser or add at the "add ingredient" or "mix in" signal
Coconut, shredded	Place in the dispenser or add at the "add ingredient" or "mix in" signal
Flavored oil	Add with the liquid ingredients
Dried fruits	Place in the dispenser or add at the "add ingredient" or "mix in" signal
Fresh fruits	Add with the liquid ingredients
Herbs, fresh or dried	Add with the flour
Garlic, roasted and mashed	Add with the liquid ingredients
Onion, chopped and sautéed	Add with the liquid ingredients
Pesto	Knead into the dough by hand
Saffron	Steep in the liquid ingredients for 30 minutes
Seeds	Add with the flour
Spices	Add with the liquid ingredients or the flour
Sun-dried tomatoes	Finely chop and stir into the liquid ingredients
Vegetables, fresh or dried	Add with the liquid ingredients or place in the dispenser or add at the "add ingredient" or "mix in" signal
Vegetables, puréed	Add with the liquid ingredients

Pesto Bread

Packaged sauce or soup mixes (such as the Knorr brand) are a great way to add flavor to a basic white bread recipe. The method is a bit unusual — the yeast is mixed with sugar and warm water *before* the dry ingredients are added — but it works. You'll get a high-rising, tender, airy loaf with a homemade flavor and texture.

Tips

Warm the water in the microwave or in a saucepan on the stove, and check the temperature with an instant-read thermometer.

Look for dry pesto sauce mix or basil Parmesan pasta seasoning mix with the packaged sauce and seasoning mixes at the supermarket. The packages are different sizes. A ¹/₂-oz (14 g) package is about 2 tbsp (30 mL) and a ²/₃-oz (22 g) package is about 2¹/₂ tbsp (37 mL).

1 lb (500 g)

4 tsp	granulated sugar	20 mL
1¹/₂ tsp	instant or bread machine yeast	7 mL
²/₃ cup	warm water (110°F/43°C)	150 mL
2¹/₂ tbsp	vegetable oil	37 mL
2 cups	bread flour	500 mL
2 tbsp	dry pesto mix (see tip, at left)	30 mL
¹/₂ tsp	salt	2 mL

1¹/₂ lb (750 g)

2 tbsp	granulated sugar	30 mL
1¹/₂ tsp	instant or bread machine yeast	7 mL
1 cup	warm water (110°F/43°C)	250 mL
¹/₄ cup	vegetable oil	60 mL
3 cups	bread flour	750 mL
3 tbsp	dry pesto mix (see tip, at left)	45 mL
1 tsp	salt	5 mL

2 lb (1 kg)

8 tsp	granulated sugar	40 mL
1¹/₂ tsp	instant or bread machine yeast	7 mL
1¹/₃ cups + 2 tbsp	warm water (110°F/43°C)	355 mL
¹/₃ cup	vegetable oil	75 mL
4 cups	bread flour	1 L
¹/₄ cup	dry pesto mix (see tip, at left)	60 mL
1 tsp	salt	5 mL

3 lb (1.5 kg)

¹/₄ cup	granulated sugar	60 mL
1³/₄ tsp	instant or bread machine yeast	8 mL
2¹/₄ cups	warm water (110°F/43°C)	550 mL
¹/₂ cup	vegetable oil	125 mL
5 cups	bread flour	1.25 L
¹/₃ cup	dry pesto mix (see tip, at left)	75 mL
1¹/₂ tsp	salt	7 mL

Tips

When making the smallest loaf allowed by your machine, check the dough a few minutes after kneading starts to make sure the ingredients are incorporated. You may need to help the machine along by using a rubber spatula to scrape the corners of the pan.

If your dough does not form a ball during the first few minutes of kneading, do one of two things: if the dough looks dry and crumbly, add 1 tbsp (15 mL) water at 1-minute intervals until the dough forms a ball; if the dough looks wet, add 1 tbsp (15 mL) bread flour at 1-minute intervals until the dough forms a ball.

1. Add sugar, yeast and water to the bread pan. Let stand for 10 minutes or until yeast starts to bubble.

2. Add oil. Spoon flour on top of liquid. Add pesto mix and salt.

3. Select the Basic/White cycle and the Light Crust setting and press Start.

Whole Wheat Pesto Bread
Replace half the bread flour with white whole wheat flour or regular whole wheat flour.

Easy Oatmeal Apple Bread

Makes 1 loaf

Packaged instant oatmeal flavored with dried apples is another great way to add flavor to basic white bread. This tender loaf has a gentle apple flavor — and more vitamins and fiber!

Tips

Warm the water in the microwave or in a saucepan on the stove, and check the temperature with an instant-read thermometer.

A 1-oz (31 g) package of instant oatmeal yields about ⅓ cup (75 mL). It is important to measure the volume to make sure you have the correct amount of dry ingredients.

1 lb (500 g)

1½ tbsp	packed light or dark brown sugar	22 mL
1 tsp	instant or bread machine yeast	5 mL
½ cup + 1 tbsp	warm water (110°F/43°C)	140 mL
¼ cup	unsweetened applesauce	60 mL
2½ tbsp	vegetable oil	37 mL
2 cups	bread flour	500 mL
⅓ cup	apple-flavored instant oatmeal (see tip, at left)	75 mL
1 tsp	salt	5 mL
½ tsp	ground cinnamon	2 mL

1½ lb (750 g)

2 tbsp	packed light or dark brown sugar	30 mL
1 tsp	instant or bread machine yeast	5 mL
¾ cup	warm water (110°F/43°C)	175 mL
⅓ cup	unsweetened applesauce	75 mL
3 tbsp	vegetable oil	45 mL
2½ cups	bread flour	625 mL
½ cup	apple-flavored instant oatmeal (see tip, at left)	125 mL
1¼ tsp	salt	6 mL
1 tsp	ground cinnamon	5 mL

2 lb (1 kg)

3 tbsp	packed light or dark brown sugar	45 mL
1 tsp	instant or bread machine yeast	5 mL
1 cup	warm water (110°F/43°C)	250 mL
½ cup	unsweetened applesauce	125 mL
3 tbsp	vegetable oil	45 mL
3½ cups	bread flour	875 mL
⅔ cup	apple-flavored instant oatmeal (see tip, at left)	150 mL
1½ tsp	salt	7 mL
1½ tsp	ground cinnamon	7 mL

Try other flavors of instant oatmeal in this bread.

For more apple flavor, use apple juice or cider in place of the water.

When making the smallest loaf allowed by your machine, check the dough a few minutes after kneading starts to make sure the ingredients are incorporated. You may need to help the machine along by using a rubber spatula to scrape the corners of the pan.

If your dough does not form a ball during the first few minutes of kneading, do one of two things: if the dough looks dry and crumbly, add 1 tbsp (15 mL) water at 1-minute intervals until the dough forms a ball; if the dough looks wet, add 1 tbsp (15 mL) bread flour at 1-minute intervals until the dough forms a ball.

3 lb (1.5 kg)

¼ cup	packed light or dark brown sugar	60 mL
1¼ tsp	instant or bread machine yeast	6 mL
1⅓ cups	warm water (110°F/43°C)	325 mL
⅔ cup	unsweetened applesauce	150 mL
¼ cup	vegetable oil	60 mL
4½ cups	bread flour	1.125 L
1 cup	apple-flavored instant oatmeal (see tip, page 88)	250 mL
2 tsp	salt	10 mL
2 tsp	ground cinnamon	10 mL

1. Add brown sugar, yeast and water to the bread pan. Let stand for 10 minutes or until yeast starts to bubble.

2. Add applesauce and oil. Spoon flour and oatmeal on top of liquid. Add salt and cinnamon.

3. Select the Basic/White cycle and the Light Crust setting and press Start.

Béarnaise Bread

This tarragon-flecked bread with the flavor of béarnaise sauce is wonderful for chicken or shrimp salad sandwiches — especially those made with tarragon. You can also cut off the crusts and serve this bread toasted under a grilled filet mignon or salmon fillet, dolloped with homemade béarnaise sauce.

Tips

Warm the water in the microwave or in a saucepan on the stove, and check the temperature with an instant-read thermometer.

Look for dry béarnaise sauce mix with the packaged sauce and seasoning mixes at the supermarket. One 1.4 oz (40 g) package is about 3$\frac{1}{2}$ tbsp (52 mL).

1 lb (500 g)

4 tsp	granulated sugar	20 mL
1$\frac{1}{2}$ tsp	instant or bread machine yeast	7 mL
$\frac{2}{3}$ cup	warm water (110°F/43°C)	150 mL
2$\frac{1}{2}$ tbsp	vegetable oil	37 mL
2 tbsp	tarragon-flavored vinegar or white wine vinegar	30 mL
2 cups	bread flour	500 mL
$\frac{1}{4}$ cup	dry béarnaise sauce mix	60 mL
2 tsp	dried tarragon	10 mL
$\frac{1}{2}$ tsp	salt	2 mL

1$\frac{1}{2}$ lb (750 g)

2 tbsp	granulated sugar	30 mL
1$\frac{1}{2}$ tsp	instant or bread machine yeast	7 mL
1 cup	warm water (110°F/43°C)	250 mL
3 tbsp	vegetable oil	45 mL
3 tbsp	tarragon-flavored vinegar or white wine vinegar	45 mL
3 cups	bread flour	750 mL
$\frac{1}{3}$ cup	dry béarnaise sauce mix	75 mL
1 tbsp	dried tarragon	15 mL
1 tsp	salt	5 mL

2 lb (1 kg)

3 tbsp	granulated sugar	45 mL
1$\frac{1}{2}$ tsp	instant or bread machine yeast	7 mL
1 cup + 2 tbsp	warm water (110°F/43°C)	280 mL
3 tbsp	vegetable oil	45 mL
$\frac{1}{4}$ cup	tarragon-flavored vinegar or white wine vinegar	60 mL
3$\frac{3}{4}$ cups	bread flour	925 mL
$\frac{1}{2}$ cup	dry béarnaise sauce mix	125 mL
1$\frac{1}{2}$ tbsp	dried tarragon	22 mL
1$\frac{1}{2}$ tsp	salt	7 mL

Tips

When making the smallest loaf allowed by your machine, check the dough a few minutes after kneading starts to make sure the ingredients are incorporated. You may need to help the machine along by using a rubber spatula to scrape the corners of the pan.

If your dough does not form a ball during the first few minutes of kneading, do one of two things: if the dough looks dry and crumbly, add 1 tbsp (15 mL) water at 1-minute intervals until the dough forms a ball; if the dough looks wet, add 1 tbsp (15 mL) bread flour at 1-minute intervals until the dough forms a ball.

3 lb (1.5 kg)

¼ cup	granulated sugar	60 mL
1¾ tsp	instant or bread machine yeast	8 mL
1¾ cups	warm water (110°F/43°C)	425 mL
¼ cup	vegetable oil	60 mL
⅓ cup	tarragon-flavored vinegar or white wine vinegar	75 mL
5¾ cups	bread flour	1.425 L
⅔ cup	dry béarnaise sauce mix	150 mL
2 tbsp	dried tarragon	30 mL
1¾ tsp	salt	8 mL

1. Add sugar, yeast and water to the bread pan. Let stand for 10 minutes or until yeast starts to bubble.

2. Add oil and vinegar. Spoon flour on top of liquid. Add béarnaise sauce mix, tarragon and salt.

3. Select the Basic/White cycle and the Light Crust setting and press Start.

> ### Whole Wheat Béarnaise Bread
> Replace half the bread flour with white whole wheat flour or regular whole wheat flour.

Sour Cream and Onion Bread

Makes 1 loaf

If you like sour cream and onion potato chips, you'll love this bread. It's great for sandwiches, and is also delectable as monkey bread (see box, opposite).

Tips

Full-fat sour cream works best in this recipe, adding richness, moisture and golden color.

For the best results, let the sour cream warm to room temperature before adding it to the bread pan. Cold ingredients will decrease the activity of the yeast.

When making the smallest loaf allowed by your machine, check the dough a few minutes after kneading starts to make sure the ingredients are incorporated. You may need to help the machine along by using a rubber spatula to scrape the corners of the pan.

1 lb (500 g)

²⁄₃ cup	finely chopped green onions	150 mL
1 tbsp	granulated sugar	15 mL
³⁄₄ tsp	salt	3 mL
¹⁄₄ tsp	freshly ground white pepper	1 mL
³⁄₄ cup	sour cream	175 mL
1 tbsp	water	15 mL
2 cups	bread flour	500 mL
1¹⁄₄ tsp	instant or bread machine yeast	6 mL
¹⁄₄ tsp	baking soda	1 mL

1¹⁄₂ lb (750 g)

1 cup	finely chopped green onions	250 mL
1¹⁄₂ tbsp	granulated sugar	22 mL
1 tsp	salt	5 mL
¹⁄₄ tsp	freshly ground white pepper	1 mL
1 cup + 2 tbsp	sour cream	280 mL
2 tbsp	water	30 mL
2³⁄₄ cups	bread flour	675 mL
1¹⁄₄ tsp	instant or bread machine yeast	6 mL
¹⁄₄ tsp	baking soda	1 mL

2 lb (1 kg)

1¹⁄₃ cups	finely chopped green onions	325 mL
2¹⁄₂ tbsp	granulated sugar	37 mL
1¹⁄₂ tsp	salt	7 mL
³⁄₄ tsp	freshly ground white pepper	3 mL
1¹⁄₂ cups	sour cream	375 mL
3 tbsp	water	45 mL
4 cups	bread flour	1 L
1³⁄₄ tsp	instant or bread machine yeast	8 mL
¹⁄₂ tsp	baking soda	2 mL

3 lb (1.5 kg)

1³⁄₄ cups	finely chopped green onions	425 mL
¹⁄₄ cup	granulated sugar	60 mL
2¹⁄₂ tsp	salt	12 mL
1 tsp	freshly ground white pepper	5 mL
1³⁄₄ cups	sour cream	425 mL
¹⁄₂ cup	water	125 mL
5¹⁄₃ cups	bread flour	1.325 L
2 tsp	instant or bread machine yeast	10 mL
1 tsp	baking soda	5 mL

Tips

If your dough does not form a ball during the first few minutes of kneading, do one of two things: if the dough looks dry and crumbly, add 1 tbsp (15 mL) water at 1-minute intervals until the dough forms a ball; if the dough looks wet, add 1 tbsp (15 mL) bread flour at 1-minute intervals until the dough forms a ball.

When you're making the monkey bread, if your bread machine doesn't have a Pause button, simply raise the lid, remove the dough, form the balls and add the toppings, then remove the kneading paddle(s) from the pan, place the balls in the pan and close the lid again. Work quickly, as the rising cycle will continue even without the bread in the pan.

1. Add green onions, sugar, salt, pepper, sour cream and water to the bread pan. Spoon flour on top of liquid. Add yeast and baking soda.

2. Select the Basic/White cycle and press Start.

Sour Cream and Onion Monkey Bread

Prepare the recipe through step 2. At the start of the final rise (see "Timing It Right," page 13), press Pause. Remove dough from bread pan and transfer to a floured surface. Divide dough into 12 pieces and form each piece into a ball. Dip each ball in 1/2 cup (125 mL) melted butter, then roll in 1/2 cup (125 mL) finely chopped green onions. Remove kneading paddle(s) from bread pan. Arrange balls in pan and press Start to continue the cycle.

Italian Cheese Bread

Packaged Italian-blend shredded cheese (mozzarella, provolone, Asiago, Pecorino and Parmesan) is an easy way to imbue bread with wonderful flavor. Use it for meatball or meatloaf sandwiches, spread with pizza sauce or ketchup.

Tip

Ideally, the water should be between 86°F and 95°F (30°C and 35°C), the temperature range in which yeast is most active. Warm it in the microwave or in a saucepan on the stove, and check the temperature with an instant-read thermometer.

1 lb (500 g)

¼ cup	chopped fresh basil	60 mL
1 tbsp	granulated sugar	15 mL
1 tsp	salt	5 mL
1 cup	lukewarm water (see tip, at left)	250 mL
1 tbsp	vegetable oil	15 mL
2¼ cups	bread flour	550 mL
¾ cup	lightly packed finely shredded Italian-blend cheese (about 2¼ oz/68 g)	175 mL
1 tsp	instant or bread machine yeast	5 mL

1½ lb (750 g)

⅓ cup	chopped fresh basil	75 mL
4 tsp	granulated sugar	20 mL
1½ tsp	salt	7 mL
1⅓ cups	lukewarm water (see tip, at left)	325 mL
4 tsp	vegetable oil	20 mL
3 cups	bread flour	750 mL
1 cup	lightly packed finely shredded Italian-blend cheese (about 3 oz/90 g)	250 mL
1¼ tsp	instant or bread machine yeast	6 mL

2 lb (1 kg)

6 tbsp	chopped fresh basil	90 mL
5 tsp	granulated sugar	25 mL
2 tsp	salt	10 mL
1½ cups	lukewarm water (see tip, at left)	375 mL
2 tbsp	vegetable oil	30 mL
3¾ cups	bread flour	925 mL
1¼ cups	lightly packed finely shredded Italian-blend cheese (about 3½ oz/105 g)	300 mL
1¼ tsp	instant or bread machine yeast	6 mL

3 lb (1.5 kg)

½ cup	chopped fresh basil	125 mL
2 tbsp	granulated sugar	30 mL
2½ tsp	salt	12 mL
1½ cups	lukewarm water (see tip, at left)	375 mL
2 tbsp	vegetable oil	30 mL
4½ cups	bread flour	1.125 L
1½ cups	lightly packed finely shredded Italian-blend cheese (about 4½ oz/140 g)	375 mL
1¾ tsp	instant or bread machine yeast	8 mL

Tips

If your dough does not form a ball during the first few minutes of kneading, do one of two things: if the dough looks dry and crumbly, add 1 tbsp (15 mL) water at 1-minute intervals until the dough forms a ball; if the dough looks wet, add 1 tbsp (15 mL) bread flour at 1-minute intervals until the dough forms a ball.

Bread machine breads tend to be best within a day or two of baking, but if you want to store them for longer, wrap and freeze loaves or slices in labeled and dated freezer-proof packages for up to 3 months. Cut large loaves to fit freezer storage bags.

1. Add basil, sugar, salt, water and oil to the bread pan. Spoon flour on top of liquid. Add cheese and yeast.

2. Select the Basic/White cycle and press Start.

Whole Wheat Italian Cheese Bread
Replace half the bread flour with white whole wheat flour or regular whole wheat flour.

Cheddar Chive Bread

Whether you get your herbs from the garden or the grocery store, this simple bread is a good excuse to use them. Use an aged Cheddar for its depth of flavor. If you're new to baking yeast bread, the results will have you hooked.

Tip

Ideally, the water should be between 86°F and 95°F (30°C and 35°C), the temperature range in which yeast is most active. Warm it in the microwave or in a saucepan on the stove, and check the temperature with an instant-read thermometer.

1 lb (500 g)

¼ cup	snipped fresh chives	60 mL
1 tbsp	granulated sugar	15 mL
1 tsp	salt	5 mL
1 cup	lukewarm water (see tip, at left)	250 mL
1 tbsp	vegetable oil	15 mL
2¼ cups	bread flour	550 mL
¾ cup	lightly packed finely shredded aged (old) Cheddar cheese (about 2¼ oz/68 g)	175 mL
1 tsp	instant or bread machine yeast	5 mL

1½ lb (750 g)

⅓ cup	snipped fresh chives	75 mL
4 tsp	granulated sugar	20 mL
1½ tsp	salt	7 mL
1⅓ cups	lukewarm water (see tip, at left)	325 mL
4 tsp	vegetable oil	20 mL
3 cups	bread flour	750 mL
1 cup	lightly packed finely shredded aged (old) Cheddar cheese (about 3 oz/90 g)	250 mL
1¼ tsp	instant or bread machine yeast	6 mL

2 lb (1 kg)

6 tbsp	snipped fresh chives	90 mL
5 tsp	granulated sugar	25 mL
2 tsp	salt	10 mL
1½ cups	lukewarm water (see tip, at left)	375 mL
2 tbsp	vegetable oil	30 mL
3¾ cups	bread flour	925 mL
1¼ cups	lightly packed finely shredded aged (old) Cheddar cheese (about 3½ oz/105 g)	300 mL
1¼ tsp	instant or bread machine yeast	6 mL

Tip

If your dough does not form a ball during the first few minutes of kneading, do one of two things: if the dough looks dry and crumbly, add 1 tbsp (15 mL) water at 1-minute intervals until the dough forms a ball; if the dough looks wet, add 1 tbsp (15 mL) bread flour at 1-minute intervals until the dough forms a ball.

3 lb (1.5 kg)

½ cup	snipped fresh chives	125 mL
2 tbsp	granulated sugar	30 mL
2½ tsp	salt	12 mL
1½ cups	lukewarm water (see tip, page 96)	375 mL
2 tbsp	vegetable oil	30 mL
4½ cups	bread flour	1.125 L
1½ cups	lightly packed finely shredded aged (old) Cheddar cheese (about 4½ oz/140 g)	375 mL
1¾ tsp	instant or bread machine yeast	8 mL

1. Add chives, sugar, salt, water and oil to the bread pan. Spoon flour on top of liquid. Add cheese and yeast.

2. Select the Basic/White cycle and press Start.

> **Whole Wheat Cheddar Chive Bread**
> Replace half the bread flour with white whole wheat flour or regular whole wheat flour.

Chipotle, Cilantro and Pepper Jack Bread

Your taste buds will say "ole!" when you try this bread. It's great for a Monterey Jack grilled cheese and avocado sandwich, it makes fabulous toast with scrambled eggs and salsa, or it's a good alternative to corn tortillas with huevos rancheros. Any leftover bread can be turned into a Southwest-style breakfast casserole with chorizo and eggs.

Tips

The amount of chipotle powder called for in the recipes gives a subtle smoky touch to the bread. For a more pronounced flavor, you can double it.

In place of chipotle powder, try ancho chile powder or smoked paprika.

Ideally, the water should be between 86°F and 95°F (30°C and 35°C), the temperature range in which yeast is most active. Warm it in the microwave or in a saucepan on the stove, and check the temperature with an instant-read thermometer.

1 lb (500 g)

2 tsp	granulated sugar	10 mL
1 tsp	salt	5 mL
¼ tsp	chipotle powder	1 mL
1 cup	lukewarm water (see tip, at left)	250 mL
1 tbsp	vegetable oil	15 mL
2¼ cups	bread flour	550 mL
¾ cup	lightly packed finely shredded pepper Jack cheese (about 2¼ oz/68 g)	175 mL
¼ cup	snipped fresh cilantro	60 mL
1 tsp	instant or bread machine yeast	5 mL

1½ lb (750 g)

1 tbsp	granulated sugar	15 mL
1½ tsp	salt	7 mL
¼ tsp	chipotle powder	1 mL
1 cup + 2 tbsp	lukewarm water (see tip, at left)	280 mL
1½ tbsp	vegetable oil	22 mL
3 cups	bread flour	750 mL
1¼ cups	lightly packed finely shredded pepper Jack cheese (about 3 oz/90 g)	300 mL
⅓ cup	snipped fresh cilantro	75 mL
1 tsp	instant or bread machine yeast	5 mL

2 lb (1 kg)

1½ tbsp	granulated sugar	22 mL
1½ tsp	salt	7 mL
½ tsp	chipotle powder	2 mL
1⅓ cups	lukewarm water (see tip, at left)	325 mL
2 tbsp	vegetable oil	30 mL
3¾ cups	bread flour	925 mL
1⅓ cups	lightly packed finely shredded pepper Jack cheese (about 3½ oz/105 g)	325 mL
½ cup	snipped fresh cilantro	125 mL
1 tsp	instant or bread machine yeast	6 mL

If your dough does not form a ball during the first few minutes of kneading, do one of two things: if the dough looks dry and crumbly, add 1 tbsp (15 mL) water at 1-minute intervals until the dough forms a ball; if the dough looks wet, add 1 tbsp (15 mL) bread flour at 1-minute intervals until the dough forms a ball.

3 lb (1.5 kg)

2 tbsp	granulated sugar	30 mL
1½ tsp	salt	7 mL
1 tsp	chipotle powder	5 mL
1¾ cups	lukewarm water (see tip, page 98)	425 mL
3 tbsp	vegetable oil	45 mL
5 cups	bread flour	1.25 L
1½ cups	lightly packed finely shredded pepper Jack cheese (about 4½ oz/140 g)	375 mL
⅔ cup	snipped fresh cilantro	150 mL
1¼ tsp	instant or bread machine yeast	6 mL

1. Add sugar, salt, chipotle powder, water and oil to the bread pan. Spoon flour on top of liquid. Add cheese, cilantro and yeast.

2. Select the Basic/White cycle and press Start.

Cornmeal Pepper Bread

This contemporary version of yeast-risen cornbread is great for hors d'oeuvres or bite-sized buffet sandwiches. You can bake a loaf in the bread machine or make the dough on the Dough cycle, then bake small loaves in clean soup cans or mini loaf pans. Try a cornmeal pepper bread round topped with fresh goat cheese, strips of roasted red bell pepper and arugula, or with unsalted butter and paper-thin slices of prosciutto and ripe, sweet melon.

Tip

Ideally, the water and milk should be between 86°F and 95°F (30°C and 35°C), the temperature range in which yeast is most active. Warm them in the microwave or in a saucepan on the stove, and check the temperature with an instant-read thermometer.

1 lb (500 g)

1 1/2 tsp	granulated sugar	7 mL
1 tsp	salt	5 mL
3/4 tsp	paprika	3 mL
1/2 tsp	freshly ground black pepper	2 mL
1/2 tsp	freshly ground white pepper	2 mL
1	small egg, beaten	1
1/4 cup	lukewarm water (see tip, at left)	60 mL
1/3 cup	unsalted butter, melted	75 mL
1/4 cup	lukewarm milk	60 mL
2 cups	bread flour	500 mL
1/3 cup	yellow cornmeal	75 mL
1 1/2 tsp	instant or bread machine yeast	7 mL

1 1/2 lb (750 g)

2 tsp	granulated sugar	10 mL
1 1/2 tsp	salt	7 mL
1 tsp	paprika	5 mL
3/4 tsp	freshly ground black pepper	3 mL
3/4 tsp	freshly ground white pepper	3 mL
1	large egg, beaten	1
2/3 cup	lukewarm water (see tip, at left)	150 mL
6 tbsp	unsalted butter, melted	90 mL
1/3 cup	lukewarm milk	75 mL
3 cups	bread flour	750 mL
1/2 cup	yellow cornmeal	125 mL
1 1/2 tsp	instant or bread machine yeast	7 mL

2 lb (1 kg)

1 tbsp	granulated sugar	15 mL
1 3/4 tsp	salt	8 mL
1 1/4 tsp	paprika	6 mL
1 tsp	freshly ground black pepper	5 mL
1 tsp	freshly ground white pepper	5 mL
2	small eggs, beaten	2
3/4 cup	lukewarm water (see tip, at left)	175 mL
1/2 cup	unsalted butter, melted	125 mL
1/3 cup	lukewarm milk	75 mL
3 3/4 cups	bread flour	925 mL
6 tbsp	yellow cornmeal	90 mL
1 1/2 tsp	instant or bread machine yeast	7 mL

Tips

If you're adventurous, replace half the paprika with smoked paprika, ancho chile powder or chipotle powder.

When you're making the 1-lb (500 g) loaf, if you can't find small eggs, beat 1 large egg until blended, then measure 2 tbsp + 1 tsp (35 mL) to equal the volume of 1 small egg, reserving any remaining egg for another use. When you're making the 2-lb (1 kg) loaf, beat 2 large eggs until blended, then measure 1/4 cup + 2 tsp (70 mL) to equal the volume of 2 small eggs.

If your dough does not form a ball during the first few minutes of kneading, do one of two things: if the dough looks dry and crumbly, add 1 tbsp (15 mL) water at 1-minute intervals until the dough forms a ball; if the dough looks wet, add 1 tbsp (15 mL) bread flour at 1-minute intervals until the dough forms a ball.

3 lb (1.5 kg)

1½ tbsp	granulated sugar	22 mL
2½ tsp	salt	12 mL
2 tsp	paprika	10 mL
1½ tsp	freshly ground black pepper	7 mL
1½ tsp	freshly ground white pepper	7 mL
2	large eggs, beaten	2
1 cup	lukewarm water (see tip, page 100)	250 mL
⅔ cup	unsalted butter, melted	150 mL
½ cup	lukewarm milk	125 mL
5 cups	bread flour	1.25 L
⅔ cup	yellow cornmeal	150 mL
1¼ tsp	instant or bread machine yeast	6 mL

1. Add sugar, salt, paprika, black pepper, white pepper, eggs, water, butter and milk to the bread pan. Spoon flour and cornmeal on top of liquid. Add yeast.

2. Select the Whole Wheat cycle and press Start.

Oven-Baked Cornmeal Pepper Mini Loaves

Prepare the 1½-lb (750 g) recipe through step 1, then select the Dough cycle and press Start. Heavily oil the insides of four 10-oz (284 mL) clean, empty soup cans that have been opened only at one end or 5¾- by 3-inch (14 by 7.5 cm) mini loaf pans. When the cycle is finished, transfer dough to a floured surface and punch down gently. Cut into 4 equal pieces and shape into loaves to fit cans or loaf pans (the dough should fill the can or pan a little less than halfway). Cover with a clean towel and let rise in a warm, draft-free place for 30 to 60 minutes or until dough has risen to within 1 inch (2.5 cm) of the top. Meanwhile, preheat oven to 375°F (190°C). Place cans at least 1 inch (2.5 cm) apart on a baking sheet. Bake for 30 to 35 minutes or until tops are browned and a wooden skewer inserted in the center of a loaf comes out clean. Run a thin spatula or knife around the inside of each can to loosen the breads, invert the breads onto wire racks and let cool. (You can also use the 3-lb/1.5 kg dough to make 8 mini loaves.)

Summertime Basil and Garlic Bread

When the garden is full of fresh basil, make Basil and Garlic Oil, the secret of this herb-flecked bread. The aroma of this bread as it rises and bakes is absolutely wonderful.

Tips

Ideally, the water should be between 86°F and 95°F (30°C and 35°C), the temperature range in which yeast is most active. Warm it in the microwave or in a saucepan on the stove, and check the temperature with an instant-read thermometer.

Try other olive oils flavored with garlic, herbs, sun-dried tomatoes or chile peppers in place of the Basil and Garlic Oil.

1 lb (500 g)

1 tsp	granulated sugar	5 mL
1 tsp	salt	5 mL
¾ cup	lukewarm water (see tip, at left)	175 mL
⅓ cup	Basil and Garlic Oil (page 279)	75 mL
2½ cups	all-purpose flour	625 mL
1½ tsp	instant or bread machine yeast	7 mL

1½ lb (750 g)

2 tsp	granulated sugar	10 mL
1½ tsp	salt	7 mL
1 cup	lukewarm water (see tip, at left)	250 mL
½ cup	Basil and Garlic Oil (page 279)	125 mL
3½ cups	all-purpose flour	875 mL
1½ tsp	instant or bread machine yeast	7 mL

2 lb (1 kg)

1 tbsp	granulated sugar	15 mL
2 tsp	salt	10 mL
1¼ cups	lukewarm water (see tip, at left)	300 mL
⅔ cup	Basil and Garlic Oil (page 279)	150 mL
4½ cups	all-purpose flour	1.125 L
2 tsp	instant or bread machine yeast	10 mL

3 lb (1.5 kg)

1½ tbsp	granulated sugar	22 mL
2½ tsp	salt	12 mL
1¾ cups	lukewarm water (see tip, at left)	425 mL
¾ cup	Basil and Garlic Oil (page 279)	175 mL
6 cups	all-purpose flour	1.5 L
1¼ tsp	instant or bread machine yeast	6 mL

1. Add sugar, salt, water and oil to the bread pan. Spoon flour on top of liquid. Add yeast.

2. Select the Basic/White cycle and press Start.

Tips

Make an easy substitution for the Basil and Garlic Oil by mixing half the specified amount of prepared pesto with an equal amount of olive oil.

When you're making the monkey bread, if your bread machine doesn't have a Pause button, simply raise the lid, remove the dough, form the balls and brush with oil, then remove the kneading paddle(s) from the pan, place the balls in the pan, sprinkle with cheese and close the lid again. Work quickly, as the rising cycle will continue even without the bread in the pan.

Basil and Garlic Monkey Bread

Prepare the recipe through step 2. At the start of the final rise (see "Timing It Right," page 13), press Pause. Remove dough from bread pan and transfer to a floured surface. Divide dough into 12 pieces and form each piece into a ball. Brush each ball with olive oil. Remove kneading paddle(s) from bread pan. Arrange balls in pan and sprinkle with 2 tbsp (30 mL) freshly grated Parmesan cheese. Press Start to resume the cycle.

Basil and Garlic Rolls

Prepare the 1½ lb (750 g) recipe through step 1, then select the Dough cycle and press Start. Grease a 9-inch (23 cm) round metal cake pan. When the cycle is finished, transfer dough to a floured surface and punch down gently. Flour your hands and pinch off 12 portions of dough. Form each portion into a ball. Place in prepared pan and sprinkle with 2 tbsp (30 mL) freshly grated Parmesan cheese. Cover with a clean towel and let rise in a warm, draft-free place for 30 minutes. Meanwhile, preheat oven to 350°F (180°C). Bake for 15 to 20 minutes or until risen and lightly browned on top and an instant-read thermometer inserted in the center of a roll registers 190°F (90°C). Remove from pan and let cool on a wire rack.

Roasted Bell Pepper and Kalamata Olive Bread

This bread, delicious with a creamy goat cheese spread slathered on it, has a beautiful sunset color flecked with dark purple, and a fabulous flavor.

Tip

Ideally, the water should be between 86°F and 95°F (30°C and 35°C), the temperature range in which yeast is most active. Warm it in the microwave or in a saucepan on the stove, and check the temperature with an instant-read thermometer.

1 lb (500 g)

1 tsp	salt	5 mL
7 tbsp	lukewarm water (see tip, at left)	105 mL
4 tsp	olive oil	20 mL
1/3 cup	finely chopped drained roasted red and/or yellow bell peppers, patted dry	75 mL
2 cups	bread flour	500 mL
1 tsp	instant or bread machine yeast	5 mL
1/3 cup	finely chopped pitted kalamata olives, patted dry	75 mL

1½ lb (750 g)

1½ tsp	salt	7 mL
2/3 cup	lukewarm water (see tip, at left)	150 mL
2 tbsp	olive oil	30 mL
1/2 cup	finely chopped drained roasted red and/or yellow bell peppers, patted dry	125 mL
3 cups	bread flour	750 mL
1 tsp	instant or bread machine yeast	5 mL
1/2 cup	finely chopped kalamata olives, patted dry	125 mL

2 lb (1 kg)

2 tsp	salt	10 mL
3/4 cup + 2 tbsp	lukewarm water (see tip, at left)	205 mL
2½ tbsp	olive oil	37 mL
2/3 cup	finely chopped drained roasted red and/or yellow bell peppers, patted dry	150 mL
4 cups	bread flour	1 L
1¼ tsp	instant or bread machine yeast	6 mL
2/3 cup	finely chopped kalamata olives, patted dry	150 mL

Tips

You can roast fresh red and yellow bell peppers or use prepared ones from a jar or the deli section of your supermarket. Drain them first, then chop and measure, then pat dry to make sure they don't add too much moisture to the dough.

If your machine has a dispenser, check the manual for the correct operating instructions.

If your dough does not form a ball during the first few minutes of kneading, do one of two things: if the dough looks dry and crumbly, add 1 tbsp (15 mL) water at 1-minute intervals until the dough forms a ball; if the dough looks wet, add 1 tbsp (15 mL) bread flour at 1-minute intervals until the dough forms a ball.

3 lb (1.5 kg)

2¼ tsp	salt	11 mL
1 cup + 3 tbsp	lukewarm water (see tip, page 104)	295 mL
3 tbsp	olive oil	45 mL
¾ cup	finely chopped drained roasted red and/or yellow bell peppers, patted dry	175 mL
5 cups	bread flour	1.25 L
1 tsp	instant or bread machine yeast	5 mL
¾ cup	finely chopped kalamata olives, patted dry	175 mL

1. Add salt, water, oil and roasted peppers to the bread pan. Spoon flour on top of liquid. Add yeast. Place olives in the dispenser (or add at the "add ingredient" or "mix in" signal).

2. Select the Basic/White cycle and press Start.

Savory Sun-Dried Tomato Bread

Makes 1 loaf

On a gray February weekend, when August seems far away, open a jar of sun-dried tomatoes preserved in oil to make this bread tasting of hot sun, ripe tomatoes and summer herbs. Then brush the snow off the grill and cook a steak — along with the first early-season asparagus — to cast a culinary spell for warmer weather to come.

Tips

Try fresh basil in place of the flat-leaf (Italian) parsley.

Ideally, the water should be between 86°F and 95°F (30°C and 35°C), the temperature range in which yeast is most active. Warm it in the microwave or in a saucepan on the stove, and check the temperature with an instant-read thermometer.

1 lb (500 g)

1 tsp	salt	5 mL
1	small clove garlic, minced	1
¼ cup	coarsely chopped drained oil-packed sun-dried tomatoes	60 mL
1 tsp	oil from the sun-dried tomatoes	5 mL
1 tbsp	finely chopped fresh flat-leaf (Italian) parsley	15 mL
2 tsp	finely chopped green onion	10 mL
1	small egg, beaten	1
⅔ cup	lukewarm water (see tip, at left)	150 mL
2 cups	all-purpose flour	500 mL
1 tsp	instant or bread machine yeast	5 mL

1½ lb (750 g)

1½ tsp	salt	7 mL
2	small cloves garlic, minced	2
⅓ cup	coarsely chopped drained oil-packed sun-dried tomatoes	75 mL
2 tsp	oil from the sun-dried tomatoes	10 mL
2 tbsp	finely chopped fresh flat-leaf (Italian) parsley	30 mL
4 tsp	finely chopped green onion	20 mL
1	large egg, beaten	1
¾ cup + 2 tbsp	lukewarm water (see tip, at left)	205 mL
3 cups	all-purpose flour	750 mL
1½ tsp	instant or bread machine yeast	7 mL

2 lb (1 kg)

2 tsp	salt	10 mL
3	small cloves garlic, minced	3
½ cup	coarsely chopped drained oil-packed sun-dried tomatoes	125 mL
1 tbsp	oil from the sun-dried tomatoes	15 mL
3 tbsp	finely chopped fresh flat-leaf (Italian) parsley	45 mL
2 tbsp	finely chopped green onion	30 mL
2	small eggs, beaten	2
1 cup	lukewarm water (see tip, at left)	250 mL
3¾ cups	all-purpose flour	925 mL
1½ tsp	instant or bread machine yeast	7 mL

Tips

When you're making the 1-lb (500 g) loaf, if you can't find small eggs, beat 1 large egg until blended, then measure 2 tbsp + 1 tsp (35 mL) to equal the volume of 1 small egg, reserving any remaining egg for another use. When you're making the 2-lb (1 kg) loaf, beat 2 large eggs until blended, then measure ¼ cup + 2 tsp (70 mL) to equal the volume of 2 small eggs.

If your dough does not form a ball during the first few minutes of kneading, do one of two things: if the dough looks dry and crumbly, add 1 tbsp (15 mL) water at 1-minute intervals until the dough forms a ball; if the dough looks wet, add 1 tbsp (15 mL) all-purpose flour at 1-minute intervals until the dough forms a ball.

3 lb (1.5 kg)

2¼ tsp	salt	11 mL
4	small cloves garlic, minced	4
⅔ cup	coarsely chopped drained oil-packed sun-dried tomatoes	150 mL
1½ tbsp	oil from the sun-dried tomatoes	22 mL
¼ cup	finely chopped fresh flat-leaf (Italian) parsley	60 mL
3 tbsp	finely chopped green onion	45 mL
2	large eggs, beaten	2
1½ cups	lukewarm water (see tip, page 106)	375 mL
5½ cups	all-purpose flour	1.375 L
1¼ tsp	instant or bread machine yeast	6 mL

1. Add salt, garlic, sun-dried tomatoes, oil, parsley, green onion, egg(s) and water to the bread pan. Spoon flour on top of liquid. Add yeast.

2. Select the Basic/White cycle and the Light Crust setting and press Start.

Eat-Your-Vegetables Bread

If you buy fruit juice or snacks that include "hidden" vegetables, you'll be all over this bread. Use a dry vegetable soup mix (sometimes labeled "recipe mix") or bulk dehydrated vegetable flakes that include tomatoes, celery root, leeks, onions, carrots and cabbage for a boost of beta carotene and vitamin C. A little pumpkin purée adds golden color and even more flavor and beta carotene.

Tips

Warm the water in the microwave or in a saucepan on the stove, and check the temperature with an instant-read thermometer.

Be sure to use unsweetened canned pumpkin purée for this recipe and not pie filling, which contains added sugar and spices.

A 1.4-oz (40 g) package of dry vegetable soup mix yields about 1/2 cup (125 mL).

1 lb (500 g)

4 tsp	granulated sugar	20 mL
1 1/4 tsp	instant or bread machine yeast	6 mL
1/2 cup	warm water (110°F/43°C)	125 mL
1/3 cup	canned pumpkin purée (not pie filling)	75 mL
2 1/2 tbsp	vegetable oil	37 mL
2 cups	bread flour	500 mL
1/4 cup	dry vegetable soup mix or mixed dehydrated vegetable flakes	60 mL

1 1/2 lb (750 g)

2 tbsp	granulated sugar	30 mL
1 1/2 tsp	instant or bread machine yeast	7 mL
3/4 cup	warm water (110°F/43°C)	175 mL
1/2 cup	canned pumpkin purée (not pie filling)	125 mL
3 tbsp	vegetable oil	45 mL
3 cups	bread flour	750 mL
1/3 cup	dry vegetable soup mix or mixed dehydrated vegetable flakes	75 mL

2 lb (1 kg)

8 tsp	granulated sugar	40 mL
1 tsp	instant or bread machine yeast	5 mL
1 cup + 1 tbsp	warm water (110°F/43°C)	265 mL
2/3 cup	canned pumpkin purée (not pie filling)	150 mL
1/4 cup	vegetable oil	60 mL
4 cups	bread flour	1 L
1/2 cup	dry vegetable soup mix or mixed dehydrated vegetable flakes	125 mL

3 lb (1.5 kg)

1/4 cup	granulated sugar	60 mL
1 1/4 tsp	instant or bread machine yeast	6 mL
1 1/3 cups	warm water (110°F/43°C)	325 mL
3/4 cup	canned pumpkin purée (not pie filling)	175 mL
1/3 cup	vegetable oil	75 mL
5 cups	bread flour	1.25 L
2/3 cup	dry vegetable soup mix or mixed dehydrated vegetable flakes	150 mL

Tips

If your dry vegetable soup mix does not contain salt, add ½ tsp (2 mL) for a 1-lb (500 g) loaf; 1 tsp (5 mL) for a 1½-lb (750 g) loaf; 1½ tsp (7 mL) for a 2-lb (1 kg) loaf; or 2 tsp (10 mL) for a 3-lb (1.5 kg) loaf.

If your dough does not form a ball during the first few minutes of kneading, do one of two things: if the dough looks dry and crumbly, add 1 tbsp (15 mL) water at 1-minute intervals until the dough forms a ball; if the dough looks wet, add 1 tbsp (15 mL) bread flour at 1-minute intervals until the dough forms a ball.

1. Add sugar, yeast and water to the bread pan. Let stand for 10 minutes or until yeast starts to bubble.

2. Add pumpkin and oil. Spoon flour on top of liquid. Add vegetable soup mix.

3. Select the Basic/White cycle and the Light Crust setting and press Start.

Eat-Your-Vegetables Sweet Potato Bread
Try mashed cooked sweet potato or winter squash in place of the pumpkin purée.

Bacon, Green Onion and Blue Cheese Bread

Yum! This savory bread makes terrific BLT or grilled cheese sandwiches. Make it completely in the bread machine for sandwich bread, or make it on the Dough setting, then bake it in the oven for an artisan loaf to serve with Artisan Butter (page 280).

Tips

Warm the water in the microwave or in a saucepan on the stove, and check the temperature with an instant-read thermometer.

If your machine has a dispenser, check the manual for the correct operating instructions.

1 lb (500 g)

4 tsp	granulated sugar	20 mL
1 tsp	instant or bread machine yeast	5 mL
⅔ cup	warm water (110°F/43°C)	150 mL
¼ cup	finely chopped green onions	60 mL
2½ tbsp	vegetable oil	37 mL
2 cups	bread flour	500 mL
½ tsp	salt	2 mL
¼ cup	finely chopped crisply cooked bacon	60 mL
¼ cup	crumbled blue cheese	60 mL

1½ lb (750 g)

1½ tbsp	granulated sugar	22 mL
1 tsp	instant or bread machine yeast	5 mL
¾ cup	warm water (110°F/43°C)	175 mL
⅓ cup	finely chopped green onions	75 mL
3 tbsp	vegetable oil	45 mL
2¾ cups	bread flour	675 mL
¾ tsp	salt	3 mL
⅓ cup	finely chopped crisply cooked bacon	75 mL
⅓ cup	crumbled blue cheese	75 mL

2 lb (1 kg)

2 tbsp	granulated sugar	30 mL
¾ tsp	instant or bread machine yeast	3 mL
1 cup + 2 tbsp	warm water (110°F/43°C)	280 mL
½ cup	finely chopped green onions	125 mL
⅓ cup	vegetable oil	75 mL
3¾ cups	bread flour	925 mL
1 tsp	salt	5 mL
½ cup	finely chopped crisply cooked bacon	125 mL
½ cup	crumbled blue cheese	125 mL

3 lb (1.5 kg)

3 tbsp	granulated sugar	45 mL
¾ tsp	instant or bread machine yeast	3 mL
1⅔ cups	warm water (110°F/43°C)	400 mL
⅔ cup	finely chopped green onions	150 mL
½ cup	vegetable oil	125 mL
5½ cups	bread flour	1.375 L

Tips

When making the smallest loaf allowed by your machine, check the dough a few minutes after kneading starts to make sure the ingredients are incorporated. You may need to help the machine along by using a rubber spatula to scrape the corners of the pan.

Bread machine breads tend to be best within a day or two of baking, but if you want to store them for longer, wrap and freeze loaves or slices in labeled and dated freezer-proof packages for up to 3 months. Cut large loaves to fit freezer storage bags.

1 1/4 tsp	salt	6 mL
2/3 cup	finely chopped crisply cooked bacon	150 mL
2/3 cup	crumbled blue cheese	150 mL

1. Add sugar, yeast and water to the bread pan. Let stand for 10 minutes or until yeast starts bubble.

2. Add green onions and oil. Spoon flour on top of liquid. Add salt, bacon and cheese.

3. Select the Basic/White cycle and press Start.

Bacon, Green Onion and Blue Cheese Boule

Prepare the recipe through step 2, then select the Dough cycle and press Start. Line a baking sheet with parchment paper. When the cycle is finished, transfer dough to a floured surface and punch down gently. Form into a boule and place on prepared baking sheet. Cover with a clean towel and let rise in a warm, draft-free place for 30 minutes. Meanwhile, preheat oven to 425°F (220°C). Using a serrated knife, cut 3 to 5 deep diagonal slashes across top of loaf. Spray loaf with water. Bake until risen and dark brown on top and an instant-read thermometer inserted in the center registers 190°F (90°C). Remove from pan and let cool on a wire rack.

Dough Size	Baking Time
1 lb (500 g)	25 to 27 minutes
1 1/2 lb (750 g)	28 to 30 minutes
2 lb (1 kg)	30 to 33 minutes
3 lb (1.5 kg)	35 to 37 minutes

Ham, Leek and Gruyère Bread

Use smoked ham in place of the bacon, leeks (white and light green parts only) in place of the green onions and shredded Gruyère cheese in place of the blue cheese.

Cheddar Beer Bread

Cheese and beer, great
go-togethers, give this
bread superb flavor and
texture. It's great with a
hearty soup, stew or chili.

Tips

When you're making the 2-lb
(1 kg) loaf, if you can't find
small eggs, beat 3 large eggs
until blended, then measure
7 tbsp (105 mL) to equal the
volume of 3 small eggs. You
can use the leftover beaten
whole egg for the topping or
use a large egg yolk.

Lager beers are best for
bread. The darker the beer,
the more bitterness it adds
to the dough.

To make beer go flat, simply
pour it into a glass and let it
stand at room temperature
for an hour or microwave it
until it boils, then let it cool
before use. Alternatively, you
can whisk the granulated
sugar from the recipe into
the measured beer and let it
stand for about 15 minutes
or until the bubbles subside.

You can use regular whole
wheat flour in place of the
white whole wheat flour.

1 lb (500 g)

3 tbsp	packed brown sugar	45 mL
1/2 tsp	granulated sugar	2 mL
1/2 tsp	salt	2 mL
1	large egg, beaten	1
1/3 cup	flat lager beer (see tips, at left)	75 mL
3 tbsp	vegetable oil	45 mL
1 1/3 cups	all-purpose flour	325 mL
2/3 cup	white whole wheat flour	150 mL
3/4 cup	lightly packed shredded aged (old) Cheddar cheese (about 2 1/4 oz/68 g)	175 mL
3/4 tsp	instant or bread machine yeast	3 mL

Topping

1	large egg yolk, beaten	1
2 tbsp	shredded aged (old) Cheddar cheese	30 mL

1 1/2 lb (750 g)

3 tbsp	packed brown sugar	45 mL
1 tsp	granulated sugar	5 mL
1 tsp	salt	5 mL
1	large egg, beaten	1
1/2 cup	flat lager beer (see tips, at left)	125 mL
3 tbsp	vegetable oil	45 mL
1 3/4 cups	all-purpose flour	425 mL
2/3 cup	white whole wheat flour	150 mL
1 cup + 2 tbsp	lightly packed shredded aged (old) Cheddar cheese (about 3 1/2 oz/105 g)	280 mL
1 tsp	instant or bread machine yeast	5 mL

Topping

1	large egg yolk, beaten	1
3 tbsp	shredded aged (old) Cheddar cheese	45 mL

2 lb (1 kg)

1/4 cup	packed brown sugar	60 mL
1 1/2 tsp	granulated sugar	7 mL
1 1/2 tsp	salt	7 mL
3	small eggs, beaten	3
3/4 cup + 1 tbsp	flat lager beer (see tips, at left)	190 mL
1/4 cup	vegetable oil	60 mL
2 1/2 cups	all-purpose flour	625 mL
1 1/2 cups	white whole wheat flour	375 mL
1 1/2 cups	lightly packed shredded aged (old) Cheddar cheese (about 5 oz/150 g)	375 mL
1 tsp	instant or bread machine yeast	5 mL

If your dough does not form
a ball during the first few
minutes of kneading, do one
of two things: if the dough
looks dry and crumbly, add
1 tbsp (15 mL) water at
1-minute intervals until the
dough forms a ball; if the
dough looks wet, add 1 tbsp
(15 mL) all-purpose flour at
1-minute intervals until the
dough forms a ball.

If your bread machine doesn't
have a Pause button, simply
raise the lid, brush with egg
yolk and sprinkle with cheese,
then close the lid again. Work
quickly, as the rising cycle will
continue even without the
bread in the pan.

Topping

1	small egg yolk, beaten	1
¼ cup	shredded aged (old) Cheddar cheese	60 mL

3 lb (1.5 kg)

⅓ cup	packed brown sugar	75 mL
2 tsp	granulated sugar	10 mL
2 tsp	salt	10 mL
2	large eggs, beaten	2
1 cup + 2 tbsp	flat lager beer (see tips, page 112)	280 mL
⅓ cup	vegetable oil	75 mL
3 cups	all-purpose flour	750 mL
2 cups	white whole wheat flour	500 mL
1¾ cups	lightly packed shredded aged (old) Cheddar cheese (about 6½ oz/195 g)	425 mL
1 tsp	instant or bread machine yeast	5 mL

Topping

1	large egg yolk, beaten	1
¼ cup	shredded aged (old) Cheddar cheese	50 mL

1. Add brown sugar, granulated sugar, salt, egg(s), beer and oil to the bread pan. Spoon all-purpose flour and whole wheat flour on top of liquid. Add cheese and yeast.

2. Select the Basic/White cycle and the Light Crust setting and press Start.

3. *Topping*: At the start of the final rise (see "Timing It Right," page 13), press Pause. Raise the lid, brush the top of the loaf with egg yolk and sprinkle with cheese. Close the lid and press Start to continue the cycle.

Oven-Baked Cheddar Beer Braid

Prepare the recipe through step 1, then select the Dough cycle and press Start. Line a large baking sheet with parchment paper. When the cycle is finished, transfer dough to a floured surface and divide into thirds. Roll each third into a 16-inch (40 cm) long rope. Braid ropes together, tucking ends under. Place on prepared baking sheet. Cover with a clean towel and let rise in a warm, draft-free place for 1 to 1½ hours or until doubled in bulk. Meanwhile, preheat oven to 350°F (180°C). Brush braid with egg yolk and sprinkle with cheese, pressing the cheese into the dough. Bake until lightly browned on top and an instant-read thermometer inserted in the center registers 190°F (90°C). Remove from pan and let cool on a wire rack.

Dough Size	Baking Time
1 lb (500 g)	30 to 34 minutes
1½ lb (750 g)	32 to 36 minutes
2 lb (1 kg)	35 to 40 minutes
3 lb (1.5 kg)	38 to 45 minutes

The Miller's Cinnamon and Raisin Bread

"People love my cinnamon and raisin bread because it's got a very soft, tender crumb," says Alvin Brensing, the octogenarian miller in charge of producing Hudson Cream Flour, a premium all-purpose flour from Stafford County, Kansas. His home economist daughter helped him perfect this recipe. If you wish, you can substitute bread flour and omit the vital wheat gluten, but the bread won't be as tender. The cinnamon turns this bread a rich, warm brown. Any leftovers make delicious French toast or bread pudding.

Tips

When you're making the 1-lb (500 g) loaf, if you can't find small eggs, beat 2 large eggs until blended, then measure 1/4 cup + 2 tsp (70 mL) to equal the volume of 2 small eggs, reserving any remaining egg for another use.

To plump raisins, place them in a bowl and add enough hot water to cover. Let stand for 15 minutes or until plump. Drain well and let cool, then pat dry.

1 lb (500 g)

3/4 cup	milk	175 mL
1 1/2 tbsp	unsalted butter, softened	22 mL
2 tbsp	packed light or dark brown sugar	30 mL
1 tsp	salt	5 mL
2	small eggs, beaten	2
2 cups	all-purpose flour	500 mL
4 tsp	vital wheat gluten	20 mL
4 tsp	ground cinnamon	20 mL
1 tsp	instant or bread machine yeast	5 mL
1/2 cup	raisins, plumped and drained (see tip, at left)	125 mL

1 1/2 lb (750 g)

3/4 cup	milk	175 mL
2 1/2 tbsp	unsalted butter, softened	37 mL
3 tbsp	packed light or dark brown sugar	45 mL
1 1/2 tsp	salt	7 mL
2	large eggs, beaten	2
2 2/3 cups	all-purpose flour	650 mL
1 1/2 tbsp	vital wheat gluten	22 mL
1 1/2 tbsp	ground cinnamon	22 mL
1 1/2 tsp	instant or bread machine yeast	7 mL
2/3 cup	raisins, plumped and drained (see tip, at left)	150 mL

2 lb (1 kg)

1 cup	milk	250 mL
3 tbsp	unsalted butter, softened	45 mL
1/4 cup	packed light or dark brown sugar	60 mL
2 tsp	salt	10 mL
3	large eggs, beaten	3
3 3/4 cups	all-purpose flour	925 mL
2 tbsp	vital wheat gluten	30 mL
2 tbsp	ground cinnamon	30 mL
1 1/2 tsp	instant or bread machine yeast	7 mL
3/4 cup	raisins, plumped and drained (see tip, at left)	175 mL

Tips

For a more delicate cinnamon flavor, decrease the amount called for by half.

If your machine has a dispenser, check the manual for the correct operating instructions.

If your dough does not form a ball during the first few minutes of kneading, do one of two things: if the dough looks dry and crumbly, add 1 tbsp (15 mL) water at 1-minute intervals until the dough forms a ball; if the dough looks wet, add 1 tbsp (15 mL) all-purpose flour at 1-minute intervals until the dough forms a ball.

3 lb (1.5 kg)

1²⁄₃ cups	milk	400 mL
¼ cup	unsalted butter, softened	60 mL
⅓ cup	packed light or dark brown sugar	75 mL
2½ tsp	salt	12 mL
3	large eggs, beaten	3
5 cups	all-purpose flour	1.25 L
8 tsp	vital wheat gluten	40 mL
8 tsp	ground cinnamon	40 mL
1¾ tsp	instant or bread machine yeast	8 mL
1 cup	raisins, plumped and drained (see tip, page 114)	250 mL

1. In a medium saucepan, scald milk over medium-high heat until bubbles form around the edge. Remove from heat and stir in butter and brown sugar. Transfer to the bread pan and let cool to lukewarm (between 86°F and 95°F/30°C and 35°C).

2. Add salt and eggs to the bread pan. Spoon flour on top of liquid. Add wheat gluten, cinnamon and yeast. Place raisins in the dispenser (or add at the "add ingredient" or "mix in" signal).

3. Select the Basic/White cycle and the Light Crust setting and press Start.

Lemon Poppy Seed Bread

This bread has just enough sweetness to marry the flavors of lemon and poppy seed, but not enough to merit baking it on the Sweet cycle. It makes fabulous French toast, sprinkled with a little confectioners' (icing) sugar, and makes a chicken or shrimp salad sandwich much more interesting.

Tips

When you're making the 1-lb (500 g) loaf, if you can't find small eggs, beat 2 large eggs until blended, then measure ¼ cup + 2 tsp (70 mL) to equal the volume of 2 small eggs, reserving any remaining egg for another use.

If you're a lemon lover, try the bread this way first, then add more lemon zest if you like.

1 lb (500 g)

⅔ cup	milk	150 mL
1½ tbsp	unsalted butter, softened	22 mL
2 tbsp	granulated sugar	30 mL
1 tsp	salt	5 mL
1 tsp	grated lemon zest	5 mL
2	small eggs, beaten	2
2 cups	all-purpose flour	500 mL
2 tbsp	poppy seeds	30 mL
4 tsp	vital wheat gluten	20 mL
1 tsp	instant or bread machine yeast	5 mL

1½ lb (750 g)

¾ cup + 2 tbsp	milk	205 mL
2½ tbsp	unsalted butter, softened	37 mL
3 tbsp	granulated sugar	45 mL
1½ tsp	salt	7 mL
1½ tsp	grated lemon zest	7 mL
2	large eggs, beaten	2
2¾ cups	all-purpose flour	675 mL
3 tbsp	poppy seeds	45 mL
2 tbsp	vital wheat gluten	30 mL
1½ tsp	instant or bread machine yeast	7 mL

2 lb (1 kg)

1 cup + 2 tbsp	milk	280 mL
3 tbsp	unsalted butter, softened	45 mL
¼ cup	granulated sugar	60 mL
2 tsp	salt	10 mL
2 tsp	grated lemon zest	10 mL
3	large eggs, beaten	3
3¾ cups	all-purpose flour	925 mL
¼ cup	poppy seeds	60 mL
2 tbsp	vital wheat gluten	30 mL
1½ tsp	instant or bread machine yeast	7 mL

If your dough does not form a ball during the first few minutes of kneading, do one of two things: if the dough looks dry and crumbly, add 1 tbsp (15 mL) water at 1-minute intervals until the dough forms a ball; if the dough looks wet, add 1 tbsp (15 mL) all-purpose flour at 1-minute intervals until the dough forms a ball.

Bread machine breads tend to be best within a day or two of baking, but if you want to store them for longer, wrap and freeze loaves or slices in labeled and dated freezer-proof packages for up to 3 months. Cut large loaves to fit freezer storage bags.

3 lb (1.5 kg)

1²⁄₃ cups	milk	400 mL
¼ cup	unsalted butter, softened	60 mL
⅓ cup	granulated sugar	75 mL
2½ tsp	salt	12 mL
1 tbsp	grated lemon zest	15 mL
3	large eggs, beaten	3
5 cups	all-purpose flour	1.25 L
⅓ cup	poppy seeds	75 mL
8 tsp	vital wheat gluten	40 mL
1½ tsp	instant or bread machine yeast	7 mL

1. In a medium saucepan, scald milk over medium-high heat until bubbles form around the edge. Remove from heat and stir in butter and sugar. Transfer to the bread pan and let cool to lukewarm (between 86°F and 95°F/30°C and 35°C).

2. Add salt, lemon zest and eggs. Spoon flour on top of liquid. Add poppy seeds, wheat gluten and yeast.

3. Select the Basic/White cycle and the Light Crust setting and press Start.

Banana Walnut Bread with Blueberries

Bananas, walnuts, dried blueberries and flax seeds make this bread a great way to start your day. It's packed with flavor — as well as potassium, antioxidants and omega-3 fatty acids — without being sweet.

Tips

Use very ripe bananas (yellow with brown spots) for the best flavor and texture in this bread.

If you can't find dried blueberries, use chopped dried cherries or cranberries. You can even try blueberry-flavored dried cranberries.

To toast walnut halves, place on a microwave-safe plate and microwave on High for 2 to 3 minutes or until fragrant. Or toast on a baking sheet in a 350°F (180°C) oven for about 8 minutes. Let cool, then chop and measure.

1 lb (500 g)

6 tbsp	milk	90 mL
1 tbsp	unsalted butter, softened	15 mL
1½ tbsp	granulated or raw sugar	22 mL
1 tsp	salt	5 mL
1	large egg, beaten	1
⅓ cup	mashed ripe banana	75 mL
1⅔ cups	all-purpose flour	400 mL
2 tsp	ground flax seeds	10 mL
1½ tsp	vital wheat gluten	7 mL
1 tsp	ground cinnamon	10 mL
1½ tsp	instant or bread machine yeast	7 mL
⅓ cup	dried blueberries	75 mL
3 tbsp	chopped toasted walnuts (see tip, at left)	45 mL

1½ lb (750 g)

½ cup	milk	125 mL
1½ tbsp	unsalted butter, softened	22 mL
2 tbsp	granulated or raw sugar	30 mL
1½ tsp	salt	7 mL
1	large egg, beaten	1
1	large egg yolk, beaten	1
½ cup	mashed ripe banana (about 1 large)	125 mL
2⅓ cups	all-purpose flour	575 mL
1 tbsp	ground flax seeds	15 mL
2 tsp	vital wheat gluten	10 mL
1½ tsp	ground cinnamon	7 mL
1½ tsp	instant or bread machine yeast	7 mL
½ cup	dried blueberries	125 mL
¼ cup	chopped toasted walnuts (see tip, at left)	60 mL

2 lb (1 kg)

¾ cup	milk	175 mL
2½ tbsp	unsalted butter, softened	37 mL
3 tbsp	granulated or raw sugar	45 mL
1¾ tsp	salt	8 mL
2	large eggs, beaten	2
⅔ cup	mashed ripe bananas (about 1½ large)	150 mL
3⅓ cups	all-purpose flour	825 mL

Tips

If your dough does not form a ball during the first few minutes of kneading, do one of two things: if the dough looks dry and crumbly, add 1 tbsp (15 mL) water at 1-minute intervals until the dough forms a ball; if the dough looks wet, add 1 tbsp (15 mL) all-purpose flour at 1-minute intervals until the dough forms a ball.

Bread machine breads tend to be best within a day or two of baking, but if you want to store them for longer, wrap and freeze loaves or slices in labeled and dated freezer-proof packages for up to 3 months. Cut large loaves to fit freezer storage bags.

1½ tbsp	ground flax seeds	22 mL
1 tbsp	vital wheat gluten	15 mL
2 tsp	ground cinnamon	10 mL
2 tsp	instant or bread machine yeast	10 mL
¾ cup	dried blueberries	175 mL
⅓ cup	chopped toasted walnuts (see tip, page 118)	75 mL

3 lb (1.5 kg)

⅔ cup	milk	150 mL
3 tbsp	unsalted butter, softened	45 mL
¼ cup	granulated or raw sugar	60 mL
2¼ tsp	salt	11 mL
3	large eggs, beaten	3
1 cup	mashed ripe bananas (about 2 large)	250 mL
4 cups	all-purpose flour	1 L
2 tbsp	ground flax seeds	30 mL
1½ tbsp	vital wheat gluten	22 mL
2½ tsp	ground cinnamon	12 mL
2¼ tsp	instant or bread machine yeast	11 mL
1 cup	dried blueberries	250 mL
½ cup	chopped toasted walnuts (see tip, page 118)	125 mL

1. In a medium saucepan, scald milk over medium-high heat until bubbles form around the edge. Remove from heat and stir in butter and sugar. Transfer to the bread pan and let cool to lukewarm (between 85 to 95°F/30°C and 35°C).

2. Add salt, egg(s) and banana(s). Spoon flour on top of liquid. Add flax seeds, wheat gluten, cinnamon and yeast. Place blueberries and walnuts in the dispenser (or add at the "add ingredient" or "mix in" signal).

3. Select the Basic/White cycle and the Light Crust setting and press Start.

> ### Whole Wheat Banana Walnut Bread with Blueberries
> Replace half the all-purpose flour with white whole wheat flour or regular whole wheat flour.

Spiced Applesauce Bread

Applesauce, fresh apple and spices make this white loaf a natural for breakfast toast. But it's also delicious in French toast, bread pudding or a fruity stuffing for roast chicken or turkey. The more flavorful the applesauce, the more flavorful the bread, so use the good stuff.

Tip

Ideally, the applesauce, apple juice and milk should be between 86°F and 95°F (30°C and 35°C), the temperature range in which yeast is most active. Warm them in the microwave or in a saucepan on the stove, and check the temperature with an instant-read thermometer.

1 lb (500 g)

1½ tsp	salt	7 mL
1 tsp	ground cinnamon	5 mL
⅓ cup	chopped peeled Golden Delicious or other sweet apple	75 mL
⅓ cup	lukewarm Honey Spice Applesauce (page 283) or other sweetened spiced applesauce (see tip, at left)	75 mL
¼ cup	lukewarm unsweetened apple juice or cider	60 mL
3 tbsp	lukewarm milk	45 mL
1 tsp	vegetable oil	5 mL
2 cups	bread flour	500 mL
1¼ tsp	instant or bread machine yeast	6 mL

1½ lb (750 g)

2 tsp	salt	10 mL
1½ tsp	ground cinnamon	7 mL
½ cup	chopped peeled Golden Delicious or other sweet apple	125 mL
½ cup	lukewarm Honey Spice Applesauce (page 283) or other sweetened spiced applesauce (see tip, at left)	125 mL
⅓ cup	lukewarm unsweetened apple juice or cider	75 mL
¼ cup	lukewarm milk	60 mL
1½ tsp	vegetable oil	7 mL
3 cups	bread flour	750 mL
1½ tsp	instant or bread machine yeast	7 mL

2 lb (2 kg)

2½ tsp	salt	12 mL
2 tsp	ground cinnamon	10 mL
⅔ cup	chopped peeled Golden Delicious or other sweet apple	150 mL
⅔ cup	lukewarm Honey Spice Applesauce (page 283) or other sweetened spiced applesauce (see tip, at left)	150 mL
⅓ cup	lukewarm unsweetened apple juice or cider	75 mL
⅓ cup	lukewarm milk	75 mL
2 tsp	vegetable oil	10 mL
3¾ cups	bread flour	925 mL
1½ tsp	instant or bread machine yeast	7 mL

Tip

If your dough does not form a ball during the first few minutes of kneading, do one of two things: if the dough looks dry and crumbly, add 1 tbsp (15 mL) water at 1-minute intervals until the dough forms a ball; if the dough looks wet, add 1 tbsp (15 mL) bread flour at 1-minute intervals until the dough forms a ball. Keep in mind that the apple will add some moisture once it gets chopped and incorporated as the machine kneads the dough, so don't be too quick to add more liquid.

3 lb (1.5 kg)

2¾ tsp	salt	13 mL
2½ tsp	ground cinnamon	12 mL
¾ cup	chopped peeled Golden Delicious or other sweet apple	175 mL
1 cup	lukewarm Honey Spice Applesauce (page 283) or other sweetened spiced applesauce (see tip, page 120)	250 mL
½ cup	lukewarm unsweetened apple juice or cider	125 mL
⅓ cup	lukewarm milk	75 mL
1 tbsp	vegetable oil	15 mL
5 cups	bread flour	1.25 L
1½ tsp	instant or bread machine yeast	7 mL

1. Add salt, cinnamon, apple, applesauce, apple juice, milk and oil to the bread pan. Spoon flour on top of liquid. Add yeast.

2. Select the Basic/White cycle and press Start.

Honey Pumpkin Bread

Golden and delicious, with more beta carotene and vitamin A than a regular white loaf, this gently flavored and colored bread can be a salute to Thanksgiving all year long when you use it for turkey sandwiches. It has just a touch of honey for sweetness.

Tips

Be sure to use unsweetened canned pumpkin purée for this recipe and not pie filling, which contains added sugar and spices.

Ideally, the milk and water should be between 86°F and 95°F (30°C and 35°C), the temperature range in which yeast is most active. Warm them in the microwave or in a saucepan on the stove, and check the temperature with an instant-read thermometer.

1 lb (500 g)

1½ tsp	salt	7 mL
½ tsp	pumpkin pie spice	2 mL
½ cup	canned pumpkin purée (not pie filling)	125 mL
¼ cup	lukewarm milk (see tip, at left)	60 mL
¼ cup	lukewarm water	60 mL
2 tbsp	liquid honey	30 mL
1 tsp	vegetable oil	5 mL
2½ cups	bread flour	625 mL
1¼ tsp	instant or bread machine yeast	6 mL

1½ lb (750 g)

2 tsp	salt	10 mL
1 tsp	pumpkin pie spice	5 mL
⅔ cup	canned pumpkin purée (not pie filling)	150 mL
½ cup	lukewarm milk (see tip, at left)	125 mL
¼ cup	lukewarm water	60 mL
3 tbsp	liquid honey	45 mL
2 tsp	vegetable oil	10 mL
3½ cups	bread flour	875 mL
1¼ tsp	instant or bread machine yeast	6 mL

2 lb (1 kg)

2½ tsp	salt	12 mL
2 tsp	pumpkin pie spice	10 mL
1 cup	canned pumpkin purée (not pie filling)	250 mL
½ cup	lukewarm milk (see tip, at left)	125 mL
⅓ cup	lukewarm water	75 mL
¼ cup	liquid honey	60 mL
2½ tsp	vegetable oil	12 mL
4½ cups	bread flour	1.125 mL
1½ tsp	instant or bread machine yeast	7 mL

Tip

If your dough does not form a ball during the first few minutes of kneading, do one of two things: if the dough looks dry and crumbly, add 1 tbsp (15 mL) water at 1-minute intervals until the dough forms a ball; if the dough looks wet, add 1 tbsp (15 mL) bread flour at 1-minute intervals until the dough forms a ball.

3 lb (1.5 kg)

2¾ tsp	salt	13 mL
2½ tsp	pumpkin pie spice	12 mL
1⅓ cups	canned pumpkin purée (not pie filling)	325 mL
⅔ cup	lukewarm milk (see tip, page 122)	150 mL
¼ cup	lukewarm water	60 mL
⅓ cup	liquid honey	75 mL
1 tbsp	vegetable oil	15 mL
5½ cups	bread flour	1.375 L
1¾ tsp	instant or bread machine yeast	8 mL

1. Add salt, pumpkin pie spice, pumpkin, milk, water, honey and oil to the bread pan. Spoon flour on top of liquid. Add yeast.

2. Select the Basic/White cycle and press Start.

Sweet Breads

SWEET DOUGHS, usually deliciously rich with sugar and dairy products, have their own special Sweet cycle on the bread machine. This cycle bakes the bread at a slightly lower temperature so it doesn't get too brown. Once you get to know how your machine bakes, you may wish to choose the Light Crust setting to make sure the crust isn't too thick and dark. If your machine doesn't have a Sweet cycle, choose the Basic/White and Light Crust setting.

One way to get a big flavor boost from sweet bread is to add a filling, which is spread on dough that has been rolled out. You then roll up the dough, making a swirled loaf, before baking the bread in the oven. Once the baked loaf has cooled, you can gild the lily by adding a glaze that complements the flavor of the filling. I've provided a wonderful selection of glazes for you to choose from on page 291 (including all of the glazes mentioned below). Here are a few fabulous filling/glaze flavor pairings:

Filling Flavor	Glaze Flavor
Cinnamon	Vanilla
Orange	Orange or almond
Apple	Cider or vanilla
Coconut	Lime, orange or vanilla
Apricot	Almond or vanilla
Sweet cheese	Vanilla, almond, orange or lemon
Pumpkin butter	Cider or orange
Poppy seeds	Vanilla, almond or lemon

For filled loaves, it's best to use the Dough cycle to make the dough, then bake the filled and formed loaf in the oven. Baking filled loaves in the machine can be tricky, since you can't adjust the rising or baking time; they tend to rise too much, and the filling can spill out and burn.

Once you get the hang of making sweet breads in the bread machine, you can use the recipes from this chapter as templates to customize your own loaves. Here are some mix-and-match flavor combinations that work well:

Dough Flavoring	Accent Flavors
Almond	Dried apricots, blueberries, cranberries or cherries, poppy seeds, chocolate chips
Banana	Dried blueberries, cranberries or cherries, crystallized ginger
Cardamom	Orange juice or orange zest
Cinnamon	Dried apples, blueberries or cranberries, maple syrup or maple sugar, apple cider
Lemon zest	Dried blueberries, poppy seeds, crystallized ginger
Lime zest	Sweetened flaked coconut, semisweet or white chocolate chips
Orange zest	Dried cranberries or blueberries, pistachios, chocolate chips

Sugar and Spice

The type of sugar — granulated, raw or brown — you choose to add to a sweet bread partially depends on what other flavorings are in the loaf. All three types of sugar work well with cinnamon, cake spice or pumpkin pie spice. Granulated or raw sugar blend well with cardamom and citrus zest, while brown sugar works better with allspice and ginger.

Lemon Blueberry Bread

The key to a blueberry bread that doesn't turn blue is to use dried blueberries instead of fresh or frozen. Without icing, this loaf makes incredible stuffed French toast with a lemon curd filling (see tip, opposite), finished off with warm blueberry sauce or syrup. You can also toast slices of the iced loaf, then slather them with Artisan Butter (page 280) and blueberry jam.

Tip

If your dough does not form a ball during the first few minutes of kneading, do one of two things: if the dough looks dry and crumbly, add 1 tbsp (15 mL) water at 1-minute intervals until the dough forms a ball; if the dough looks wet, add 1 tbsp (15 mL) all-purpose flour at 1-minute intervals until the dough forms a ball.

1 lb (500 g)

6 tbsp	milk	90 mL
2 tbsp	unsalted butter, softened	30 mL
1/4 cup	granulated sugar	60 mL
2 tsp	grated lemon zest	10 mL
1 tbsp	freshly squeezed lemon juice	15 mL
1/4 tsp	salt	1 mL
1	large egg	1
1 3/4 cup	all-purpose flour	425 mL
1 1/4 tsp	instant or bread machine yeast	6 mL
1/2 cup	dried blueberries	125 mL

Lemon Icing

2/3 cup	confectioners' (icing) sugar	150 mL
1 1/2 tsp	unsalted butter, softened	7 mL
1 tbsp	freshly squeezed lemon juice	15 mL

1 1/2 lb (750 g)

2/3 cup	milk	150 mL
3 tbsp	unsalted butter, softened	45 mL
1/3 cup	granulated sugar	75 mL
1/4 tsp	salt	1 mL
1 tbsp	grated lemon zest	15 mL
2 tbsp	freshly squeezed lemon juice	30 mL
1	large egg, beaten	1
1	large egg yolk, beaten	1
2 3/4 cups	all-purpose flour	675 mL
1 1/2 tsp	instant or bread machine yeast	7 mL
2/3 cup	dried blueberries	150 mL

Lemon Icing

2/3 cup	confectioners' (icing) sugar	150 mL
1 1/2 tsp	unsalted butter, softened	7 mL
1 tbsp	freshly squeezed lemon juice	15 mL

2 lb (1 kg)

3/4 cup	milk	175 mL
1/4 cup	unsalted butter, softened	60 mL
1/2 cup	granulated sugar	125 mL
1/2 tsp	salt	2 mL
1 1/2 tbsp	grated lemon zest	22 mL
2 tbsp	freshly squeezed lemon juice	30 mL
2	large eggs, beaten	2
3 1/2 cups	all-purpose flour	875 mL
1 1/2 tsp	instant or bread machine yeast	7 mL
3/4 cup	dried blueberries	175 mL

Tips

Bread machine breads tend to be best within a day or two of baking, but if you want to store them for longer, wrap and freeze un-iced loaves in labeled and dated freezer-proof packages for up to 3 months. Cut large loaves to fit freezer storage bags. Thaw, then ice the bread before serving.

To make stuffed French toast, cut day-old bread into 1/2-inch (1 cm) thick slices. Spread half the slices with lemon curd and sandwich with another slice. Dip filled sandwiches in the egg mixture of your favorite French toast recipe and cook as directed.

Lemon Icing

1 1/4 cups	confectioners' (icing) sugar	300 mL
1 tbsp	unsalted butter, softened	15 mL
2 tbsp	freshly squeezed lemon juice	30 mL

3 lb (1.5 kg)

1 cup	milk	250 mL
6 tbsp	unsalted butter, softened	90 mL
2/3 cup	granulated sugar	150 mL
1 tsp	salt	5 mL
1 tbsp	grated lemon zest	15 mL
3 tbsp	freshly squeezed lemon juice	45 mL
3	large eggs, beaten	3
5 1/2 cups	all-purpose flour	1.375 L
1 1/4 tsp	instant or bread machine yeast	6 mL
1 1/4 cups	dried blueberries	300 mL

Lemon Icing

1 1/4 cups	confectioners' (icing) sugar	300 mL
1 tbsp	unsalted butter, softened	15 mL
2 tbsp	freshly squeezed lemon juice	30 mL

1. In a small saucepan, scald milk over medium-high heat until small bubbles form around the edges. Remove from heat and stir in butter and sugar. Transfer to the bread pan and let cool to lukewarm (between 86°F and 95°F/30°C and 35°C).

2. Add salt, lemon zest, lemon juice and eggs to the bread pan. Spoon flour on top of liquid. Add yeast. Place blueberries in the dispenser (or add at the "add ingredient" or "mix in" signal).

4. Select the Sweet or Fruit & Nut cycle and press Start. When the cycle is finished, transfer the loaf to a wire rack and let cool for 1 hour.

5. *Icing:* In a bowl, whisk together confectioners' sugar, butter and lemon juice. Spread icing over loaf. Let set for 30 minutes before slicing.

Banana Chocolate Chip Bread

With this versatile dough, you can make a simple bread machine loaf or a glazed swirl loaf.

Tips

Use very ripe bananas (yellow with brown spots) for the best flavor and texture in this bread.

You can use milk, semisweet or dark chocolate chips in this recipe — whatever you prefer.

To toast pecans, spread pecan halves on a baking sheet and toast in a 350°F (180°C) oven for about 8 minutes, stirring once, until golden and fragrant. Immediately transfer to a bowl and let cool.

1 lb (500 g)

2½ tbsp	milk	37 mL
1 tbsp	unsalted butter, softened	15 mL
3 tbsp	granulated or raw sugar	45 mL
1 tsp	salt	5 mL
1	large egg, beaten	1
1	large egg yolk, beaten	1
6 tbsp	mashed ripe banana (about 1)	90 mL
1¾ cups	all-purpose flour	425 mL
1 tbsp	vital wheat gluten	15 mL
¾ tsp	ground cinnamon (optional)	3 mL
1¼ tsp	instant or bread machine yeast	6 mL
⅓ cup	chocolate chips	75 mL
¼ cup	toasted chopped pecans (see tip, at left)	60 mL

1½ lb (750 g)

¼ cup	milk	60 mL
2 tbsp	unsalted butter, softened	30 mL
¼ cup	granulated or raw sugar	60 mL
1½ tsp	salt	7 mL
2	large eggs, beaten	2
⅔ cup	mashed ripe bananas (about 1½)	150 mL
2⅔ cups	all-purpose flour	650 mL
1½ tbsp	vital wheat gluten	22 mL
1¼ tsp	ground cinnamon (optional)	6 mL
1½ tsp	instant or bread machine yeast	7 mL
½ cup	chocolate chips	125 mL
⅓ cup	toasted chopped pecans (see tip, at left)	75 mL

2 lb (1 kg)

7 tbsp	milk	105 mL
3 tbsp	unsalted butter, softened	45 mL
⅓ cup	granulated or raw sugar	75 mL
2¼ tsp	salt	11 mL
2	large eggs, beaten	2
1	large egg yolk, beaten	1
¾ cup	mashed ripe bananas (about 2)	175 mL
3½ cups	all-purpose flour	875 mL
2 tbsp	vital wheat gluten	30 mL
1½ tsp	ground cinnamon (optional)	7 mL
2 tsp	instant or bread machine yeast	10 mL
¾ cup	semisweet chocolate chips	175 mL
½ cup	toasted chopped pecans (see tip, at left)	125 mL

continued after photos…

Oven-Baked Wheat and Walnut Boule (page 163)

Sour Dark Rye Bread with Caraway (page 156)

Authentic Focaccia (page 176)

Roasted Chicken, Pancetta and Potato Pizza (page 190)

Tips

When making the smallest loaf allowed by your machine, check the dough a few minutes after kneading starts to make sure the ingredients are incorporated. You may need to help the machine along by using a rubber spatula to scrape the corners of the pan.

If your dough does not form a ball during the first few minutes of kneading, do one of two things: if the dough looks dry and crumbly, add 1 tbsp (15 mL) water at 1-minute intervals until the dough forms a ball; if the dough looks wet, add 1 tbsp (15 mL) all-purpose flour at 1-minute intervals until the dough forms a ball.

3 lb (1.5 kg)

½ cup	milk	125 mL
¼ cup	unsalted butter, softened	60 mL
6 tbsp	granulated or raw sugar	90 mL
2½ tsp	salt	12 mL
3	large eggs, beaten	3
1 cup	mashed ripe bananas (about 2½)	250 mL
4¼ cups	all-purpose flour	1.06 L
3 tbsp	vital wheat gluten	45 mL
2 tsp	ground cinnamon (optional)	10 mL
2¼ tsp	instant or bread machine yeast	11 mL
1 cup	chocolate chips	250 mL
⅔ cup	toasted chopped pecans (see tip, page 128)	150 mL

1. In a small saucepan, scald milk over medium-high heat until small bubbles form around the edges. Remove from heat and stir in butter and sugar. Transfer to the bread pan and let cool to lukewarm (between 86°F and 95°F/30°C and 35°C).

2. Add salt, eggs and banana(s) to the bread pan. Spoon flour on top of liquid. Add wheat gluten, cinnamon (if using) and yeast. Place chocolate chips and pecans in the dispenser (or add at the "add ingredient" or "mix in" signal).

3. Select the Sweet or Fruit & Nut cycle and press Start.

Chocolate-Glazed Banana Coconut Swirl Loaf

Prepare the basic recipe for the 1½-lb (750 g) or 2-lb (1 kg) dough. Grease a 9- by 5-inch (23 by 12.5 cm) metal loaf pan or line with parchment paper. At the start of the final rise (see "Timing It Right," page 13), press Pause. Transfer dough to a floured surface and punch down gently. Roll out into a 12- by 9-inch (30 by 23 cm) rectangle. Spread ½ recipe Coconut Cream Cheese Filling (variation, page 288) over dough, leaving a 1-inch (2.5 cm) perimeter. Starting with a short end, roll dough into a tight cylinder. Pinch the seam and ends closed. Place loaf, seam side down, in the prepared loaf pan. Cover with a clean towel and let rise in a warm, draft-free place for 30 minutes. Meanwhile, preheat oven to 350°F (180°C). Bake for about 50 minutes or until browned, risen and an instant-read thermometer inserted in the center of the loaf registers 190°F (90°C). Let cool in pan on a wire rack for 15 minutes, then transfer loaf to rack and let cool for 30 minutes. Brush or drizzle bread with ½ cup (125 mL) Chocolate Glaze (page 292). Let set for 30 minutes before slicing.

Apricot Almond Loaf

This sunny loaf with a tender, feathery crumb and nuggets of apricot makes a delicious breakfast bread or fantastic French toast.

Tips

When you're making the 1-lb (500 g) loaf, if you can't find small eggs, beat 2 large eggs until blended, then measure $1/4$ cup + 2 tsp (70 mL) to equal the volume of 2 small eggs, reserving any remaining egg for another use.

Ideally, the buttermilk should be between 86°F and 95°F (30°C and 35°C), the temperature range in which yeast is most active. Warm it in the microwave or in a saucepan on the stove, and check the temperature with an instant-read thermometer.

To toast almonds, spread sliced almonds on a baking sheet and toast in a 350°F (180°C) oven for 4 to 6 minutes, stirring once, or until golden and fragrant. Immediately transfer to a bowl and let cool.

1 lb (500 g)

3 tbsp	granulated sugar	45 mL
1 tsp	salt	5 mL
2	small eggs, beaten	2
6 tbsp	lukewarm buttermilk (see tip, at left)	90 mL
3 tbsp	unsalted butter, softened	45 mL
1 tsp	almond extract	5 mL
2 cups	all-purpose flour	500 mL
1 tsp	instant or bread machine yeast	5 mL
$1/2$ cup	finely snipped dried apricots	125 mL

Glaze

$1/4$ cup	Almond Glaze (variation, page 291)	60 mL
2 tbsp	toasted sliced almonds (see tip, at left)	30 mL

$1^{1}/_{2}$ lb (750 g)

$1/4$ cup	granulated sugar	60 mL
$1^{1}/_{4}$ tsp	salt	6 mL
2	large eggs, beaten	2
$2/3$ cup	lukewarm buttermilk (see tip, at left)	150 mL
$1/4$ cup	unsalted butter, softened	60 mL
$1^{1}/_{2}$ tsp	almond extract	7 mL
3 cups	all-purpose flour	750 mL
$1^{1}/_{2}$ tsp	instant or bread machine yeast	7 mL
$2/3$ cup	finely snipped dried apricots	150 mL

Glaze

$1/4$ cup	Almond Glaze (variation, page 291)	60 mL
3 tbsp	toasted sliced almonds (see tip, at left)	45 mL

2 lb (1 kg)

$1/3$ cup	granulated sugar	75 mL
$1^{1}/_{2}$ tsp	salt	7 mL
3	large eggs, beaten	3
$3/4$ cup	lukewarm buttermilk (see tip, at left)	175 mL
$1/3$ cup	unsalted butter, softened	75 mL
2 tsp	almond extract	10 mL
$3^{3}/_{4}$ cups	all-purpose flour	925 mL
$1^{1}/_{4}$ tsp	instant or bread machine yeast	6 mL
$3/4$ cup	finely snipped dried apricots	175 mL

Glaze

$1/2$ cup	Almond Glaze (variation, page 291)	125 mL
$1/4$ cup	toasted sliced almonds (see tip, at left)	60 mL

Tips

When making the smallest loaf allowed by your machine, check the dough a few minutes after kneading starts to make sure the ingredients are incorporated. You may need to help the machine along by using a rubber spatula to scrape the corners of the pan.

If your dough does not form a ball during the first few minutes of kneading, do one of two things: if the dough looks dry and crumbly, add 1 tbsp (15 mL) buttermilk at 1-minute intervals until the dough forms a ball; if the dough looks wet, add 1 tbsp (15 mL) all-purpose flour at 1-minute intervals until the dough forms a ball.

Use any leftovers (as if!) to make a fabulous bread pudding with an apricot sauce laced with a little amaretto or rum.

3 lb (1.5 kg)

6 tbsp	granulated sugar	90 mL
2 tsp	salt	10 mL
4	large eggs, beaten	4
1 cup	lukewarm buttermilk (see tip, page 130)	250 mL
½ cup	unsalted butter, softened	125 mL
2½ tsp	almond extract	12 mL
5 cups	all-purpose flour	1.25 L
1¾ tsp	instant or bread machine yeast	8 mL
1 cup	finely snipped dried apricots	250 mL

Glaze

½ cup	Almond Glaze (variation, page 291)	125 mL
¼ cup	toasted sliced almonds (see tip, page 130)	60 mL

1. Add sugar, salt, eggs, buttermilk, butter and almond extract to the bread pan. Spoon flour on top of liquid. Add yeast. Place apricots in the dispenser (or add at the "add ingredient" or "mix in" signal).

2. Select the Sweet or Fruit & Nut cycle and press Start. When the cycle is finished, transfer the loaf to a wire rack and let cool for 1 hour.

3. *Glaze:* Brush or drizzle bread with glaze. Sprinkle with almonds. Let set for 30 minutes before slicing.

Apricot Almond Sweet Rolls

Prepare the recipe for the 1½-lb (750 g) dough through step 3, then select the Dough cycle and press Start. Line a large baking sheet with parchment paper. When the cycle is finished, transfer dough to a floured surface and punch down gently. Roll out dough into a 12- by 10-inch (30 by 25 cm) rectangle. Spread ½ cup (125 mL) apricot preserves over dough, leaving a 1-inch (2.5 cm) perimeter. Starting with a long end, roll dough into a tight cylinder. Using dental floss or a sharp knife, cut cylinder into 1-inch (2.5 cm) slices. Place slices, spiral side up, 2 inches (5 cm) apart on prepared baking sheet. Let rise while preheating oven to 350°F (180°C). Bake for 15 to 20 minutes or until risen and lightly browned on top and an instant-read thermometer inserted in the center of a roll registers 190°F (90°C). Let cool on pan on a wire rack for 30 minutes, then brush or drizzle with glaze and sprinkle with almonds.

Chocolate Almond Loaf

Substitute chocolate chips for the apricots.

Swedish Cardamom Bread

Makes 1 loaf

Also known as Swedish coffee bread or vetebröd, this sweet bread has all the flavor of a Swedish tea ring. Make it as a simple bread machine loaf or as a braid. Vanilla Glaze adds a final touch of sweetness.

Tip

Ideally, the buttermilk should be between 86°F and 95°F (30°C and 35°C), the temperature range in which yeast is most active. Warm it in the microwave or in a saucepan on the stove, and check the temperature with an instant-read thermometer.

1 lb (500 g)

2 tbsp	granulated sugar	30 mL
1 tsp	salt	5 mL
1	large egg, beaten	1
1	large egg yolk, beaten	1
½ cup	lukewarm buttermilk (see tip, at left)	125 mL
¼ cup	unsalted butter, softened	60 mL
2½ cups	all-purpose flour	625 mL
1 tsp	ground cardamom	5 mL
1 tsp	ground cinnamon	5 mL
1 tsp	instant or bread machine yeast	5 mL
Glaze		
¼ cup	Vanilla Glaze (page 291)	60 mL
2 tbsp	pearl sugar (optional)	30 mL

1½ lb (750 g)

3 tbsp	granulated sugar	45 mL
1½ tsp	salt	7 mL
2	large eggs, beaten	2
⅔ cup	lukewarm buttermilk (see tip, at left)	150 mL
⅓ cup	unsalted butter, softened	75 mL
3½ cups	all-purpose flour	875 mL
1½ tsp	ground cardamom	7 mL
1½ tsp	ground cinnamon	7 mL
1 tsp	instant or bread machine yeast	5 mL
Glaze		
¼ cup	Vanilla Glaze (page 291)	60 mL
2 tbsp	pearl sugar (optional)	30 mL

2 lb (1 kg)

⅓ cup	granulated sugar	75 mL
1¼ tsp	salt	6 mL
3	large eggs, beaten	3
¾ cup	lukewarm buttermilk (see tip, at left)	175 mL
6 tbsp	unsalted butter, softened	90 mL
4¼ cups	all-purpose flour	1.06 L
2 tsp	ground cardamom	10 mL
2 tsp	ground cinnamon	10 mL
1¼ tsp	instant or bread machine yeast	6 mL
Glaze		
½ cup	Vanilla Glaze (page 291)	125 mL
¼ cup	pearl sugar (optional)	60 mL

Tips

If your dough does not form a ball during the first few minutes of kneading, do one of two things: if the dough looks dry and crumbly, add 1 tbsp (15 mL) buttermilk at 1-minute intervals until the dough forms a ball; if the dough looks wet, add 1 tbsp (15 mL) all-purpose flour at 1-minute intervals until the dough forms a ball.

3 lb (1.5 kg)

½ cup	granulated sugar	125 mL
1¼ tsp	salt	6 mL
4	large eggs, beaten	4
1⅓ cups	lukewarm buttermilk (see tip, page 132)	325 mL
½ cup	unsalted butter, softened	125 mL
5½ cups	all-purpose flour	1.375 L
2 tsp	ground cardamom	10 mL
2 tsp	ground cinnamon	10 mL
1¼ tsp	instant or bread machine yeast	6 mL

Glaze

½ cup	Vanilla Glaze (page 291)	125 mL
¼ cup	pearl sugar (optional)	60 mL

1. Add sugar, salt, eggs, buttermilk and butter to the bread pan. Spoon flour on top of liquid. Add cardamom, cinnamon and yeast.

2. Select the Sweet cycle and press Start. When the cycle is finished, transfer the loaf to a wire rack and let cool for 1 hour.

3. *Glaze:* Brush or drizzle bread with glaze. Sprinkle with pearl sugar, if desired. Let set for 30 minutes before slicing.

Oven-Baked Swedish Cardamom Braid

Prepare the recipe through step 1, then select the Dough cycle and press Start. Line a large baking sheet with parchment paper. When the cycle is finished, transfer dough to a floured surface and punch down gently. Divide dough into thirds. Roll each third into a 16-inch (40 cm) long rope. Braid ropes together, tucking ends under. Place on prepared baking sheet. Cover with a clean towel and let rise in a warm, draft-free place for 30 minutes. Meanwhile, preheat oven to 350°F (180°C). Bake until risen and an instant-read thermometer inserted in the center registers 190°F (90°C). Remove from pan and let cool on a wire rack for 1 hour. Brush or drizzle bread with glaze. Sprinkle with pearl sugar, if desired. Let set for 30 minutes before slicing.

Loaf Size	Baking Time
1 lb (500 g)	30 to 34 minutes
1½ lb (750 g)	34 to 36 minutes
2 lb (1 kg)	35 to 40 minutes
3 lb (1.5 kg)	38 to 42 minutes

Polish Lemon Poppy Seed Bread

Makes 1 loaf

The crunch of poppy seeds and the tang of lemon combine to make an addictive breakfast or teatime loaf.

Tip

Ideally, the buttermilk should be between 86°F and 95°F (30°C and 35°C), the temperature range in which yeast is most active. Warm it in the microwave or in a saucepan on the stove, and check the temperature with an instant-read thermometer.

1 lb (500 g)

1/4 cup	granulated sugar	60 mL
2 tsp	grated lemon zest	10 mL
1 tsp	salt	5 mL
1	large egg, beaten	1
1	large egg yolk, beaten	1
6 tbsp	lukewarm buttermilk (see tip, at left)	90 mL
3 tbsp	unsalted butter, softened	45 mL
2 cups	all-purpose flour	500 mL
3 tbsp	poppy seeds	45 mL
1 tsp	instant or bread machine yeast	5 mL
Glaze		
1/4 cup	Lemon Glaze (variation, page 291)	60 mL
1 tsp	poppy seeds	5 mL

1 1/2 lb (750 g)

1/3 cup	granulated sugar	75 mL
1 tbsp	grated lemon zest	15 mL
1 1/2 tsp	salt	7 mL
2	large eggs, beaten	2
2/3 cup	lukewarm buttermilk (see tip, at left)	150 mL
1/4 cup	unsalted butter, softened	60 mL
3 1/2 cups	all-purpose flour	875 mL
1/4 cup	poppy seeds	60 mL
2 tsp	instant or bread machine yeast	7 mL
Glaze		
1/4 cup	Lemon Glaze (variation, page 291)	60 mL
1 tsp	poppy seeds	5 mL

2 lb (1 kg)

6 tbsp	granulated sugar	90 mL
1 1/2 tbsp	grated lemon zest	22 mL
1 1/4 tsp	salt	6 mL
3	large eggs, beaten	3
3/4 cup + 1 tbsp	lukewarm buttermilk (see tip, at left)	190 mL
1/3 cup	unsalted butter, softened	75 mL
3 3/4 cups	all-purpose flour	925 mL
1/3 cup	poppy seeds	75 mL
1 1/2 tsp	instant or bread machine yeast	7 mL

Tips

When making the smallest loaf allowed by your machine, check the dough a few minutes after kneading starts to make sure the ingredients are incorporated. You may need to help the machine along by using a rubber spatula to scrape the corners of the pan.

If your dough does not form a ball during the first few minutes of kneading, do one of two things: if the dough looks dry and crumbly, add 1 tbsp (15 mL) buttermilk at 1-minute intervals until the dough forms a ball; if the dough looks wet, add 1 tbsp (15 mL) all-purpose flour at 1-minute intervals until the dough forms a ball.

Glaze

½ cup	Lemon Glaze (variation, page 291)	125 mL
1½ tsp	poppy seeds	7 mL

3 lb (1.5 kg)

½ cup	granulated sugar	125 mL
2 tbsp	grated lemon zest	30 mL
1¼ tsp	salt	6 mL
4	large eggs, beaten	4
1¼ cups	lukewarm buttermilk (see tip, page 134)	300 mL
½ cup	unsalted butter, softened	125 mL
5½ cups	all-purpose flour	1.375 L
6 tbsp	poppy seeds	90 mL
1¾ tsp	instant or bread machine yeast	8 mL

Glaze

½ cup	Lemon Glaze (variation, page 291)	125 mL
1½ tsp	poppy seeds	7 mL

1. Add sugar, lemon zest, salt, eggs, buttermilk and butter to the bread pan. Spoon flour on top of liquid. Add poppy seeds and yeast.

2. Select the Sweet cycle and press Start. When the cycle is finished, transfer the loaf to a wire rack and let cool for 1 hour.

3. *Glaze:* Brush or drizzle bread with glaze. Sprinkle with poppy seeds. Let set for 30 minutes before slicing.

Sweet Orange Swirl Bread

Equipment

- Bread machine with a 2-lb (1 kg) capacity
- 9- by 5-inch (23 by 12.5 cm) metal loaf pan, greased or lined with parchment paper

There's something sunny and energizing about the flavor of fresh orange, which permeates this sweet bread. You'll only find this swirl loaf in your own kitchen bakery — now that's signature.

Tips

Ideally, the buttermilk should be between 86°F and 95°F (30°C and 35°C), the temperature range in which yeast is most active. Warm it in the microwave or in a saucepan on the stove, and check the temperature with an instant-read thermometer.

If your dough does not form a ball during the first few minutes of kneading, do one of two things: if the dough looks dry and crumbly, add 1 tbsp (15 mL) buttermilk at 1-minute intervals until the dough forms a ball; if the dough looks wet, add 1 tbsp (15 mL) all-purpose flour at 1-minute intervals until the dough forms a ball.

½ cup	granulated sugar	125 mL
¾ tsp	salt	3 mL
2	large eggs, beaten	2
⅔ cup	lukewarm buttermilk (see tip, at left)	150 mL
⅓ cup	unsalted butter, softened	75 mL
3½ cups	all-purpose flour	875 mL
1½ tsp	instant or bread machine yeast	7 mL

Orange Filling

¼ cup	granulated sugar	60 mL
1 tbsp	grated orange zest	15 mL
⅛ tsp	salt	0.5 mL
¼ cup	unsalted butter, softened	60 mL

Glaze

¼ cup	Orange Glaze (variation, page 291)	60 mL

1. Add sugar, salt, eggs, buttermilk and butter to the bread pan. Spoon flour on top of liquid. Add yeast.

2. Select the Dough cycle and press Start.

3. *Filling:* In a bowl, using a fork, combine sugar, orange zest, salt and butter until smooth. Set aside.

4. When the cycle is finished, transfer dough to a floured surface and punch down gently. Roll out into a 12- by 9-inch (30 by 23 cm) rectangle.

5. Spread filling over dough, leaving a ½-inch (1 cm) perimeter. Starting with a short end, roll dough into a cylinder. Pinch the seam and ends closed.

6. Place loaf, seam side down, in the prepared loaf pan. Cover with a clean towel and let rise in a warm, draft-free place for 30 minutes. Meanwhile, preheat oven to 350°F (180°C).

7. Bake for about 40 minutes or until risen and lightly browned and an instant-read thermometer inserted in the center registers 190°F (90°C). Let cool in pan on a wire rack for 15 minutes, then transfer to the rack and let cool for 1 hour.

8. *Glaze:* Brush or drizzle bread with glaze. Let set for 30 minutes before slicing.

> ### Cinnamon Swirl Loaf
> Use Cinnamon Filling (page 284) in place of the Orange Filling and use Vanilla Glaze (page 291) in place of the Orange Glaze.

Lime and Coconut Swirl Loaf

On the darkest, coldest winter morning, wouldn't it be great to wake up to flavors that remind you of sunny beaches and tropical climes? This sweet bread delivers on all counts.

Tips

Ideally, the buttermilk should be between 86°F and 95°F (30°C and 35°C), the temperature range in which yeast is most active. Warm it in the microwave or in a saucepan on the stove, and check the temperature with an instant-read thermometer.

If your dough does not form a ball during the first few minutes of kneading, do one of two things: if the dough looks dry and crumbly, add 1 tbsp (15 mL) buttermilk at 1-minute intervals until the dough forms a ball; if the dough looks wet, add 1 tbsp (15 mL) all-purpose flour at 1-minute intervals until the dough forms a ball.

½ cup	granulated sugar	125 mL
¾ tsp	salt	3 mL
2	large eggs, beaten	2
⅔ cup	lukewarm buttermilk (see tip, at left)	150 mL
⅓ cup	unsalted butter, softened	75 mL
3½ cups	all-purpose flour	875 mL
1½ tsp	instant or bread machine yeast	7 mL

Filling

⅔ cup	Coconut Lime Cream Cheese Filling (variation, page 288)	150 mL

Glaze

¼ cup	Lime Glaze (variation, page 291)	60 mL

1. Add sugar, salt, eggs, buttermilk and butter to the bread pan. Spoon flour on top of liquid. Add yeast.

2. Select the Dough cycle and press Start.

3. When the cycle is finished, transfer dough to a floured surface and punch down gently. Roll out into a 12- by 9-inch (30 by 23 cm) rectangle.

4. *Filling:* Spread filling over dough, leaving a ½-inch (1 cm) perimeter. Starting with a short end, roll dough into a cylinder. Pinch the seam and ends closed.

5. Place loaf, seam side down, in the prepared loaf pan. Cover with a clean towel and let rise in a warm, draft-free place for 30 minutes. Meanwhile, preheat oven to 350°F (180°C).

6. Bake for about 40 minutes or until risen and lightly browned and an instant-read thermometer inserted in the center registers 190°F (90°C). Let cool in pan on a wire rack for 15 minutes, then transfer to the rack and let cool for 1 hour.

7. *Glaze:* Brush or drizzle bread with glaze. Let set for 30 minutes before slicing.

German Kuchen

Kuchen is oven-baked as a coffee cake rather than a conventional loaf. Tender and yeasty, this traditional pastry is perfect for a lazy weekend breakfast.

Tip

If your dough does not form a ball during the first few minutes of kneading, do one of two things: if the dough looks dry and crumbly, add 1 tbsp (15 mL) water at 1-minute intervals until the dough forms a ball; if the dough looks wet, add 1 tbsp (15 mL) all-purpose flour at 1-minute intervals until the dough forms a ball.

1 cup	milk	250 mL
¼ cup	unsalted butter, softened	60 mL
½ cup	granulated sugar	125 mL
½ tsp	salt	2 mL
2	large eggs, beaten	2
3½ cups	all-purpose flour	875 mL
1½ tsp	instant or bread machine yeast	7 mL
Filling		
1¾ cups	Cottage Cheese Filling (page 289)	425 mL
Glaze		
½ cup	Vanilla Glaze (page 291)	125 mL

1. In a small saucepan, scald milk over medium-high heat until small bubbles form around the edges. Remove from heat and stir in butter and sugar. Transfer to the bread pan and let cool to lukewarm (between 86°F and 95°F/30°C and 35°C).

2. Add salt and eggs to the bread pan. Spoon flour on top of liquid. Add yeast.

3. Select the Dough cycle and press Start.

4. When the cycle is finished, preheat oven to 350°F (180°C). Transfer dough to a floured surface and punch down gently. Divide dough in half and roll out each half into an 11-inch (28 cm) square. Place each square in a prepared pan. Form a raised edge around the perimeter, pressing the dough against the sides of the pan to help shape it.

5. *Filling:* Add half the filling to each pan and spread evenly over dough.

6. Bake for 20 to 25 minutes or until edges are browned and risen and the filling does not shake when the pan is lightly tapped. Let cool in pans on a wire rack for 30 minutes.

7. *Glaze:* Drizzle with glaze. Let set for 30 minutes before slicing. Serve warm or at room temperature.

Sugar and Spice Monkey Bread

Equipment
- Bread machine with a 2-lb (1 kg) capacity
- 9-inch (23 cm) Bundt or tube pan, greased

Monkey bread is a pull-apart loaf formed from individual balls of dough that are dipped in butter, rolled in flavored sugar, spices or herbs, then arranged in the pan. You can go in a savory or a sweet direction with monkey bread — you just need a soft, somewhat sweet white dough. The "monkey" in monkey bread could refer to the impish grabbing of just-baked pieces this bread inspires, so be forewarned!

Tips

If your dough does not form a ball during the first few minutes of kneading, do one of two things: if the dough looks dry and crumbly, add 1 tbsp (15 mL) buttermilk at 1-minute intervals until the dough forms a ball; if the dough looks wet, add 1 tbsp (15 mL) all-purpose flour at 1-minute intervals until the dough forms a ball.

You can also make monkey bread with Sour Cream Bread dough (page 48), Fast and Easy White Bread dough (page 28), Brioche dough (page 40), Challah dough (page 38) or any of the doughs in this chapter.

½ cup	granulated sugar	125 mL
¾ tsp	salt	3 mL
2	large eggs, beaten	2
⅔ cup	lukewarm buttermilk (see tip, page 137)	150 mL
⅓ cup	unsalted butter, softened	75 mL
3½ cups	all-purpose flour	875 mL
1½ tsp	instant or bread machine yeast	7 mL

Topping

½ cup	unsalted butter, melted	125 mL
½ cup	Cinnamon Sugar (page 290)	125 mL

1. Add sugar, salt, eggs, buttermilk and butter to the bread pan. Spoon flour on top of liquid. Add yeast.

2. Select the Dough cycle and press Start.

3. When the cycle is finished, transfer dough to a floured surface and punch down gently. Divide dough into 20 pieces and form each piece into a ball.

4. *Topping:* Dip each ball in melted butter, then roll in cinnamon sugar. Arrange evenly in layers in prepared Bundt pan. Cover with a clean towel and let rise in a warm, draft-free place for 30 minutes. Meanwhile, preheat oven to 350°F (180°C).

5. Bake for about 40 minutes or until risen and lightly browned on top and an instant-read thermometer inserted in the center registers 190°F (90°C). Let cool in pan on a wire rack for 15 minutes. Invert onto a serving platter and serve warm or let cool completely.

Sticky Fingers Monkey Bread

For the topping, instead of butter and cinnamon sugar, melt ¼ cup (60 mL) unsalted butter and stir in ¾ cup (175 mL) packed light or dark brown sugar. Brush caramel onto dough balls.

Sourdough and Slow-Rise Breads

GOOD THINGS COME to those who wait — even for those of us with bread machines! Although sourdough starters need to ferment for at least 24 hours before you can use them, they do wonderful things for the flavor and texture of bread machine breads. Breads are firmer and chewier, because they don't rise as high as those that use more yeast. They have a more developed homemade bread flavor, and the crust is crisper than that of other bread machine breads, without being heavy — it sort of flakes.

Once you try these breads, you'll be hooked, especially when you see how easy they are to make in the bread machine.

Slow-Rise Cycles

Newer bread machines have a slow-rise cycle that allows dough more time to develop flavor and a crisper crust. This cycle usually has three rising times instead of two, the rising temperature is lower than on other cycles, and the baking temperature is higher. (Slow-rise breads tend to do most of their rising during baking, so don't be alarmed if, by the third rise, your somewhat slack and shiny dough doesn't seem to have risen much.)

Depending on your bread machine, the slow-rise cycle might be called French, French/Italian or Sourdough. With these cycles, the machine goes on to bake the bread after the final rise. The Cuisinart CBK-200 also features a slow-rise cycle — the Artisan Dough cycle — but it only prepares the dough. You'll need to shape the dough, let it rise and bake the loaf in the oven.

If you're not sure what cycle to use for these breads, simply look through your manual to find the chart that lists the time for each cycle; the white bread cycle that takes the longest is the one you want.

If you have an older machine, rest assured that this type of bread still tastes delicious when made using the Basic/White cycle and the Light Crust setting, as the starter has already done a good part of the flavor development.

About Slow-Rise Doughs

Doughs made with starters and sponges come together differently in the machine than do other doughs. They start out quite wet and sticky, then firm up as the flour absorbs the liquid, then get loose and sticky again. Check the dough after 5 to 8 minutes of kneading; if it hasn't formed a soft ball yet, gradually sprinkle in just enough flour for the bread to form a cohesive ball (it will still be fairly loose), scraping the edges of the pan as you sprinkle. To prevent a dry bread, it's important not to add too much flour too soon. You may also want to scrape the sides of the pan after the first long knead to remove any dough that is stuck up high on the sides.

For breads you make on the Dough cycle and bake in the oven, the dough will be softer than regular breads, so you will need an oiled or floured dough scraper or spatula to scrape the dough from the pan. As well, be sure to flour the work surface liberally and keep your hands floured while shaping the dough. Dust off any excess flour just before you transfer the loaf to the prepared pan.

Starters 101

A starter, also known as a sponge, is simply a mixture of flour, a liquid and either natural yeast in the air (naturally leavened sourdough starter) or instant or bread machine yeast (yeast-risen sponge). The mixture is covered and left to ferment at room temperature until it is doubled in size and is light and full of bubbles.

Once active, most starters will last at room temperature for about 3 days. After that, they get "hungry" — if not fed again with flour and liquid, they will start to die and will no longer be good for making dough. If your starter does not produce bubbles, turns pink or develops an "off" aroma (not clean, sour or tangy), throw it out.

Naturally Leavened Sourdough Starter

"Naturally leavened" means just that — the rising or leavening power comes from nature. Wild yeasts in the air, rather than manufactured ones, allow fermentation to take place, creating those bubbles that rise to the surface and help your bread rise.

There are many different recipes for homemade sourdough starters. Traditional artisan baker's levain, for example, starts with a simple mixture of unbleached flour, spring water and organic purple grapes; it needs to ferment for 2 weeks, then must be fed for another week or so before it can be used in baking.

The easier way to acquire sourdough starter is to buy readymade starter online, from a source such as King Arthur Flour Company (www.kingarthurflour.com) or Sourdoughs International (www.sourdo.com), or to get some from a friend — like Carl Griffith, who was famous for his 1847 Oregon Trail starter (http://home.att.net/~carlsfriends/). I use the King Arthur sourdough starter, a descendant of a 250-year-old starter.

Follow the instructions from your source for feeding your starter, and feed it until it is bubbling, active and looks ready to use for baking. Once your starter is active, you can wrap and refrigerate it for up to a week between feedings, or put it in hibernation in the freezer until you're ready to thaw, feed and bake with it again.

Making Your Own Sourdough Starter

If you have difficulty finding readymade sourdough starter, you can make your own. Like any natural process, fermentation proceeds at its own pace, taking anywhere from 5 to 15 days, but it needs your attention for just a few minutes a day. It develops best in a cool environment — about 72°F (22°C). Once it ferments to a bubbly, cream-colored, batter-like mixture, you can start baking delicious artisan bread.

1 cup	bottled spring or filtered water (flat, not fizzy)	250 mL
1 cup	unbleached all-purpose or bread flour	250 mL
4 oz	purple or black grapes, chopped plums or crabapples (preferably organic), rinsed and patted dry	125 g

Day 1: Make the Starter

In a 6- to 8-cup (1.5 to 2 L) earthenware, glass or ceramic bowl, whisk water into flour until just blended. Place grapes in a double thickness of cheesecloth and tie the corners together to make a pouch. Holding the pouch over the flour mixture, crush the grapes with your hands until about 1 tsp (5 mL) of juice falls into the bowl. Whisk juice into flour mixture, then place the pouch in the center of the mixture. Cover loosely with plastic wrap and let ferment for 24 hours at a cool room temperature (72°F/22°C).

Days 2 and 3: Stir the Starter

The starter should gradually take on a fruity, yeasty smell. By Day 3 it should start to look bubbly and will start to develop a pinkish beige liquid on top called the hooch. Each day, stir the hooch back into the starter. If at any point in the fermentation process the starter develops mold or smells rancid, throw it away and start again.

Days 4 and 5: Feed the Starter

The hooch may deepen in color to a dark pink. Remove and discard the bag of grapes. Each day, stir the hooch back into the starter. Remove and discard half the starter. Stir in 1 cup (250 mL) bottled spring or filtered water and 1 cup (250 mL) unbleached all-purpose or bread flour.

Days 6 to 15: Monitor and Feed the Starter

Continue to check on your starter each day. You'll know it's ready for use when bubbles are slowly rising and bursting on top and it has a frothy appearance and a pleasantly tangy, beery aroma. If it's not ready yet, stir the hooch back in. Remove and discard half the starter and feed as above.

Sourdough Starter Maintenance

You've gone to all this trouble to make sourdough starter, so be sure to keep some for ongoing use.

To Keep the Starter Going

Store, loosely covered with plastic wrap, in the refrigerator and maintain a once-a-week feeding schedule. To feed, remove and discard half the starter. Stir in 1 cup (250 mL) bottled spring or filtered water and 1 cup (250 mL) unbleached all-purpose or bread flour. To revive a refrigerated starter, let it come to room temperature. Feed it once a day, if necessary, until it is ready.

To Freeze the Starter

Place 1 cup (250 mL) starter in an airtight container and freeze indefinitely.

To revive a frozen starter, let it thaw to room temperature. Feed it once a day, if necessary, until it is ready.

What to Do with Extra Starter

You can use your sourdough starter to make bread, of course, but you can also make sourdough pancakes or waffles. Simply stir the starter into your favorite pancake or waffle mix along with the egg and oil, according to your recipe. Add just enough milk or water to make a batter-like consistency. If you want a more pronounced sourdough flavor, cover and refrigerate overnight before making pancakes and waffles.

There are many other recipes available online that use sourdough starter, including crumpets, cakes and scones. It's fun to experiment with these in between batches of bread!

Yeast-Risen Sponge

With a yeast-risen sponge, you'll be ready to make bread in 24 hours. For the liquid component, you can simply use water, or you can choose yogurt, lager beer or buttermilk to add nuances of flavor to the bread. To make the sponge, you stir the flour, yeast and liquid together, cover the bowl, let the mixture ferment at room temperature for 24 hours, then transfer the starter to the bread pan and add the remaining ingredients for your dough.

Sponge Ingredient	What It Does for the Bread
Water	Adds moisture, helps yeast work
Yogurt	Adds a medium sourness, helps yeast work, helps bread stay moist
Lager beer	Adds a slight bitterness, helps yeast work, adds a malty flavor
Buttermilk	Adds a slight sourness, helps yeast work, helps bread stay moist
Flour	Feeds the sponge and helps fermentation
Yeast	Starts the fermentation

If you're patient enough to let a buttermilk sponge ferment for about 3 days, it will develop a much more pronounced sourness that's perfect for my Really, Really Slow-Rise breads (pages 166 to 171). When a clear beige liquid — called the hooch — rises to the top, it's ready; just stir the hooch back into the sponge.

Following are some master sponge recipes that are used to make many of the breads in this chapter.

Sour Sponge

The yogurt at the bottom of the container is sometimes thicker; if necessary, add enough additional water to your starter to make a very thick, batter-like mixture.

Ingredients	For a 1-lb (500 g) loaf	For a 1½-lb (750 g) loaf	For a 2-lb (1 kg) loaf	For a 3-lb (1.5 kg) loaf
All-purpose flour	⅔ cup (150 mL)	1 cup (250 mL)	1½ cups (375 mL)	2¼ cups (550 mL)
Instant or bread machine yeast	¼ tsp (1 mL)	¼ tsp (1 mL)	½ tsp (2 mL)	¾ tsp (3 mL)
Low-fat plain yogurt	½ cup (125 mL)	¾ cup (175 mL)	1¼ cups (300 mL)	1¾ cups (425 mL)
Water	2½ tbsp (37 mL)	¼ cup (60 mL)	¼ cup (60 mL)	½ cup (125 mL)

In a large bowl, combine flour, yeast and yogurt. Cover with plastic wrap and let rise in a warm place for at least 12 hours or for up to 24 hours, until the sponge has doubled in size and is light and full of bubbles. Then use to make bread.

Sour Rye Sponge

The yogurt at the bottom of the container is sometimes thicker; if necessary, add enough additional water to your starter to make a very thick, batter-like mixture.

Ingredients	For a 1-lb (500 g) loaf	For a 1½-lb (750 g) loaf	For a 2-lb (1 kg) loaf	For a 3-lb (1.5 kg) loaf
Bread flour	6 tbsp (90 mL)	½ cup (125 mL)	¾ cup (175 mL)	1 cup + 2 tbsp (280 mL)
Dark rye flour, preferably stone-ground or coarse	¼ cup (60 mL)	⅓ cup (75 mL)	⅔ cup (150 mL)	¾ cup + 2 tbsp (205 mL)
Instant or bread machine yeast	¼ tsp (1 mL)	¼ tsp (1 mL)	½ tsp (2 mL)	½ tsp (2 mL)
Low-fat plain yogurt	½ cup (125 mL)	¾ cup (175 mL)	1 cup + 2 tbsp (280 mL)	1⅔ cups (400 mL)
Water	2 tbsp (30 mL)	3 tbsp (45 mL)	¼ cup (60 mL)	⅓ cup (75 mL)

Slow-Rise Sour Rye Sponge

In a large bowl, combine bread flour, rye flour, yeast, yogurt and water. Cover with plastic wrap and let rise in a warm place for at least 12 hours or for up to 24 hours, until the sponge has doubled in size and is light and full of bubbles. Then use to make bread.

Really, Really Slow-Rise Sour Rye Sponge

In a large bowl, combine bread flour, rye flour, yeast, yogurt and water. Cover with plastic wrap and let rise in a warm place for 2 to 3 days or until the sponge has developed a clear beige liquid (the hooch) on top. Then use to make bread.

Buttermilk Sponge

The buttermilk at the bottom of the container is sometimes thicker; if necessary, add enough additional water to your starter to make a very thick, batter-like mixture.

Ingredients	For a 1-lb (500 g) loaf	For a 1½-lb (750 g) loaf	For a 2-lb (1 kg) loaf	For a 3-lb (1.5 kg) loaf
All-purpose or bread flour	1 cup (250 mL)	1½ cups (375 mL)	2 cups (500 mL)	2½ cups (625 mL)
Instant or bread machine yeast	¼ tsp (1 mL)	½ tsp (2 mL)	½ tsp (2 mL)	½ tsp (2 mL)
Buttermilk	½ cup (125 mL)	¾ cup + 1 tbsp (190 mL)	1 cup (250 mL)	1¼ cups (300 mL)
Water	6 tbsp (90 mL)	½ cup (125 mL)	¾ cup (175 mL)	¾ cup (175 mL)

Slow-Rise Buttermilk Sponge

In a large bowl, combine flour, yeast, buttermilk and water. Cover with plastic wrap and let rise in a warm place for at least 12 hours or for up to 24 hours, until the sponge has doubled in size and is light and full of bubbles. Then use to make bread.

Really, Really Slow-Rise Buttermilk Sponge

In a large bowl, combine flour, yeast, buttermilk and water. Cover with plastic wrap and let rise in a warm place for 2 to 3 days or until the sponge has developed a clear beige liquid (the hooch) on top. Then use to make bread.

Sourdough Sandwich Loaf

The tangy flavor of sourdough starter will give your sandwich bread a lift. Make sure your starter is bubbling before using it in this recipe.

Tips

Ideally, the water should be between 86°F and 95°F (30°C and 35°C), the temperature range in which yeast is most active. Warm it in the microwave or in a saucepan on the stove, and check the temperature with an instant-read thermometer.

Check the dough after 5 to 8 minutes of kneading; if it hasn't formed a soft ball yet, gradually sprinkle in just enough flour for the bread to form a cohesive ball (it will still be fairly loose), scraping the edges of the pan as you sprinkle. To prevent a dry bread, it's important not to add too much flour too soon.

1 cup	active prepared sourdough starter (see page 141)	250 mL
2 tsp	salt	10 mL
1 cup	lukewarm water (see tip, at left)	250 mL
1¾ cups	bread flour	425 mL
1½ cups	whole wheat flour	375 mL
1 tsp	instant or bread machine yeast	5 mL

1. Transfer starter to the bread pan. Add salt and water. Spoon flour on top of liquid. Add yeast.

2. Select your machine's slow-rise cycle (see page 140) or the Basic/White cycle and press Start.

Oven-Baked Sourdough Sandwich Loaf

Prepare the recipe through step 1, then select the Artisan Dough or Dough cycle and press Start. Line a large baking sheet with parchment paper. When the cycle is finished, transfer dough to a floured surface and punch down gently. Form dough into an oval loaf about 10 inches (25 cm) long and place on prepared baking sheet. Cover with a clean towel and let rise for 30 minutes. Meanwhile, preheat oven to 425°F (220°C). Using a serrated knife, cut 3 deep diagonal slashes across top of loaf. Spray loaf lightly with water. Bake for about 25 minutes or until risen and browned and an instant-read thermometer inserted in the center registers 190°F (90°C). Remove from pan and let cool on a wire rack.

Sourdough Buns

Prepare the recipe through step 1, then select your machine's Artisan Dough or Dough cycle and press Start. Line a large baking sheet with parchment paper. When the cycle is finished, transfer dough to a floured surface and punch down gently. Divide dough in half. Cut each half into 6 pieces. Form each piece into a bun. Place buns 2 inches (5 cm) apart on prepared baking sheet. Cover with a clean towel and let rise in a warm, draft-free place for 30 minutes. Meanwhile, preheat oven to 425°F (220°C). Using a serrated knife, cut a slash across the top of buns. Spray tops of buns lightly with water. Bake for about 20 minutes or until risen and lightly browned and an instant-read thermometer inserted in the center registers 190°F (90°C). Remove from pan and let cool on a wire rack.

Ciabatta

Equipment

- Bread machine with a 2-lb (1 kg) capacity
- Large baking sheet, lined with parchment paper and sprinkled with cornmeal
- Baking stone
- Broiler pan

This narrow oval Italian bread has a crisp crust, a somewhat chewy crumb and a honeycomb texture. Ciabatta dough remains soft and batter-like, and it is mixed rather than kneaded. The combination of naturally leavened starter with a yeast dough adds a wonderful depth of flavor.

Tips

Room temperature water slows down the action of the yeast, allowing it to act more gradually and develop more flavor, particularly on the long Artisan Dough cycle. If you use the shorter Dough cycle, heat the water to lukewarm (between 86°F and 95°F/30°C and 35°C) for faster rising.

Check the dough after 5 to 8 minutes of kneading; if it hasn't formed a soft ball yet, gradually sprinkle in just enough flour for the bread to form a cohesive ball (it will still be fairly loose), scraping the edges of the pan as you sprinkle. To prevent a dry bread, it's important not to add too much flour too soon.

1 cup	active prepared sourdough starter (see page 141)	250 mL
2 tsp	fine sea salt	10 mL
1 cup	water, at room temperature	250 mL
3 tbsp	milk	45 mL
1 tbsp	olive oil	15 mL
3¼ cups	bread flour	800 mL
2 tsp	instant or bread machine yeast	10 mL

1. Transfer starter to the bread pan. Add salt, water, milk and oil. Spoon flour on top of liquid. Add yeast.

2. Select the Artisan Dough or Dough cycle and press Start.

3. When the cycle is finished, use a floured spatula to scrape the slack dough out of the pan onto a well floured surface. Using floured hands, form dough into an oval loaf about 10 inches (25 cm) long. Using your hands or two dough scrapers, carefully transfer loaf to prepared baking sheet. Cover with a clean towel and let rise in a warm, draft-free place for 40 minutes.

4. Meanwhile, preheat oven to 450°F (230°C). Place baking stone on the middle rack and broiler pan on the bottom rack.

5. Add 2 cups (500 mL) hot water to the broiler pan. Place baking sheet on baking stone. Bake for about 30 minutes or until risen and deep brown and an instant-read thermometer inserted in the center registers 190°F (90°C). Remove from pan and let cool on a wire rack.

Italian Scali Bread

Equipment
- Bread machine with a
  1½-lb (750 g) capacity

The Scali family of Boston once specialized in this bread, which is now a fixture in grocery stores, bakeries and cafés in the area. It has a wonderful yeasty flavor that is complemented by the wealth of sesame seeds on its braided crust. If your bread machine makes horizontal loaves, you can bake this loaf in the machine; otherwise, you'll bake it in the oven. On the slow-rise cycle, the loaf comes out slightly chewy with a golden crust. In the oven, it ends up with a more tender crumb and a burnished crust.

Tip

If your bread machine doesn't have a Pause button, simply raise the lid, remove the dough, form and top it, then remove the kneading paddle(s) from the pan, place the braid in the pan and close the lid again. Work quickly, as the rising cycle will continue even without the bread in the pan.

Bread Machine Italian Scali Bread

Starter

1 cup	all-purpose flour	250 mL
½ cup	water, at room temperature	125 mL
¼ tsp	instant or bread machine yeast	1 mL

Dough

⅓ cup	lukewarm water (see tip, at right)	75 mL
⅓ cup	lukewarm milk	75 mL
2 tbsp	olive oil	30 mL
1¼ tsp	salt	6 mL
2 cups	all-purpose flour	500 mL
¾ tsp	instant or bread machine yeast	3 mL

Topping

1	large egg, beaten	1
1 tbsp	sesame seeds	15 mL

1. *Starter:* In a bowl, combine flour, water and yeast. Cover with plastic wrap and let rise at room temperature for 12 hours or overnight.

2. *Dough:* Transfer starter to the bread pan. Add water, milk, oil and salt. Spoon flour on top of liquid. Add yeast.

3. Select your machine's slow-rise cycle (see page 140), or the Basic/White cycle and the Light Crust setting, and press Start.

4. At the start of the final rise (see "Timing It Right," page 13), press Pause. Remove dough from bread pan and transfer to a floured surface and punch down gently. Divide dough into thirds. Roll each third into a 10-inch (25 cm) long rope. Lay the three ropes out parallel to each other on a floured surface so that they are very close but not touching. Braid ropes together snugly. Tuck ends under to form an oblong loaf.

5. *Topping:* Brush braid with beaten egg and sprinkle with sesame seeds, pressing the seeds into the dough.

6. Remove kneading paddle(s) from bread pan. Place braid in pan and press Start to continue the cycle.

Tips

Ideally, the water and milk should be between 86°F and 95°F (30°C and 35°C), the temperature range in which yeast is most active. Warm them in the microwave or in a saucepan on the stove, and check the temperature with an instant-read thermometer.

If your dough does not form a ball during the first few minutes of kneading, do one of two things: if the dough looks dry and crumbly, add 1 tbsp (15 mL) water at 1-minute intervals until the dough forms a ball; if the dough looks wet, add 1 tbsp (15 mL) all-purpose flour at 1-minute intervals until the dough forms a ball.

For an untraditional but dramatic effect, use black sesame seeds in place of pale brown.

Oven-Baked Braided Scali Bread

Starter

1 cup	all-purpose flour	250 mL
½ cup	water, at room temperature	125 mL
¼ tsp	instant or bread machine yeast	1 mL

Dough

⅓ cup	lukewarm water (see tip, at left)	75 mL
⅓ cup	lukewarm milk	75 mL
2 tbsp	olive oil	30 mL
1¼ tsp	salt	6 mL
2 cups	all-purpose flour	500 mL
2 tsp	instant or bread machine yeast	10 mL

Topping

1	large egg, beaten	1
2 tbsp	sesame seeds	30 mL

1. *Starter:* In a bowl, combine flour, water and yeast. Cover with plastic wrap and let rise at room temperature for 12 hours or overnight.

2. *Dough:* Transfer starter to the bread pan. Add water, milk, oil and salt. Spoon flour on top of liquid. Add yeast.

3. Select the Artisan Dough or Dough cycle and press Start.

4. When the cycle is finished, transfer dough to a floured surface and punch down gently. Divide dough into thirds. Roll each third into a 16-inch (40 cm) long rope. Braid ropes together, tucking ends under. Place on prepared baking sheet. Cover with a clean towel and let rise for 30 minutes. Meanwhile, preheat oven to 425°F (220°C).

5. *Topping:* Brush braid with beaten egg and sprinkle with sesame seeds, pressing the seeds into the dough.

6. Bake for about 25 minutes or until risen and dark brown and an instant-read thermometer inserted in the center registers 190°F (90°C). Remove from pan and let cool on a wire rack.

Oven-Baked Italian Scali Knots

Prepare the oven-baked recipe through step 3. When the cycle is finished, transfer dough to a floured surface and punch down gently. Divide dough into thirds. Roll each third into a 24-inch (60 cm) long rope. Cut ropes into 6-inch (15 cm) lengths and tie each length into a knot. Place knots at least 3 inches (7.5 cm) apart on prepared baking sheet. Let rise, add topping and bake as for loaf, decreasing the baking time to 15 to 20 minutes.

Semolina Bread

Semolina flour is made from hard spring wheat — the hardest variety of wheat, with the highest protein content — and is thus a very high-gluten flour. It can be found with other specialty flours in better grocery stores and in health food stores, specialty food markets, some Italian markets and mail-order baking catalogs. When you find it, run home and make this delicious, fine-textured artisanal bread that practically says "Amore!"

Tip

Ideally, the water should be between 86°F and 95°F (30°C and 35°C), the temperature range in which yeast is most active. Warm it in the microwave or in a saucepan on the stove, and check the temperature with an instant-read thermometer.

1 lb (500 g)

	Active prepared Sour Sponge for a 1-lb (500 g) loaf (see page 144)	
1/3 cup	lukewarm water (see tip, at left)	75 mL
1 cup	semolina flour	250 mL
1/2 cup	all-purpose flour	125 mL
1 tsp	salt	5 mL
Topping		
1 tbsp	sesame seeds	15 mL

1½ lb (750 g)

	Active prepared Sour Sponge for a 1½-lb (750 g) loaf (see page 144)	
7 tbsp	lukewarm water (see tip, at left)	105 mL
1½ cups	semolina flour	375 mL
3/4 cup	all-purpose flour	175 mL
2 tsp	salt	10 mL
Topping		
1 tbsp	sesame seeds	15 mL

2 lb (1 kg)

	Active prepared Sour Sponge for a 2-lb (1 kg) loaf (see page 144)	
7 tbsp	lukewarm water (see tip, at left)	105 mL
2 cups	semolina flour	500 mL
3/4 cup	all-purpose flour	175 mL
2½ tsp	salt	12 mL
Topping		
1 tbsp	sesame seeds	15 mL

3 lb (1.5 kg)

	Active prepared Sour Sponge for a 3-lb (1.5 kg) loaf (see page 144)	
6 tbsp	lukewarm water (see tip, at left)	90 mL
2½ cups	semolina flour	625 mL
1 cup	all-purpose flour	250 mL
2¾ tsp	salt	13 mL
Topping		
1 tbsp	sesame seeds	15 mL

Tips

Check the dough after 5 to 8 minutes of kneading; if it hasn't formed a soft ball yet, gradually sprinkle in just enough flour for the bread to form a cohesive ball (it will still be fairly loose), scraping the edges of the pan as you sprinkle. To prevent a dry bread, it's important not to add too much flour too soon.

If your bread machine doesn't have a Pause button, simply raise the lid, remove the dough, pat the seeds into the surface of the dough, then remove the kneading paddle(s) from the pan, return the dough to the pan and close the lid again. Work quickly, as the rising cycle will continue even without the bread in the pan.

This bread makes wonderful bruschetta. Slice the loaf, brush slices on both sides with olive oil, then grill on both sides, either outside on the barbecue or using a grill pan on the stovetop. Spoon or spread bruschetta toppings of your choice over the warm bread.

1. Transfer sponge to the bread pan. Add water. Spoon semolina flour and all-purpose flour on top of liquid. Add salt.

2. Select your machine's slow-rise cycle (see page 140), or the Basic/White cycle and the Light Crust setting, and press Start.

3. *Topping:* At the start of the final rise (see "Timing It Right," page 13), press Pause. Remove dough from bread pan and transfer to a floured surface. Pat sesame seeds into surface of dough.

4. Remove kneading paddle(s) from bread pan. Return dough to pan and press Start to continue the cycle.

Oven-Baked Semolina Baguette

Prepare the recipe through step 1, then select the Artisan Dough or Dough cycle and press Start. Line a large baking sheet with parchment paper. When the cycle is finished, transfer dough to a floured surface and punch down gently. Form dough into one or more 10- to 12-inch (25 to 30 cm) cylinders (see chart, below) and place on prepared baking sheet. Cover with a clean towel and let rise while oven is preheating. Preheat oven to 425°F (220°C). Using a serrated knife, cut 3 deep diagonal slashes across top of loaf. Spray loaf lightly with water and sprinkle with sesame seeds. Bake until risen and browned and an instant-read thermometer inserted in the center registers 190°F (90°C). Remove from pan and let cool on a wire rack.

Dough Size	Number of Baguettes	Baking Time
1 lb (500 g)	1	20 to 22 minutes
1½ lb (750 g)	1	22 to 24 minutes
2 lb (1 kg)	2	20 to 22 minutes
3 lb (1.5 kg)	3	20 to 22 minutes

Rosemary and Olive Bread

This bread machine version of an artisan bakery specialty allows you to make and enjoy this bread at home. Make sure to wait until the start of the second knead before adding the olives. You can also simply make the dough on the slow-rise cycle and bake it in the oven for a darker, crisper crust.

Tips

Ideally, the water should be between 86°F and 95°F (30°C and 35°C), the temperature range in which yeast is most active. Warm it in the microwave or in a saucepan on the stove, and check the temperature with an instant-read thermometer.

Check the dough after 5 to 8 minutes of kneading; if it hasn't formed a soft ball yet, gradually sprinkle in just enough bread flour for the bread to form a cohesive ball (it will still be fairly loose), scraping the edges of the pan as you sprinkle. To prevent a dry bread, it's important not to add too much flour too soon.

1 lb (500 g)

	Active prepared Sour Sponge for a 1-lb (500 g) loaf (see page 144)	
¼ cup	lukewarm water (see tip, at left)	60 mL
¾ cup	bread flour	175 mL
⅔ cup	whole-meal or whole wheat flour	150 mL
1 tsp	dried rosemary	5 mL
¾ tsp	salt	3 mL
½ cup	chopped kalamata olives, patted dry	125 mL

1½ lb (750 g)

	Active prepared Sour Sponge for a 1½-lb (750 g) loaf (see page 144)	
⅓ cup	lukewarm water (see tip, at left)	75 mL
1 cup + 2 tbsp	bread flour	280 mL
¾ cup	whole-meal or whole wheat flour	175 mL
1½ tsp	dried rosemary	7 mL
1 tsp	salt	5 mL
⅔ cup	chopped kalamata olives, patted dry	150 mL

2 lb (1 kg)

	Active prepared Sour Sponge for a 2-lb (1 kg) loaf (see page 144)	
⅓ cup	lukewarm water (see tip, at left)	75 mL
1½ cups	bread flour	375 mL
1 cup	whole-meal or whole wheat flour	250 mL
2 tsp	dried rosemary	10 mL
1½ tsp	salt	7 mL
¾ cup	chopped kalamata olives, patted dry	175 mL

3 lb (1.5 kg)

	Active prepared Sour Sponge for a 3-lb (1.5 kg) loaf (see page 144)	
¼ cup	lukewarm water (see tip, at left)	60 mL
2 cups	bread flour	500 mL
1¼ cups	whole-meal or whole wheat flour	300 mL
2½ tsp	dried rosemary	12 mL
2 tsp	salt	10 mL
1 cup	chopped kalamata olives, patted dry	250 mL

1. Transfer sponge to the bread pan. Add water. Spoon bread flour and whole-meal flour on top of liquid. Add rosemary and salt.

Tips

If you prefer to knead in the olives by hand (to keep them from getting chopped too much) in step 3, press Pause. Remove dough from bread pan and transfer to a floured surface. Press dough into an oval and sprinkle half the olives on the top half of the oval. Fold the bottom half over the top, rotate the dough a quarter turn and press with the heel of your hand or your knuckles to flatten it into an oval again. Repeat with the remaining olives. Remove kneading paddle(s) from bread pan. Return dough to pan and press Start to continue the cycle.

Placing a pan of water in the bottom of the oven while the bread is baking creates steam that helps form a good crust.

2. Select your machine's slow-rise cycle (see page 140), or the Basic/White cycle and the Light Crust setting, and press Start.

3. At the start of the second knead (see "Timing It Right," page 13), lift the lid and add olives. Close the lid to continue the cycle.

Oven-Baked Rosemary and Olive Boule

Prepare the recipe through step 1, then select the Artisan Dough or Dough cycle and press Start. Line a baking sheet with parchment paper. When the cycle is finished, transfer dough to a floured surface and punch down gently. Knead in olives. Let dough rest for 5 minutes. Form into a boule and place on prepared baking sheet. Cover with a clean towel and let rise for 30 minutes. Meanwhile, preheat oven to 425°F (220°C) and place a broiler pan on the bottom rack. Using a serrated knife, cut 3 deep slashes across top of loaf. Add 2 cups (500 mL) hot water to the broiler pan. Place baking sheet on the middle rack. Bake until risen and browned and an instant-read thermometer inserted in the center registers 190°F (90°C). Remove from pan and let cool on a wire rack.

Dough Size	Baking Time
1 lb (500 g)	20 to 25 minutes
1½ lb (750 g)	25 to 30 minutes
2 lb (1 kg)	30 to 40 minutes
3 lb (1.5 kg)	40 to 50 minutes

Cheddar and Green Olive Bread

Makes 1 loaf

This wonderfully tangy bread with the flavor of cheese and olives needs only the barest fillings to make a great sandwich. Make sure to wait until the start of the second knead before adding the cheese and olives.

Tips

Ideally, the water should be between 86°F and 95°F (30°C and 35°C), the temperature range in which yeast is most active. Warm it in the microwave or in a saucepan on the stove, and check the temperature with an instant-read thermometer.

Check the dough after 5 to 8 minutes of kneading; if it hasn't formed a soft ball yet, gradually sprinkle in just enough bread flour for the bread to form a cohesive ball (it will still be fairly loose), scraping the edges of the pan as you sprinkle. To prevent a dry bread, it's important not to add too much flour too soon.

1 lb (500 g)

	Active prepared Sour Sponge for a 1-lb (500 g) loaf (see page 144)	
¼ cup	lukewarm water (see tip, at left)	60 mL
¾ cup	bread flour	175 mL
⅔ cup	whole-meal or whole wheat flour	150 mL
½ tsp	salt	2 mL
⅓ cup	lightly packed shredded aged (old) Cheddar cheese	75 mL
⅓ cup	chopped pimento-stuffed green olives, patted dry	75 mL

1½ lb (750 g)

	Active prepared Sour Sponge for a 1½-lb (750 g) loaf (see page 144)	
⅓ cup	lukewarm water (see tip, at left)	75 mL
1 cup + 2 tbsp	bread flour	280 mL
¾ cup	whole-meal or whole wheat flour	175 mL
¾ tsp	salt	3 mL
½ cup	lightly packed shredded aged (old) Cheddar cheese	125 mL
½ cup	chopped pimento-stuffed green olives, patted dry	125 mL

2 lb (1 kg)

	Active prepared Sour Sponge for a 2-lb (1 kg) loaf (see page 144)	
⅓ cup	lukewarm water (see tip, at left)	75 mL
1½ cups	bread flour	375 mL
1 cup	whole-meal or whole wheat flour	250 mL
1¼ tsp	salt	6 mL
⅔ cup	lightly packed shredded aged (old) Cheddar cheese	150 mL
⅔ cup	chopped pimento-stuffed green olives, patted dry	150 mL

3 lb (1.5 kg)

	Active prepared Sour Sponge for a 3-lb (1.5 kg) loaf (see page 144)	
¼ cup	lukewarm water (see tip, at left)	60 mL
2 cups	bread flour	500 mL
1¼ cups	whole-meal or whole wheat flour	300 mL

Tips

If you prefer to knead in the cheese and olives by hand in step 3 (to keep them from getting chopped too much), press Pause. Remove dough from bread pan and transfer to a floured surface. Press dough into an oval and sprinkle half the cheese and half the olives on the top half of the oval. Fold the bottom half over the top, rotate the dough a quarter turn and press with the heel of your hand or your knuckles to flatten it into an oval again. Repeat with the remaining cheese and olives. Remove kneading paddle(s) from bread pan. Return dough to pan and press Start to continue the cycle.

If you're making the oven-baked version and kneading in the cheese and olives by hand, you can cut the cheese into small cubes, instead of shredding, so the cheese is more visible in the baked loaf. Shredded cheese is best for machine-baked bread, as cubes melt and weigh the dough down.

Placing a pan of water in the bottom of the oven while the bread is baking creates steam that helps form a good crust.

1¾ tsp	salt	8 mL
¾ cup	lightly packed shredded aged (old) Cheddar cheese	175 mL
¾ cup	chopped pimento-stuffed green olives, patted dry	175 mL

1. Transfer sponge to the bread pan. Add water. Spoon bread flour and whole-meal flour on top of liquid. Add salt.

2. Select your machine's slow-rise cycle (see page 140), or the Basic/White cycle and the Light Crust setting, and press Start.

3. At the start of the second knead (see "Timing It Right," page 13), lift the lid and add cheese and olives. Close the lid to continue the cycle.

Oven-Baked Cheddar and Green Olive Boule

Prepare the recipe through step 1, then select the Artisan Dough or Dough cycle and press Start. Line a baking sheet with parchment paper. When the cycle is finished, transfer dough to a floured surface and punch down gently. Knead in cheese and olives. Let dough rest for 5 minutes. Form into a boule and place on prepared baking sheet. Cover with a clean towel and let rise for 30 minutes. Meanwhile, preheat oven to 425°F (220°C) and place a broiler pan on the bottom rack. Using a serrated knife, cut 3 deep slashes across top of loaf. Add 2 cups (500 mL) hot water to the broiler pan. Place baking sheet on the middle rack. Bake until risen and browned and an instant-read thermometer inserted in the center registers 190°F (90°C). Remove from pan and let cool on a wire rack.

Dough Size	Baking Time
1 lb (500 g)	20 to 25 minutes
1½ lb (750 g)	25 to 30 minutes
2 lb (1 kg)	30 to 40 minutes
3 lb (1.5 kg)	40 to 50 minutes

Sour Dark Rye Bread with Caraway

Makes 1 loaf

Slices of this compact, somewhat shaggy-textured loaf with a gentle sourness make a wonderful ham sandwich with a little Dijon mustard or good mayonnaise.

Tip

Ideally, the water for the dough should be between 86°F and 95°F (30°C and 35°C), the temperature range in which yeast is most active. Warm it in the microwave or in a saucepan on the stove, and check the temperature with an instant-read thermometer.

1 lb (500 g)

	Active prepared Sour Rye Sponge for a 1-lb (500 g) loaf (see page 144)	
¼ cup	lukewarm water (see tip, at left)	60 mL
1½ tbsp	light (fancy) molasses	22 mL
¾ cup	bread flour	175 mL
⅔ cup	dark rye flour, preferably stone-ground or coarse	150 mL
1½ tbsp	unsweetened cocoa powder	22 mL
1 tsp	caraway seeds	5 mL
1¼ tsp	salt	6 mL

1½ lb (750 g)

	Active prepared Sour Rye Sponge for a 1½-lb (750 g) loaf (see page 144)	
½ cup	lukewarm water (see tip, at left)	125 mL
2 tbsp	light (fancy) molasses	30 mL
1 cup + 2 tbsp	bread flour	280 mL
1 cup	dark rye flour, preferably stone-ground or coarse	250 mL
2 tbsp	unsweetened cocoa powder	30 mL
1½ tsp	caraway seeds	7 mL
1¾ tsp	salt	8 mL

2 lb (1 kg)

	Active prepared Sour Rye Sponge for a 2-lb (1 kg) loaf (see page 144)	
7 tbsp	lukewarm water (see tip, at left)	105 mL
3 tbsp	light (fancy) molasses	45 mL
1½ cups	bread flour	375 mL
1 cup	dark rye flour, preferably stone-ground or coarse	250 mL
3 tbsp	unsweetened cocoa powder	45 mL
2 tsp	caraway seeds	10 mL
2¼ tsp	salt	11 mL

Tips

Check the dough after 5 to 8 minutes of kneading; if it hasn't formed a soft ball yet, gradually sprinkle in just enough bread flour for the bread to form a cohesive ball (it will still be fairly loose), scraping the edges of the pan as you sprinkle. To prevent a dry bread, it's important not to add too much flour too soon.

For a smoother-textured bread that can be thinly sliced for Scandinavian-style smørrebrød or open-face sandwiches, select the Whole Wheat cycle in step 3.

Placing a pan of water in the bottom of the oven while the bread is baking creates steam that helps form a good crust.

3 lb (1.5 kg)

	Active prepared Sour Rye Sponge for a 3-lb (1.5 kg) loaf (see page 144)	
7 tbsp	lukewarm water (see tip, page 156)	105 mL
⅓ cup	light (fancy) molasses	75 mL
2 cups	bread flour	500 mL
1½ cups	dark rye flour, preferably stone-ground or coarse	375 mL
¼ cup	unsweetened cocoa powder	60 mL
1 tbsp	caraway seeds	15 mL
2¾ tsp	salt	13 mL

1. Transfer sponge to the bread pan. Add water and molasses. Spoon bread flour and rye flour on top of liquid. Add cocoa, caraway seeds and salt.

2. Select your machine's slow-rise cycle (see page 140), or the Basic/White cycle and the Light Crust setting, and press Start.

Oven-Baked Sour Dark Rye with Caraway

Prepare the recipe through step 1, then select the Artisan Dough or Dough cycle and press Start. Line a baking sheet with parchment paper. When the cycle is finished, transfer dough to a floured surface and punch down gently. Form into an oblong loaf (see chart, below) and place on prepared baking sheet. Cover with a clean towel and let rise for 45 minutes. Meanwhile, preheat oven to 425°F (220°C) and place a broiler pan on the bottom rack. Using a serrated knife, cut 3 deep diagonal slashes across top of loaf. Add 2 cups (500 mL) hot water to the broiler pan. Place baking sheet on the middle rack. Bake until risen and browned and an instant-read thermometer inserted in the center registers 190°F (90°C). Remove from pan and let cool on a wire rack.

Dough Size	Loaf Size	Baking Time
1 lb (500 g)	10 inches (25 cm) long	20 to 25 minutes
1½ lb (750 g)	11 inches (28 cm) long	20 to 25 minutes
2 lb (1 kg)	12 inches (30 cm) long	25 to 30 minutes
3 lb (1.5 kg)	14 inches (35 cm) long	30 to 40 minutes

Brewhouse Bread

Makes 1 loaf

This hearty slow-rise loaf, enriched by the malty flavor of beer, is the perfect foil to a grilled bratwurst and a jolt of horseradish. Or try it with an aged Cheddar and pickled onions.

Tips

Don't be tempted to use a darker beer, as this will produce an unpleasantly bitter flavor in the starter.

To make beer go flat, simply pour it into a glass and let it stand at room temperature for an hour or microwave it until it boils, then let it cool before use. Alternatively, you can whisk the granulated sugar from the recipe into the measured beer and let it stand for about 15 minutes or until the bubbles subside.

Ideally, the water should be between 86°F and 95°F (30°C and 35°C), the temperature range in which yeast is most active. Warm it in the microwave or in a saucepan on the stove, and check the temperature with an instant-read thermometer.

1 lb (500 g)

Brewhouse Sponge

1 cup	all-purpose flour	250 mL
¾ tsp	granulated sugar	3 mL
¼ tsp	instant or bread machine yeast	1 mL
⅔ cup	flat lager beer	150 mL

Dough

¼ cup	lukewarm water (see tip, at left)	60 mL
⅔ cup	bread flour	150 mL
½ cup	whole wheat flour	125 mL
1 tsp	salt	5 mL

1½ lb (750 g)

Brewhouse Sponge

1½ cups	all-purpose flour	375 mL
1 tsp	granulated sugar	5 mL
¼ tsp	instant or bread machine yeast	1 mL
1 cup	flat lager beer	250 mL

Dough

⅓ cup	lukewarm water (see tip, at left)	75 mL
1 cup	bread flour	250 mL
¾ cup	whole wheat flour	175 mL
1½ tsp	salt	7 mL

2 lb (1 kg)

Brewhouse Sponge

1⅔ cups	all-purpose flour	400 mL
1½ tsp	granulated sugar	7 mL
½ tsp	instant or bread machine yeast	2 mL
1¼ cups	flat lager beer	300 mL

Dough

⅓ cup	lukewarm water (see tip, at left)	75 mL
1⅓ cups	bread flour	325 mL
1 cup	whole wheat flour	250 mL
2 tsp	salt	10 mL

3 lb (1.5 kg)

Brewhouse Sponge

2½ cups	all-purpose flour	625 mL
2 tsp	granulated sugar	10 mL
½ tsp	instant or bread machine yeast	2 mL
1¾ cups	flat lager beer	425 mL

Tips

Check the dough after 5 to 8 minutes of kneading; if it hasn't formed a soft ball yet, gradually sprinkle in just enough bread flour for the bread to form a cohesive ball (it will still be fairly loose), scraping the edges of the pan as you sprinkle. To prevent a dry bread, it's important not to add too much flour too soon.

Placing a pan of water in the bottom of the oven while the bread is baking creates steam that helps form a good crust.

Dough

½ cup + 1 tbsp	lukewarm water (see tip, page 158)	140 mL
2 cups	bread flour	500 mL
1½ cups	whole wheat flour	375 mL
2½ tsp	salt	12 mL

1. *Sponge:* In a large bowl, combine flour, sugar, yeast and beer. Cover with plastic wrap and let rise in a warm place for about 24 hours or until the sponge has doubled in size and is light and full of bubbles.

2. *Dough:* Transfer sponge to the bread pan. Add water. Spoon bread flour and whole wheat flour on top of liquid. Add salt.

3. Select your machine's slow-rise cycle (see page 140) or the Basic/White cycle and press Start.

Oven-Baked Brewhouse Boule

Prepare the recipe through step 2, then select the Artisan Dough or Dough cycle and press Start. Line a baking sheet with parchment paper. When the cycle is finished, transfer dough to a floured surface and punch down gently. Form into a boule and place on prepared baking sheet. Cover with a clean towel and let rise for 30 minutes. Meanwhile, preheat oven to 425°F (220°C) and place a broiler pan on the bottom rack. Using a serrated knife, cut 3 deep slashes across top of loaf. Add 2 cups (500 mL) hot water to the broiler pan. Place baking sheet on the middle rack. Bake until risen and browned and an instant-read thermometer inserted in the center registers 190°F (90°C). Remove from pan and let cool on a wire rack.

Dough Size	Baking Time
1 lb (500 g)	20 to 25 minutes
1½ lb (750 g)	25 to 30 minutes
2 lb (1 kg)	30 to 40 minutes
3 lb (1.5 kg)	40 to 50 minutes

Herbed Brewhouse Bread

Add mixed dried herbs (dillweed, chives, celery flakes, etc.) equivalent to the amount of salt with the flour in step 2.

Old-Fashioned Buttermilk Bread

Makes 1 loaf

My inspiration for this loaf came from *Buckeye Cookery and Practical Housekeeping*, published in Minneapolis in 1876. I'm sure the original authors would applaud our 21st-century improvements. We can mix the sponge 24 hours ahead, then finish mixing and baking the bread in the bread machine. The result is a high, light, crusty loaf with a somewhat honeycombed crumb. Serve it with the finest accompaniments: Artisan Butter (page 280) and Sour Cherry Preserves (page 293).

Tip

Ideally, the water for the dough should be between 86°F and 95°F (30°C and 35°C), the temperature range in which yeast is most active. Warm it in the microwave or in a saucepan on the stove, and check the temperature with an instant-read thermometer.

1 lb (500 g)

	Active prepared Buttermilk Sponge for a 1-lb (500 g) loaf (see page 145), made with all-purpose flour	
2½ tbsp	lukewarm water (see tip, at left)	37 mL
1¼ cups	bread flour	300 mL
1 tsp	salt	5 mL

1½ lb (750 g)

	Active prepared Buttermilk Sponge for a 1½-lb (750 g) loaf (see page 145), made with all-purpose flour	
3 tbsp	lukewarm water (see tip, at left)	45 mL
1¾ cups	bread flour	425 mL
1½ tsp	salt	7 mL

2 lb (1 kg)

	Active prepared Buttermilk Sponge for a 2-lb (1 kg) loaf (see page 145), made with all-purpose flour	
¼ cup	lukewarm water (see tip, at left)	60 mL
2⅓ cups	bread flour	575 mL
2 tsp	salt	10 mL

3 lb (1.5 kg)

	Active prepared Buttermilk Sponge for a 3-lb (1.5 kg) loaf (see page 145), made with all-purpose flour	
⅓ cup	lukewarm water (see tip, at left)	75 mL
3½ cups	bread flour	875 mL
2¾ tsp	salt	13 mL

1. Transfer sponge to the bread pan. Add water. Spoon flour on top of liquid. Add salt.

2. Select your machine's slow-rise cycle (see page 140), or the Basic/White cycle and the Light Crust setting, and press Start.

Tips

Check the dough after 5 to 8 minutes of kneading; if it hasn't formed a soft ball yet, gradually sprinkle in just enough bread flour for the bread to form a cohesive ball (it will still be fairly loose), scraping the edges of the pan as you sprinkle. To prevent a dry bread, it's important not to add too much flour too soon.

Placing a pan of water in the bottom of the oven while the bread is baking creates steam that helps form a good crust.

If you have a large machine, you can prepare the 3-lb (1.5 kg) recipe and make 24 crescents.

Oven-Baked Buttermilk Boule

Prepare the recipe through step 1, then select the Artisan Dough or Dough cycle and press Start. Line a baking sheet with parchment paper. When the cycle is finished, transfer dough to a floured surface and punch down gently. Form into a boule and place on prepared baking sheet. Cover with a clean towel and let rise for 30 minutes. Meanwhile, preheat oven to 425°F (220°C) and place a broiler pan on the bottom rack. Using a serrated knife, cut 3 deep slashes across top of loaf. Add 2 cups (500 mL) hot water to the broiler pan. Place baking sheet on the middle rack. Bake until risen and browned and an instant-read thermometer inserted in the center registers 190°F (90°C). Remove from pan and let cool on a wire rack.

Dough Size	Baking Time
1 lb (500 g)	20 to 25 minutes
1½ lb (750 g)	25 to 30 minutes
2 lb (1 kg)	30 to 40 minutes
3 lb (1.5 kg)	40 to 50 minutes

Old-Fashioned Buttermilk Crescents

Prepare the 1½-lb (750 g) recipe through step 1, then select the Artisan Dough or Dough cycle and press Start. Line a large baking sheet with parchment paper. When the cycle is finished, transfer dough to a floured surface and punch down gently. Dust lightly with flour and roll out into a 10- to 12-inch (25 to 30 cm) circle. Using a pizza wheel or a sharp knife, cut circle into 12 triangles. Starting with the wide end, roll up each triangle. Place rolls, seam side down, at least 2 inches (5 cm) apart on prepared baking sheet and form into crescents. Cover with a clean towel and let rise while oven is preheating. Preheat oven to 375°F (190°C). Brush crescents with 1 large egg, beaten. Bake for 20 minutes or until puffed and browned and an instant-read thermometer inserted in the center of a crescent registers 190°F (90°C). Serve hot.

French Canadian Wheat and Walnut Bread

Makes 1 loaf		

Versions of this country-style bread have traveled from central France to Quebec, and then on to the southernmost tip of Lake Michigan and down the Kankakee River to the village of Bourbonnais in northern Illinois. With its honeycomb crumb, chewy bite and nutty flavor, it's perfect with an aged cheese or a pungent blue, along with thin slices of fresh apple or pear.

Tip

To toast whole walnuts, spread them on a microwave-safe plate and microwave on High for 2 to 3 minutes or until they begin to give off a nutty aroma. Let cool, then chop.

1 lb (500 g)

	Active prepared Buttermilk Sponge for a 1-lb (500 g) loaf (see page 145), made with all-purpose flour	
2½ tbsp	pure maple syrup (preferably Grade B or Dark)	37 mL
¾ cup	bread flour	175 mL
½ cup	stone-ground or coarse whole wheat flour	125 mL
1 tsp	salt	1 mL
½ cup	finely chopped toasted walnuts (see tip, at left)	125 mL

1½ lb (750 g)

	Active prepared Buttermilk Sponge for a 1½-lb (750 g) loaf (see page 145), made with all-purpose flour	
¼ cup	pure maple syrup (preferably Grade B or Dark)	60 mL
1¼ cups	bread flour	300 mL
⅔ cup	stone-ground or coarse whole wheat flour	150 mL
1½ tsp	salt	7 mL
⅔ cup	finely chopped toasted walnuts (see tip, at left)	150 mL

2 lb (1 kg)

	Active prepared Buttermilk Sponge for a 2-lb (1 kg) loaf (see page 145), made with all-purpose flour	
⅓ cup	pure maple syrup (preferably Grade B or Dark)	75 mL
1½ cups	bread flour	375 mL
1 cup	stone-ground or coarse whole wheat flour	250 mL
2 tsp	salt	10 mL
¾ cup	finely chopped toasted walnuts (see tip, at left)	175 mL

3 lb (1.5 kg)

	Active prepared Buttermilk Sponge for a 3-lb (1.5 kg) loaf (see page 145), made with all-purpose flour	

Tips

If you prefer to knead in the walnuts by hand (to keep them from getting chopped too much), instead of adding them in step 1, at the start of the final rise (see "Timing It Right," page 13) press Pause. Remove dough from bread pan and transfer to a floured surface. Press dough into an oval and sprinkle half the walnuts on the top half of the oval. Fold the bottom half over the top, rotate the dough a quarter turn and press with the heel of your hand or your knuckles to flatten it into an oval again. Repeat with the remaining walnuts. Remove kneading paddle(s) from bread pan. Return dough to pan and press Start to continue the cycle.

Placing a pan of water in the bottom of the oven while the bread is baking creates steam that helps form a good crust.

½ cup	pure maple syrup (preferably Grade B or Dark)	125 mL
1¾ cups	bread flour	425 mL
1⅓ cups	stone-ground or coarse whole wheat flour	325 mL
2½ tsp	salt	12 mL
1 cup	finely chopped toasted walnuts (see tip, page 162)	250 mL

1. Transfer sponge to the bread pan. Add maple syrup. Spoon bread flour and whole wheat flour on top of liquid. Add salt. Place walnuts in the dispenser (or add at the "add ingredient" or "mix in" signal).

2. Select your machine's slow-rise cycle (see page 140), or the Basic/White cycle and the Light Crust setting, and press Start.

Oven-Baked Wheat and Walnut Boule

Prepare the recipe through step 1 (without adding walnuts), then select the Artisan Dough or Dough cycle and press Start. Line a baking sheet with parchment paper. When the cycle is finished, transfer dough to a floured surface and punch down gently. Knead in walnuts. Let dough rest for 5 minutes. Form into a boule and place on prepared baking sheet. Cover with a clean towel and let rise for 30 minutes. Preheat oven to 400°F (200°C) and place a broiler pan on the bottom rack. Using a serrated knife, cut 3 deep slashes across top of loaf. Add 2 cups (500 mL) hot water to the broiler pan. Place baking sheet on the middle rack. Bake until boule is risen and browned and an instant-read thermometer inserted in the center registers 190°F (90°C). Remove from pan and let cool on a wire rack.

Dough Size	Baking Time
1 lb (500 g)	25 to 30 minutes
1½ lb (750 g)	30 to 35 minutes
2 lb (1 kg)	35 to 40 minutes
3 lb (1.5 kg)	45 to 55 minutes

Herbed Polenta Bread

This golden, herbed bread has a true homemade flavor. The fine cornmeal (the type used to make polenta) softens during mixing and rising, producing just the right amount of texture.

Tip

Ideally, the water for the dough should be between 86°F and 95°F (30°C and 35°C), the temperature range in which yeast is most active. Warm it in the microwave or in a saucepan on the stove, and check the temperature with an instant-read thermometer.

1 lb (500 g)

	Active prepared Buttermilk Sponge for a 1-lb (500 g) loaf (see page 145), made with all-purpose flour	
3 tbsp	lukewarm water (see tip, at left)	45 mL
3/4 cup	bread flour	175 mL
1/2 cup	fine yellow cornmeal	125 mL
1 tsp	salt	5 mL
1/2 tsp	dried rosemary	2 mL
1/2 tsp	dried basil	2 mL

1 1/2 lb (750 g)

	Active prepared Buttermilk Sponge for a 1 1/2-lb (750 g) loaf (see page 145), made with all-purpose flour	
1/3 cup	lukewarm water (see tip, at left)	75 mL
1 cup	bread flour	250 mL
2/3 cup	fine yellow cornmeal	150 mL
1 1/2 tsp	salt	7 mL
3/4 tsp	dried rosemary	3 mL
3/4 tsp	dried basil	3 mL

2 lb (1 kg)

	Active prepared Buttermilk Sponge for a 2-lb (1 kg) loaf (see page 145), made with all-purpose flour	
1/3 cup	lukewarm water (see tip, at left)	75 mL
1 1/2 cups	bread flour	375 mL
1 cup	fine yellow cornmeal	175 mL
2 1/4 tsp	salt	11 mL
1 tsp	dried rosemary	5 mL
1 tsp	dried basil	5 mL

3 lb (1.5 kg)

	Active prepared Buttermilk Sponge for a 3-lb (1.5 kg) loaf (see page 145), made with all-purpose flour	
6 tbsp	lukewarm water (see tip, at left)	90 mL
2 1/3 cups	bread flour	575 mL
1 1/3 cups	fine yellow cornmeal	325 mL
2 1/2 tsp	salt	12 mL
1 1/2 tsp	dried rosemary	7 mL
1 1/2 tsp	dried basil	7 mL

Tips

Check the dough after 5 to 8 minutes of kneading; if it hasn't formed a soft ball yet, gradually sprinkle in just enough bread flour for the bread to form a cohesive ball (it will still be fairly loose), scraping the edges of the pan as you sprinkle. To prevent a dry bread, it's important not to add too much flour too soon.

Placing a pan of water in the bottom of the oven while the bread is baking creates steam that helps form a good crust.

1. Transfer sponge to the bread pan. Add water. Spoon flour on top of liquid. Add cornmeal, salt, rosemary and basil.

2. Select your machine's slow-rise cycle (see page 140) or the Basic/White cycle and press Start.

Oven-Baked Herbed Polenta Boule

Prepare the recipe through step 1, then select the Artisan Dough or Dough cycle and press Start. Line a baking sheet with parchment paper. When the cycle is finished, transfer dough to a floured surface and punch down gently. Form into a boule and place on prepared baking sheet. Cover with a clean towel and let rise for 30 minutes. Preheat oven to 400°F (200°C) and place a broiler pan on the bottom rack. Using a serrated knife, cut 3 deep slashes across top of loaf. Add 2 cups (500 mL) hot water to the broiler pan. Place baking sheet on the middle rack. Bake until boule is risen and browned and an instant-read thermometer inserted in the center registers 190°F (90°C). Remove from pan and let cool on a wire rack.

Dough Size	Baking Time
1 lb (500 g)	25 to 30 minutes
1½ lb (750 g)	30 to 35 minutes
2 lb (1 kg)	35 to 40 minutes
3 lb (1.5 kg)	45 to 55 minutes

Really, Really Slow-Rise Sour Wheat Bread

Tip

Ideally, the water for the dough should be between 86°F and 95°F (30°C and 35°C), the temperature range in which yeast is most active. Warm it in the microwave or in a saucepan on the stove, and check the temperature with an instant-read thermometer.

1 lb (500 g)

	Active prepared Buttermilk Sponge for a 1-lb (500 g) loaf (see page 145), made with bread flour and fermented for 3 days	
1 tbsp	lukewarm water (see tip, at left)	15 mL
1 cup + 2 tbsp	white whole wheat or whole wheat flour	280 mL
1 tsp	salt	5 mL

1½ lb (750 g)

	Active prepared Buttermilk Sponge for a 1½-lb (750 g) loaf (see page 145), made with bread flour and fermented for 3 days	
1½ tbsp	lukewarm water (see tip, at left)	22 mL
1½ cups	white whole wheat or whole wheat flour	375 mL
1½ tsp	salt	7 mL

2 lb (1 kg)

	Active prepared Buttermilk Sponge for a 2-lb (1 kg) loaf (see page 145), made with bread flour and fermented for 3 days	
2 tbsp	lukewarm water (see tip, at left)	30 mL
2 cups	white whole wheat or whole wheat flour	500 mL
2 tsp	salt	10 mL

3 lb (1.5 kg)

	Active prepared Buttermilk Sponge for a 3-lb (1.5 kg) loaf (see page 145), made with bread flour and ¼ tsp (1 mL) yeast and fermented for 3 days	
⅓ cup	lukewarm water (see tip, at left)	75 mL
3⅔ cups	white whole wheat or whole wheat flour	900 mL
2½ tsp	salt	12 mL

1. Stir the hooch back into the sponge and transfer sponge to the bread pan. Add water. Spoon flour on top of liquid. Add salt.

Tips

Check the dough after 5 to 8 minutes of kneading; if it hasn't formed a soft ball yet, gradually sprinkle in just enough bread flour for the bread to form a cohesive ball (it will still be fairly loose), scraping the edges of the pan as you sprinkle. To prevent a dry bread, it's important not to add too much flour too soon.

When making the oven-baked boule, use a floured dough scraper or silicone spatula to remove the soft, sticky dough from the bread pan, and keep your hands and work surface well floured to prevent the dough from sticking.

2. Select your machine's slow-rise cycle (see page 140), or the Basic/White cycle and the Light Crust setting, and press Start.

Oven-Baked Really, Really Slow-Rise Wheat Boule

Prepare the recipe through step 1, then select the Artisan Dough or Dough cycle and press Start. Line a baking sheet with parchment paper. When the cycle is finished, transfer the slack dough to a floured surface and punch down gently. Form into a boule and place on prepared baking sheet. Cover with a clean towel and let rise for 45 minutes. Preheat oven to 400°F (200°C) and place a broiler pan on the bottom rack. Using a serrated knife, cut 3 deep slashes across top of loaf. Add 2 cups (500 mL) hot water to the broiler pan. Place baking sheet on the middle rack. Bake until boule is risen and browned and an instant-read thermometer inserted in the center registers 190°F (90°C). Remove from pan and let cool on a wire rack.

Dough Size	Baking Time
1 lb (500 g)	25 to 30 minutes
1½ lb (750 g)	30 to 35 minutes
2 lb (1 kg)	35 to 40 minutes
3 lb (1.5 kg)	45 to 55 minutes

Really, Really Slow-Rise Sour Rye Bread

Good things really do come to those who wait — like this tangy rye bread. Just let your sponge ferment for about 3 days, until a clear beige liquid rises to the top. Stir "the hooch" back into the sponge, and you're ready to bake.

Tip

Ideally, the water for the dough should be between 86°F and 95°F (30°C and 35°C), the temperature range in which yeast is most active. Warm it in the microwave or in a saucepan on the stove, and check the temperature with an instant-read thermometer.

1 lb (500 g)

	Active prepared Sour Rye Sponge for a 1-lb (500 g) loaf (see page 144), fermented for 3 days	
1 tsp	packed brown sugar	5 mL
1/4 cup	lukewarm water (see tip, at left)	60 mL
3/4 cup	dark rye flour, preferably stone-ground or coarse	175 mL
2/3 cup	bread flour	150 mL
1 tsp	caraway seeds	5 mL
1 tsp	vital wheat gluten	5 mL
1 tsp	salt	5 mL

1 1/2 lb (750 g)

	Active prepared Sour Rye Sponge for a 1 1/2-lb (750 g) loaf (see page 144), fermented for 3 days	
1 1/2 tsp	packed brown sugar	7 mL
1/2 cup	lukewarm water (see tip, at left)	125 mL
1 1/4 cups	dark rye flour, preferably stone-ground or coarse	300 mL
1 cup	bread flour	250 mL
1 1/2 tsp	caraway seeds	7 mL
1 1/2 tsp	vital wheat gluten	7 mL
1 1/2 tsp	salt	7 mL

2 lb (1 kg)

	Active prepared Sour Rye Sponge for a 2-lb (1 kg) loaf (see page 144), fermented for 3 days	
2 tsp	packed brown sugar	10 mL
1/2 cup	lukewarm water (see tip, at left)	125 mL
1 1/2 cups	dark rye flour, preferably stone-ground or coarse	375 mL
1 1/4 cups	bread flour	300 mL
2 tsp	caraway seeds	10 mL
2 tsp	vital wheat gluten	10 mL
2 tsp	salt	10 mL

3 lb (1.5 kg)

	Active prepared Sour Rye Sponge for a 3-lb (1.5 kg) loaf (see page 144), fermented for 3 days	

Tips

Check the dough after 5 to 8 minutes of kneading; if it hasn't formed a soft ball yet, gradually sprinkle in just enough bread flour for the bread to form a cohesive ball (it will still be fairly loose), scraping the edges of the pan as you sprinkle. To prevent a dry bread, it's important not to add too much flour too soon.

When making the oven-baked boule, use a floured dough scraper or silicone spatula to remove the soft, sticky dough from the bread pan, and keep your hands and work surface well floured to prevent the dough from sticking.

1 tbsp	packed brown sugar	15 mL
2/3 cup	lukewarm water (see tip, page 168)	150 mL
2 cups	dark rye flour, preferably stone-ground or coarse	500 mL
1¾ cups	bread flour	425 mL
1 tbsp	caraway seeds	15 mL
1 tbsp	vital wheat gluten	15 mL
2¾ tsp	salt	13 mL

1. Stir the hooch back into the sponge and transfer sponge to the bread pan. Add brown sugar and water. Spoon rye flour and bread flour on top of liquid. Add caraway seeds, wheat gluten and salt.

2. Select your machine's slow-rise cycle (see page 140), or the Basic/White cycle and the Light Crust setting, and press Start.

Oven-Baked Really, Really Slow-Rise Sour Rye Bread

Prepare the recipe through step 1, then select the Artisan Dough or Dough cycle and press Start. Line a baking sheet with parchment paper. When the cycle is finished, transfer the slack dough to a floured surface and punch down gently. Form into an oblong loaf (see chart, below) and place on prepared baking sheet. Cover with a clean towel and let rise for 45 minutes. Meanwhile, preheat oven to 425°F (220°C) and place a broiler pan on the bottom rack. Using a serrated knife, cut 3 deep diagonal slashes across top of loaf. Add 2 cups (500 mL) hot water to the broiler pan. Place baking sheet on the middle rack. Bake until risen and browned and an instant-read thermometer inserted in the center registers 190°F (90°C). Remove from pan and let cool on a wire rack.

Dough Size	Loaf Size	Baking Time
1 lb (500 g)	10 inches (25 cm) long	20 to 25 minutes
1½ lb (750 g)	11 inches (28 cm) long	20 to 25 minutes
2 lb (1 kg)	12 inches (30 cm) long	25 to 30 minutes
3 lb (1.5 kg)	14 inches (35 cm) long	30 to 40 minutes

Really, Really Slow-Rise Whole Wheat Seed Bread

Makes 1 loaf

This tangy loaf has a hearty texture thanks to the whole wheat and the seeds. No one will guess you made it in the bread machine.

Tip

Ideally, the water for the dough should be between 86°F and 95°F (30°C and 35°C), the temperature range in which yeast is most active. Warm it in the microwave or in a saucepan on the stove, and check the temperature with an instant-read thermometer.

1 lb (500 g)

	Active prepared Buttermilk Sponge for a 1-lb (500 g) loaf (see page 145), made with bread flour and fermented for 3 days	
1 tbsp	lukewarm water (see tip, at left)	15 mL
1 cup + 2 tbsp	white whole wheat or whole wheat flour	280 mL
1 tsp	salt	5 mL
2 tbsp	toasted green pumpkin seeds (pepitas)	30 mL
2 tbsp	roasted salted sunflower seeds	30 mL

1½ lb (750 g)

	Active prepared Buttermilk Sponge for a 1½-lb (750 g) loaf (see page 145), made with bread flour and fermented for 3 days	
1½ tbsp	lukewarm water (see tip, at left)	22 mL
1½ cups	white whole wheat or whole wheat flour	375 mL
1½ tsp	salt	7 mL
3 tbsp	toasted green pumpkin seeds (pepitas)	45 mL
3 tbsp	roasted salted sunflower seeds	45 mL

2 lb (1 kg)

	Active prepared Buttermilk Sponge for a 2-lb (1 kg) loaf (see page 145), made with bread flour and fermented for 3 days	
2 tbsp	lukewarm water (see tip, at left)	30 mL
2 cups	white whole wheat or whole wheat flour	500 mL
2 tsp	salt	10 mL
¼ cup	toasted green pumpkin seeds (pepitas)	60 mL
¼ cup	roasted salted sunflower seeds	60 mL

3 lb (1.5 kg)

	Active prepared Buttermilk Sponge for a 3-lb (1.5 kg) loaf (see page 145), made with bread flour and ¼ tsp (1 mL) yeast and fermented for 3 days	
⅓ cup	lukewarm water (see tip, at left)	75 mL

Check the dough after 5 to 8 minutes of kneading; if it hasn't formed a soft ball yet, gradually sprinkle in just enough bread flour for the bread to form a cohesive ball (it will still be fairly loose), scraping the edges of the pan as you sprinkle. To prevent a dry bread, it's important not to add too much flour too soon.

When making the oven-baked boule, use a floured dough scraper or silicone spatula to remove the soft, sticky dough from the bread pan, and keep your hands and work surface well floured to prevent the dough from sticking.

3²⁄₃ cups	white whole wheat or whole wheat flour	900 mL
2¹⁄₂ tsp	salt	12 mL
¹⁄₃ cup	toasted green pumpkin seeds (pepitas)	75 mL
¹⁄₃ cup	roasted salted sunflower seeds	75 mL

1. Stir the hooch back into the sponge and transfer sponge to the bread pan. Add water. Spoon flour on top of liquid. Add salt. Place pumpkin seeds and sunflower seeds in the dispenser (or add at the "add ingredient" or "mix in" signal).

2. Select your machine's slow-rise cycle (see page 140) or the Basic/White cycle and press Start.

Oven-Baked Really, Really Slow-Rise Wheat and Seed Boule

Prepare the recipe through step 1 (without adding seeds), then select the Artisan Dough or Dough cycle and press Start. Line a baking sheet with parchment paper. When the cycle is finished, transfer the slack dough to a floured surface and punch down gently. Knead in pumpkin seeds and sunflower seeds. Let dough rest for 5 minutes. Form into a boule and place on prepared baking sheet. Cover with a clean towel and let rise for 45 minutes. Preheat oven to 400°F (200°C) and place a broiler pan on the bottom rack. Using a serrated knife, cut 3 deep slashes across top of loaf. Add 2 cups (500 mL) hot water to the broiler pan. Place baking sheet on the middle rack. Bake until boule is risen and browned and an instant-read thermometer inserted in the center registers 190°F (90°C). Remove from pan and let cool on a wire rack.

Dough Size	Baking Time
1 lb (500 g)	25 to 30 minutes
1¹⁄₂ lb (750 g)	30 to 35 minutes
2 lb (1 kg)	35 to 40 minutes
3 lb (1.5 kg)	45 to 55 minutes

Flatbreads
and Pizzas

MAKING FLATBREAD AND pizza dough in the bread machine is a great way to expand your horizons. You use the machine to make a well-mixed and well-kneaded dough, then form the flatbread or pizza crust by hand and bake it in the oven. The Dough cycle usually takes about 1½ hours, so you can set the delay timer to have the dough ready in time for dinner or get the dough going while you prepare the toppings.

The type of flour you use for flatbreads and pizzas makes a big difference in the texture of the baked bread or crust:

- Bread flour and semolina flour create a dough that will crisp up nicely when you roll it thin, then bake it at a high temperature. The dough can be difficult to roll, though; if you have trouble getting it really thin on your first attempt, let it rest for 15 minutes, then give it another go. Thin, crispy pizzas and flatbreads are well suited to sleek, minimal ingredients. Try sturdy greens such as kale or Swiss chard (they taste like black olives when they're baked at a high temperature), grilled vegetables and chicken, fresh herbs and sweet corn. You can also bake the crust simply brushed with olive oil, then arrange delicate slices of prosciutto and baby arugula on top after it comes out of the oven. Avoid heavy meats and cheeses with this type of crust.

- All-purpose flour and whole-grain flour create a chewier, softer, more elastic crust that is better able to support heavy toppings such as meat and cheese. This type of crust is perfect for deep-dish pizzas and substantial flatbreads. With a deep-dish crust, it's all about indulgence: zesty pizza sauce, mushrooms, Italian sausage, pepperoni and cheeses, such as mozzarella and provolone, that will tear away in luscious strands.

- Low-protein, Italian-style flour (such as doppio zero) creates a silky dough that's easy to roll. Bake this type of crust first, then top it with sophisticated ingredients such as cream cheese, smoked salmon, prosciutto, chopped red onions or baby greens.

Flatbreads and pizzas are casual and are meant to be fun, but rolling the dough into a perfect circle can stress some bakers out. The great thing about flatbread is that no one cares if it's irregularly shaped. For pizza, though, people expect a more precise circle. No problem: if you roll out the dough for pizza and it's a bit of a wonky shape, just call it flatbread instead. It's homemade. It will taste great no matter what.

Sicilian-Style Flatbread

Delay Timer

Equipment
- Bread machine with a 1-lb (500 g) capacity
- Rolling pin
- 2 large baking sheets, lined with parchment paper

This thin, oval flatbread bakes with only a brush of olive oil for a topping. When it's cooled, add shavings of truffled pecorino or dollops of creamy goat cheese, paper-thin ribbons of prosciutto and baby arugula, or slices of Gorgonzola, tomatoes and grilled rare steak.

Tips

Ideally, the water should be between 86°F and 95°F (30°C and 35°C), the temperature range in which yeast is most active. Warm it in the microwave or in a saucepan on the stove, and check the temperature with an instant-read thermometer.

This is a small amount of dough, so it's best to check it a few minutes after kneading starts to make sure the ingredients are incorporated. You may need to use a rubber spatula to scrape the corners and help it along.

As you roll out the dough, if it feels too springy and elastic, let it rest for 2 to 3 minutes, then try again.

1 tsp	salt	5 mL
½ cup	lukewarm water (see tip, at left)	125 mL
2 tbsp	olive oil, divided	30 mL
1 tsp	liquid honey	5 mL
1½ cups	bread flour	375 mL
1 tsp	instant or bread machine yeast	5 mL

1. Add salt, water, 1 tbsp (15 mL) oil and honey to the bread pan. Spoon flour on top of liquid. Add yeast.

2. Select the Dough cycle and press Start.

3. When the cycle is finished, transfer dough to a floured surface and punch down gently. Preheat oven to 450°F (230°C).

4. Divide dough into 4 pieces and lightly dust tops with flour. Roll out 2 pieces into rough ovals, then use your hands to press and stretch each into an 8-inch (20 cm) long oval. Place 2 flatbreads on one prepared baking sheet (set the other 2 pieces aside).

5. Brush each flatbread with one-quarter of the remaining oil. Bake for 12 to 15 minutes or until light golden brown. Remove from pans and let cool on wire racks. Repeat with the remaining flatbreads, rolling out the dough while the first two bake.

Fennel and Garlic Flatbread
Add 1 tsp (5 mL) granulated garlic and ½ tsp (2 mL) fennel seed with the flour.

Griddle-Baked Pitas

Delay Timer

Equipment

- Bread machine with a 1-lb (500 g) capacity
- Large nonstick griddle or skillet
- Instant-read thermometer

For the most authentic and freshest-tasting pitas, use a combination of flours that includes atta (Indian whole wheat flour for roti, naan and chapati, found at Indian markets) or white whole wheat flour. These are the pocketless style of pita — perfect for dipping or using as the base for an open-faced sandwich.

Tips

Ideally, the water should be between 86°F and 95°F (30°C and 35°C), the temperature range in which yeast is most active. Warm it in the microwave or in a saucepan on the stove, and check the temperature with an instant-read thermometer.

This is a small amount of dough, so it's best to check it a few minutes after kneading starts to make sure the ingredients are incorporated. You may need to use a rubber spatula to scrape the corners and help it along.

¾ tsp	salt	3 mL
⅔ cup	lukewarm water (see tip, at left)	150 mL
4 tsp	vegetable oil	20 mL
1 cup	bread flour	250 mL
⅔ cup	atta, white whole wheat flour or whole wheat flour	150 mL
¾ tsp	instant or bread machine yeast	3 mL
	Olive oil	

1. Add salt, water and vegetable oil to the bread pan. Spoon bread flour and atta on top of liquid. Add yeast.

2. Select the Dough cycle and press Start.

3. When the cycle is finished, transfer dough to a floured surface and punch down gently. Divide dough into 6 pieces and form each piece into a ball. Flatten each ball with your hand to about a 6-inch (15 cm) round. Place on a baking sheet and cover with clean towels. Let rise for 30 to 45 minutes or until puffy.

4. Heat griddle over medium-high heat. Brush both sides of each pita with olive oil. Working in batches as necessary, griddle-bake pitas for 3 to 4 minutes or until browned on the bottom and puffy. Flip pitas over, reduce heat to medium and griddle-bake for 3 minutes or until risen and browned and an instant-read thermometer inserted in the center of a pita registers 190°F (90°C).

> **Grilled Pitas**
> Prepare the dough through step 3. Prepare a medium-hot fire in your grill. Brush both sides of each pita with olive oil. Place directly over the fire and grill until tops bubble up like pancakes and bottoms have good grill marks. Turn pitas over. Close the lid and grill for 1 to 2 minutes or until puffy and browned.

Authentic Focaccia

To make authentic focaccia, you need to use doppio zero flour, which is milled from a soft red wheat that has just 8% to 8.5% protein, giving the bread a lighter texture and a finer crumb. The slurry of water, olive oil and salt provides the true focaccia flavor.

Tips

Ideally, the water should be between 86°F and 95°F (30°C and 35°C), the temperature range in which yeast is most active. Warm it in the microwave or in a saucepan on the stove, and check the temperature with an instant-read thermometer.

If your dough does not form a ball during the first few minutes of kneading, do one of two things: if the dough looks dry and crumbly, add 1 tbsp (15 mL) water at 1-minute intervals until the dough forms a ball; if the dough looks wet, add 1 tbsp (15 mL) doppio zero flour at 1-minute intervals until the dough forms a ball.

Dough

1 tsp	fine kosher salt or sea salt	5 mL
¾ cup	lukewarm water (see tip, at left)	175 mL
2½ cups	doppio zero flour	625 mL
1¼ tsp	instant or bread machine yeast	6 mL

Topping

1 tbsp	water	15 mL
1 tbsp	olive oil	15 mL
½ tsp	fine kosher salt or sea salt	2 mL
1 tbsp	fresh rosemary leaves	15 mL

1. *Dough:* Add salt and water to the bread pan. Spoon flour on top of liquid. Add yeast.

2. Select the Dough cycle and press Start.

3. When the cycle is finished, transfer dough to the prepared pan. Using your hands, spread dough to fit the pan. Press the surface of the dough with your fingertip or knuckle to make random dimples. Preheat oven to 350°F (180°C).

4. *Topping:* In a small bowl, combine water, oil and salt. Brush over dough. Sprinkle with rosemary. Let rise while oven is preheating.

5. Bake for 27 to 30 minutes or until top of dough is golden brown and an instant-read thermometer inserted in the center of the loaf registers 190°F (90°C). Let cool in pan on a wire rack for 10 to 20 minutes, then cut into 8 pieces and serve.

Roasted Onion and Sage Focaccia

This version of focaccia has a more muscular crumb and is a great bread for panini.

Tips

Ideally, the water should be between 86°F and 95°F (30°C and 35°C), the temperature range in which yeast is most active. Warm it in the microwave or in a saucepan on the stove, and check the temperature with an instant-read thermometer.

If your dough does not form a ball during the first few minutes of kneading, do one of two things: if the dough looks dry and crumbly, add 1 tbsp (15 mL) water at 1-minute intervals until the dough forms a ball; if the dough looks wet, add 1 tbsp (15 mL) bread flour at 1-minute intervals until the dough forms a ball.

Dough

1 tsp	fine kosher salt or sea salt	5 mL
1 cup	lukewarm water (see tip, at left)	250 mL
2½ cups	bread flour	625 mL
1¼ tsp	instant or bread machine yeast	6 mL

Topping

1 tbsp	water	15 mL
1 tbsp	olive oil	15 mL
½ tsp	fine kosher salt or sea salt	2 mL
8	fresh sage leaves	8
2	shallots, thinly sliced	2
½ cup	thinly sliced red onion	125 mL
½ cup	freshly grated Parmesan cheese	125 mL
1 tbsp	olive oil	15 mL

1. *Dough:* Add salt and water to the bread pan. Spoon flour on top of liquid. Add yeast.

2. Select the Dough cycle and press Start.

3. When the cycle is finished, transfer dough to the prepared pan. Using your hands, spread dough to fit the pan. Press the surface of the dough with your fingertip or knuckle to make random dimples. Preheat oven to 350°F (180°C).

4. *Topping:* In a small bowl, combine water, oil and salt. Brush over dough. Top with sage, shallots and red onion. Sprinkle with Parmesan and drizzle with oil. Let rise while oven is preheating.

5. Bake for 27 to 30 minutes or until edges are golden brown and an instant-read thermometer inserted in the center of the loaf registers 190°F (90°C). Let cool in pan on a wire rack for 10 to 20 minutes, then cut into 8 pieces and serve.

Caprese-Style Focaccia

Prepare the recipe through step 4, but after brushing the slurry of water, oil and salt over the dough, spread with ¼ cup (60 mL) prepared pesto, then top with 3 thinly sliced plum (Roma) tomatoes and 4 oz (125 g) thinly sliced fresh mozzarella (bocconcini) cheese. Drizzle with 1 tbsp (15 mL) olive oil. Bake for 27 to 30 minutes or until edges are golden brown and an instant-read thermometer inserted in the center of the loaf registers 190°F (90°C).

Flatbread with Caramelized Onions and Brie

Tips

If your dough does not form a ball during the first few minutes of kneading, do one of two things: if the dough looks dry and crumbly, add 1 tbsp (15 mL) water at 1-minute intervals until the dough forms a ball; if the dough looks wet, add 1 tbsp (15 mL) all-purpose flour at 1-minute intervals until the dough forms a ball.

Once baked or grilled, this flatbread freezes well. Wrap well in plastic wrap, then in foil, or place in an airtight container and freeze for up to 2 months. To reheat, remove plastic wrap and cover the frozen flatbread with foil. Heat in a 350°F (180°C) oven for about 15 minutes.

Dough

½ tsp	salt	2 mL
1 cup	lukewarm water (see tip, page 177)	250 mL
3 tbsp	olive oil	45 mL
1 tbsp	liquid honey	15 mL
3¼ cups	all-purpose flour	800 mL
¼ cup	semolina flour	60 mL
1 tbsp	instant or bread machine yeast	15 mL

Topping

2 cups	Easy Caramelized Onions (page 282)	500 mL
8 oz	Brie cheese, cut into small cubes	250 g

1. *Dough:* Add salt, water, oil and honey to the bread pan. Spoon all-purpose flour and semolina flour on top of liquid. Add yeast.

2. Select the Dough cycle and press Start.

3. When the cycle is finished, transfer dough to a floured surface and punch down gently. Preheat oven to 375°F (190°C).

4. Lightly dust top of dough with flour. Roll out into a 12-inch (30 cm) square. Transfer to prepared baking sheet.

5. *Topping:* Spread caramelized onions over dough. Scatter Brie over onions. Let rise while oven is preheating.

6. Bake for 20 to 25 minutes or until crust is golden brown and Brie is melted. Let cool slightly on pan, then slice and serve.

Grilled Flatbread with Caramelized Onions and Brie

Prepare the dough through step 3. Divide dough into 4 pieces and lightly dust tops with flour. Roll out or pat out each piece into an oval. Prepare a medium-hot fire in one half of your grill. Brush both sides of flatbreads with olive oil. Place directly over the fire and grill until tops bubble up like pancakes and bottoms have good grill marks. Transfer to the other side of the grill and turn flatbreads over. Quickly spread caramelized onions over dough and dot with Brie, dividing evenly. Close the lid and grill for 8 to 10 minutes or until Brie is melted.

Black Pepper Taralli-Style Flatbread with Lox and Cream Cheese

Topped with cream cheese, paper-thin slices of smoked salmon and a scattering of red onion and capers, this flatbread makes a chic brunch dish or appetizer.

Tips

Together, the hot water and wine create the optimum warm temperature for mixing the dough.

Doppio zero flour is available at Italian grocery stores and online. If you can't find doppio zero flour, substitute 1¾ cups (425 mL) all-purpose flour.

Dough

1 tsp	granulated sugar	5 mL
¾ tsp	salt	3 mL
3 tbsp	olive oil, divided	45 mL
¼ cup	hot water (see tip, at left)	60 mL
¼ cup	dry white wine	60 mL
2 cups	doppio zero flour	500 mL
1½ tsp	coarsely ground black pepper	7 mL
1½ tsp	instant or bread machine yeast	7 mL

Topping

1 cup	whipped cream cheese	250 mL
4 oz	thinly sliced smoked salmon	125 g
½ cup	finely chopped red onion	125 mL
¼ cup	drained capers	60 mL

1. *Dough:* Add sugar, salt, 2 tbsp (30 mL) oil, water and wine to the bread pan. Spoon flour on top of liquid. Add pepper and yeast.

2. Select the Dough cycle and press Start.

3. When the cycle is finished, transfer dough to a floured surface and punch down gently. Preheat oven to 450°F (230°C).

4. Divide dough into 4 pieces and lightly dust tops with flour. Roll out 2 pieces into 10-inch (25 cm) long ovals. Place 2 flatbreads on one prepared baking sheet (set the other 2 pieces aside).

5. Brush each flatbread with one-quarter of the remaining oil. Bake for about 12 minutes or until bubbled, brown and slightly crisp. Remove from pan and let cool on a flat surface for 10 minutes. Repeat with the remaining flatbreads, rolling out the dough while the first two bake.

6. *Topping:* Spread cream cheese over each flatbread, dividing evenly. Top with salmon and sprinkle with red onion and capers. Using a pizza wheel or a sharp knife, cut into wedges.

White Whole Wheat Flatbread with Gorgonzola, Pear and Walnuts

This easy dough is made with white whole wheat flour for added nutrition and flavor. The toppings add sophistication. Cut into small pieces, it makes wonderful hors d'oeuvres to serve with glasses of red wine.

Tip

Ideally, the water should be between 86°F and 95°F (30°C and 35°C), the temperature range in which yeast is most active. Warm it in the microwave or in a saucepan on the stove, and check the temperature with an instant-read thermometer.

Dough

½ tsp	salt	2 mL
1½ cups	lukewarm water (see tip, at left)	375 mL
1 tbsp	olive oil	15 mL
1 tbsp	liquid honey	15 mL
1¾ cups	all-purpose flour	425 mL
1½ cups	white whole wheat flour or whole wheat flour	375 mL
1 tbsp	instant or bread machine yeast	15 mL

Topping

	Olive oil	
2 cups	Easy Caramelized Onions (page 282)	500 mL
3	large ripe pears, peeled and chopped	3
3 to 4 oz	Gorgonzola or other blue cheese, crumbled or cut into small pieces	90 to 125 g
½ cup	roughly chopped walnuts	125 mL

1. *Dough:* Add salt, water, oil and honey to the bread pan. Spoon all-purpose flour and whole wheat flour on top of liquid. Add yeast.

2. Select the Dough cycle and press Start.

3. When the cycle is finished, transfer dough to a floured surface and punch down gently. Preheat oven to 375°F (190°C).

4. Dust rolling pin with a little flour. Lightly dust top of dough with flour. Roll out into a 16- by 12-inch (40 by 30 cm) rectangle. Transfer to prepared baking sheet.

4. *Topping:* Brush dough with oil. Top with caramelized onions. Sprinkle with pears, blue cheese to taste and walnuts.

5. Bake for 15 to 17 minutes or until dough has risen and is browned around the edges and toppings are browned. Let cool slightly on pan, then slice and serve.

Tips

If your dough does not form a ball during the first few minutes of kneading, do one of two things: if the dough looks dry and crumbly, add 1 tbsp (15 mL) water at 1-minute intervals until the dough forms a ball; if the dough looks wet, add 1 tbsp (15 mL) all-purpose flour at 1-minute intervals until the dough forms a ball.

You can make this dough up to 1 day ahead. Transfer it to a large bowl, cover and refrigerate until you're ready to roll it out and make flatbread. Let warm to room temperature for 15 minutes before rolling.

Grilled Caprese Flatbread

Prepare the dough through step 3. Divide dough into 4 pieces and lightly dust tops with flour. Roll out or pat out each piece into an oval. Prepare a medium-hot fire in one half of your grill. Brush both sides of flatbreads with olive oil. Place directly over the fire and grill until tops bubble up like pancakes and bottoms have good grill marks. Transfer to the other side of the grill and turn flatbreads over. Quickly spread 2 tbsp (30 mL) prepared basil pesto over each flatbread. Top with $\frac{1}{2}$ cup (125 mL) finely chopped fresh tomatoes and 2 oz (60 g) thinly sliced fresh mozzarella (bocconcini) cheese. Close the lid and grill for 8 to 10 minutes or until mozzarella is melted. Top each flatbread with 2 tbsp (30 mL) fresh basil leaves.

Lebanese Flatbread with Spicy Lamb Topping

Equipment

- Bread machine with a 1½-lb (750 g) capacity
- 2 large baking sheets, lined with foil, foil brushed with olive oil

These open-face meat pies, known as Lahm bi' Ajeen, are the more easy-going cousins of the traditional Lebanese meat pies formed into turban-like shapes. The yogurt in the dough keeps it moist and supple. This dough is easier to work with on an oiled surface.

Tip

Ideally, the water should be between 86°F and 95°F (30°C and 35°C), the temperature range in which yeast is most active. Warm it in the microwave or in a saucepan on the stove, and check the temperature with an instant-read thermometer.

Dough

¼ tsp	granulated sugar	1 mL
1 tsp	salt	5 mL
1 cup	low-fat plain yogurt, at room temperature	250 mL
¼ cup	lukewarm water (see tip, at left)	60 mL
¼ cup	olive oil	60 mL
3½ cups	bread flour	875 mL
2 tsp	instant or bread machine yeast	10 mL

Topping

1 lb	lean ground lamb	500 g
3	large cloves garlic, minced	3
1	small onion, finely chopped	1
1 cup	finely chopped tomatoes	250 mL
½ cup	pine nuts	125 mL
3 tbsp	finely chopped flat-leaf (Italian) parsley	45 mL
½ tsp	ground allspice	2 mL
1 tbsp	freshly squeezed lemon juice	15 mL
1 tbsp	olive oil	15 mL
	Salt and freshly ground black pepper	

1. *Dough:* Add sugar, salt, yogurt, water and oil to the bread pan. Spoon flour on top of liquid. Add yeast.

2. Select the Dough cycle and press Start.

3. When the cycle is finished, transfer dough to an oiled surface and punch down gently. Preheat oven to 400°F (200°C).

4. Divide dough into 8 pieces and lightly dust tops with flour. Let rest for 10 minutes. Roll or press each piece into a 5-inch (12.5 cm) round. Place on prepared baking sheets.

5. *Topping:* In a large bowl, combine lamb, garlic, onion, tomatoes, pine nuts, parsley, allspice, lemon juice and oil. Season with salt and pepper. Spread topping evenly over dough rounds, spreading right to the edge of the dough.

6. Bake for 35 minutes or until crust is golden brown and lamb is browned.

Tips

As you roll out the dough, if it feels too springy and elastic, let it rest for 2 to 3 minutes, then try again.

Serve these flatbreads as a *mezze* (appetizer), with bowls of raita, fresh chopped tomatoes, black olives and other Middle Eastern condiments.

Lebanese Breakfast Flatbread with Za'atar

Prepare the dough through step 4. Brush dough rounds with olive oil and sprinkle with za'atar seasoning (a blend of ground thyme, sumac berries and toasted sesame seeds). Bake for 12 to 15 minutes or until crust is golden brown.

Lebanese Flatbread with Herbed Feta

Prepare the dough through step 4. Brush dough rounds with olive oil and spread 2 tbsp (30 mL) prepared herbed feta spread or labneh over each. Bake for 12 to 15 minutes or until crust is golden brown. Top with pomegranate seeds or toasted pine nuts.

Lebanese Flatbread with Hummus and Black Olives

Prepare the dough through step 4. Brush dough rounds with olive oil. Bake for 12 to 15 minutes or until crust is golden brown. Spread with 1/4 cup (60 mL) prepared hummus and sprinkle with chopped pitted kalamata olives.

Caraway Rye Flatbread with Sausage and Sauerkraut

Equipment

- Bread machine with a 2-lb (1 kg) capacity
- Rolling pin
- 12-inch (30 cm) round pizza pan or large baking sheet, greased

In this recipe with Eastern European roots, a caraway rye crust takes on a savory topping of sauerkraut, sausage and Gruyère. It makes a wonderful supper when you invite family or friends over to enjoy a casual meal in front of the fire.

Tip

You'll need about 3 cups (750 mL) sauerkraut in brine to get 2 cups (500 mL) drained.

Dough

1 cup	water	250 mL
1/3 cup	milk	75 mL
1 tbsp	granulated sugar	15 mL
2 tsp	salt	10 mL
1 tbsp	butter, softened	15 mL
2 1/3 cups	all-purpose flour	575 mL
1 cup	dark rye flour	250 mL
1 tbsp	caraway seeds	15 mL
1 1/2 tsp	instant or bread machine yeast	7 mL

Filling

2 cups	drained sauerkraut (see tip, at left)	500 mL
2 tbsp	butter	30 mL
1	large onion, thinly sliced	1
8 oz	Polish or garlic sausage (fresh or smoked), removed from casings if fresh or cut into bite-size pieces if smoked	250 g
2	large eggs, beaten	2
1 cup	heavy or whipping (35%) cream	250 mL
1/2 cup	shredded Gruyère cheese	125 mL
1/2 tsp	freshly ground white or black pepper	5 mL
1/2 tsp	freshly grated nutmeg (see tip, at right)	5 mL

1. *Dough:* In a small saucepan, scald water and milk over medium-high heat until small bubbles form around the edges. Remove from heat and stir in sugar, salt and butter. Transfer to the bread pan and let cool to lukewarm (between 86°F and 95°F/30°C and 35°C).

2. Spoon all-purpose flour and rye flour on top of liquid in the bread pan. Add caraway seeds and yeast.

3. Select the Dough cycle and press Start.

4. *Filling:* In a sieve, rinse sauerkraut under running water and drain several times to remove brine. Press out excess moisture. In a large skillet, melt butter over medium-high heat. Sauté onion for about 5 minutes or until translucent. Add sausage, breaking up any large pieces, and cook for about 5 minutes or until browned. Add sauerkraut, reduce heat and simmer, stirring often, for about 10 minutes or until mixture is very dry. Remove from heat and set aside.

Freshly grated nutmeg has a lovely, delicate flavor and adds a nice touch to this filling. You can buy whole nutmeg at specialty spice emporiums and at some supermarkets. Use a nutmeg grater or the finest holes on a box cheese grater. If you don't have whole nutmeg, use $\frac{1}{4}$ tsp (1 mL) pre-ground nutmeg.

If your dough does not form a ball during the first few minutes of kneading, do one of two things: if the dough looks dry and crumbly, add 1 tbsp (15 mL) water at 1-minute intervals until the dough forms a ball; if the dough looks wet, add 1 tbsp (15 mL) all-purpose flour at 1-minute intervals until the dough forms a ball.

5. In a bowl, whisk together eggs, cream, Gruyère, pepper and nutmeg.

6. When the cycle is finished, transfer dough to a floured surface and punch down gently. Preheat oven to 350°F (180°C).

7. Lightly dust top of dough with flour. Roll out into a 16-inch (40 cm) circle. Transfer to prepared pan and roll up the edges to form a 2-inch (5 cm) high perimeter. Spoon sauerkraut mixture over dough and pour egg mixture evenly over top.

8. Bake for 35 to 40 minutes or until filling is set and browned and a knife inserted in the center comes out clean. Let stand for 5 minutes. Cut into wedges and serve hot.

Chicago Deep-Dish Pizza

Makes 2 individual pizzas

Delay Timer

Equipment
- Bread machine with a 1½-lb (750 g) capacity
- Rolling pin
- Two 8-inch (20 cm) square or round metal baking pans, greased

Deep-dish pizza, created in Chicago in 1943, is typically eaten with a knife and fork. Although there's a lot of dough involved, it's relatively thin, patted out by hand and pulled up high on the sides of a pan to encase the delicious ingredients. The toppings are added in reverse order from a regular pizza: the cheese is sprinkled over the dough first, then ingredients such as mushrooms, onions and pepperoni are scattered on top, then the sauce is slathered on, with a little sprinkle of cheese and herbs before the pizza goes into the oven.

Dough

½ tsp	salt	2 mL
1 cup	lukewarm water (see tip, at right)	250 mL
3 tbsp	olive oil	45 mL
1 tbsp	liquid honey	15 mL
3¼ cups	all-purpose flour	800 mL
¼ cup	semolina flour	60 mL
1 tbsp	instant or bread machine yeast	15 mL

Topping

2 tbsp	olive oil	30 mL
2 cups	shredded mozzarella cheese	500 mL
1 cup	sliced mushrooms	250 mL
½ cup	finely chopped red onion	125 mL
8 oz	pepperoni, sliced, or Italian sausage, cooked and crumbled	250 g
½ cup	pizza sauce	125 mL
¼ cup	freshly grated Parmesan cheese	60 mL
2 tsp	dried Italian seasoning	10 mL

1. *Dough:* Add salt, water, oil and honey to the bread pan. Spoon all-purpose flour and semolina flour on top of liquid. Add yeast.

2. Select the Dough cycle and press Start.

3. When the cycle is finished, transfer dough to a floured surface and punch down gently. Preheat oven to 400°F (200°C).

4. Divide dough in half and lightly dust tops with flour. Roll out each half into a 10-inch (25 cm) square or circle. Place one square in each prepared baking pan. Using lightly floured hands, fit the dough into the bottom and up the sides of the pans.

5. *Topping:* Brush each crust with 1 tbsp (15 mL) oil. Sprinkle with mozzarella, then with mushrooms, onion and pepperoni, dividing evenly. Spoon sauce over top. Sprinkle with Parmesan and Italian seasoning.

6. Bake for 25 to 30 minutes or until crust is golden brown and cheese is bubbling. Let cool for 5 to 10 minutes in pans on a wire rack. Using a pie server or a metal spatula, remove pizzas from pans. Cut into wedges and serve hot.

Tips

Ideally, the water should be between 86°F and 95°F (30°C and 35°C), the temperature range in which yeast is most active. Warm it in the microwave or in a saucepan on the stove, and check the temperature with an instant-read thermometer.

As you roll out the dough, if it feels too springy and elastic, let it rest for 2 to 3 minutes, then try again.

This dough also makes delicious grilled or traditional round pizzas and flatbreads.

Veggie Lover's Deep-Dish Pizza

Substitute 1/2 cup (125 mL) chopped green bell pepper and 1/2 cup (125 mL) pitted kalamata olives for the pepperoni.

Cheeseburger, Cheeseburger Deep-Dish Pizza

Substitute mild Cheddar cheese for the mozzarella and seasoned ground beef, cooked and crumbled, for the pepperoni.

Deep-Dish Chicken and Pesto Pizza

Substitute shredded rotisserie chicken for the pepperoni and 1/4 cup (60 mL) prepared pesto for the pizza sauce. Omit the mushrooms and Italian seasoning.

Rustic Grilled Pizza with Fresh Corn, Tomatoes and Pesto

Delay Timer

Equipment

- Bread machine with a 1½-lb (750 g) capacity
- Rolling pin (optional)
- Kettle or gas barbecue grill

In late July and early August, the first tomatoes are ripening in the garden and farm stands showcase the season's first sweet corn. When it's too hot to contemplate heating the oven, make this smoky-flavored pizza. Although you get a better wood smoke flavor when you use hardwood charcoal on a kettle grill, this recipe also works on a gas grill.

Tip

Ideally, the water should be between 86°F and 95°F (30°C and 35°C), the temperature range in which yeast is most active. Warm it in the microwave or in a saucepan on the stove, and check the temperature with an instant-read thermometer.

Dough

½ tsp	salt	2 mL
1 cup	lukewarm water (see tip, at left)	250 mL
5 tbsp	olive oil, divided	75 mL
1 tbsp	liquid honey	15 mL
3¼ cups	all-purpose flour	800 mL
¼ cup	semolina flour	60 mL
1 tbsp	instant or bread machine yeast	15 mL

Topping

½ cup	prepared basil pesto	125 mL
3 cups	sweet corn kernels or thawed frozen shoepeg corn	750 mL
1⅓ cups	finely chopped fresh tomatoes	325 mL
2 cups	shredded fontina cheese	500 mL

1. *Dough:* Add salt, water, 3 tbsp (45 mL) oil and honey to the bread pan. Spoon all-purpose flour and semolina flour on top of liquid. Add yeast.

2. Select the Dough cycle and press Start.

3. Meanwhile, prepare a medium-hot fire in one half of your grill.

4. When the cycle is finished, transfer dough to a floured surface and punch down gently. Divide into 4 pieces and lightly dust tops with flour. Roll out or pat each piece into an 8-inch (20 cm) long oval. Brush both sides of crusts with the remaining oil.

5. Place crusts directly over the fire and grill until tops bubble up like pancakes and bottoms have good grill marks. Transfer to other side of the grill and turn crusts over.

6. *Topping:* Quickly spread pesto over each crust, dividing evenly. Sprinkle with corn and tomatoes, then with cheese. Close the lid and grill for 8 to 10 minutes or until cheese is melted.

Tips

If your dough does not form a ball during the first few minutes of kneading, do one of two things: if the dough looks dry and crumbly, add 1 tbsp (15 mL) water at 1-minute intervals until the dough forms a ball; if the dough looks wet, add 1 tbsp (15 mL) all-purpose flour at 1-minute intervals until the dough forms a ball.

As you roll out the dough, if it feels too springy and elastic, let it rest for 2 to 3 minutes, then try again.

Oven-Baked Rustic Pizza with Fresh Corn, Tomatoes and Pesto

Prepare the recipe through step 4, omitting step 3 and oil brushed on dough. Preheat oven to 400°F (200°C). Sprinkle 2 large baking sheets with cornmeal. Spread pesto over each crust, dividing evenly. Sprinkle with corn and tomatoes, then with cheese. Place 2 crusts on each prepared baking sheet. Bake for 15 to 20 minutes or until crust is golden brown and toppings are bubbling. Let cool slightly on pans, then slice and serve.

Roasted Chicken, Pancetta and Potato Pizza

This pizza gives you a delicious way to use up leftover grilled chicken and baked potatoes.

Tips

If your dough does not form a ball during the first few minutes of kneading, do one of two things: if the dough looks dry and crumbly, add 1 tbsp (15 mL) water at 1-minute intervals until the dough forms a ball; if the dough looks wet, add 1 tbsp (15 mL) bread flour at 1-minute intervals until the dough forms a ball.

As you roll out the dough, if it feels too springy and elastic, let it rest for 2 to 3 minutes, then try again.

To prevent the dough from rising too much and making a very thick crust, roll out and top 4 of the crusts and get them in the oven, then roll out the remaining four.

Dough

1 tsp	granulated sugar	5 mL
2 tsp	salt	10 mL
1½ cups	lukewarm water (see tip, page 192)	375 mL
2 tbsp	olive oil	30 mL
3½ cups	bread flour	875 mL
2¼ tsp	instant or bread machine yeast	11 mL

Topping

2 tbsp	olive oil	30 mL
½ tsp	hot pepper flakes	2 mL
½ tsp	dried basil	2 mL
4	small potatoes, baked and sliced	4
1	large red onion, thinly sliced	1
4 oz	pancetta, diced	125 g
2 cups	shredded rotisserie chicken	500 mL
2 cups	shredded mozzarella cheese	500 mL
2 cups	shredded provolone cheese	500 mL
1 cup	shredded Asiago cheese	125 mL
1 tbsp	chopped fresh rosemary	15 mL

1. *Dough:* Add sugar, salt, water and oil to the bread pan. Spoon flour on top of liquid. Add yeast.

2. Select the Dough cycle and press Start.

3. When the cycle is finished, transfer dough to a floured surface and punch down gently. Preheat oven to 450°F (230°C).

4. Divide dough into 8 pieces and lightly dust tops with flour. Roll out each piece into a 6-inch (15 cm) circle. Place on prepared baking sheets.

5. *Topping:* Lightly brush each crust with oil. Sprinkle with hot pepper flakes and basil. Arrange potatoes, red onion, pancetta and chicken on top, dividing evenly. Top with mozzarella, provolone and Asiago. Sprinkle with rosemary.

6. Bake one sheet at a time for 10 to 12 minutes or until pancetta is browned, cheese is bubbling and crust is golden brown. Let cool slightly on pans, then slice and serve.

Pizza with Prosciutto and Arugula

The higher protein content in bread flour contributes to this pizza's crispy crust.

Tips

If your dough does not form a ball during the first few minutes of kneading, do one of two things: if the dough looks dry and crumbly, add 1 tbsp (15 mL) water at 1-minute intervals until the dough forms a ball; if the dough looks wet, add 1 tbsp (15 mL) bread flour at 1-minute intervals until the dough forms a ball.

As you roll out the dough, if it feels too springy and elastic, let it rest for 2 to 3 minutes, then try again.

To prevent the dough from rising too much and making a very thick crust, roll out one crust and get it in the oven, then roll out the remaining crust.

If you only want to make one pizza, see tip, page 195.

Dough

1 tsp	granulated sugar	5 mL
2 tsp	salt	10 mL
1½ cups	lukewarm water (see tip, page 192)	375 mL
2 tbsp	olive oil	30 mL
3½ cups	bread flour	875 mL
2¼ tsp	instant or bread machine yeast	11 mL
	Additional olive oil	

Topping

4 oz	thinly sliced prosciutto	125 g
2 cups	baby arugula	500 mL
2 oz	Parmesan or pecorino cheese, shaved	90 g
	Olive oil (preferably extra virgin)	

1. *Dough:* Add sugar, salt, water and oil to the bread pan. Spoon flour on top of liquid. Add yeast.

2. Select the Dough cycle and press Start.

3. When the cycle is finished, transfer dough to a floured surface and punch down gently. Preheat oven to 450°F (230°C).

4. Divide dough in half. Lightly dust top of dough with flour. Roll out each half into a 10-inch (25 cm) circle. Transfer to prepared pans and brush with oil.

5. Bake one pan at a time for 10 to 12 minutes or until crust is golden brown. Let cool slightly.

6. *Topping:* Arrange prosciutto over crusts, dividing evenly. Sprinkle with arugula and cheese. Drizzle with oil, slice and serve.

Pizza Bianca

Tips

Ideally, the water should be between 86°F and 95°F (30°C and 35°C), the temperature range in which yeast is most active. Warm it in the microwave or in a saucepan on the stove, and check the temperature with an instant-read thermometer.

If your dough does not form a ball during the first few minutes of kneading, do one of two things: if the dough looks dry and crumbly, add 1 tbsp (15 mL) water at 1-minute intervals until the dough forms a ball; if the dough looks wet, add 1 tbsp (15 mL) bread flour at 1-minute intervals until the dough forms a ball.

Garlic-Herb Flavoring

2 tbsp	olive oil	30 mL
1 tbsp	minced garlic	15 mL
1 tsp	freshly ground black pepper	5 mL
¼ tsp	dried oregano	1 mL
¼ tsp	dried basil	1 mL

Dough

1 tsp	granulated sugar	5 mL
2 tsp	salt	10 mL
1½ cups	lukewarm water (see tip, at left)	375 mL
1 tbsp	olive oil	15 mL
3½ cups	bread flour	875 mL
2¼ tsp	instant or bread machine yeast	11 mL

Topping

2 tbsp	olive oil	30 mL
2 cups	shredded mozzarella cheese	500 mL
2 cups	shredded provolone cheese	500 mL
1 cup	shredded Asiago cheese	125 mL

1. *Flavoring:* In a small skillet, heat oil over medium heat. Sauté garlic, pepper, oregano and basil for 2 minutes or until garlic is softened. Transfer to the bread pan and let cool.

2. *Dough:* Add sugar, salt, water and oil to the bread pan. Spoon flour on top of liquid. Add yeast.

3. Select the Dough cycle and press Start.

4. When the cycle is finished, transfer dough to a floured surface and punch down gently. Preheat oven to 450°F (230°C).

5. Divide dough into 8 pieces and lightly dust tops with flour. Roll out each piece into a 6-inch (15 cm) circle. Place on prepared baking sheets.

6. *Topping:* Brush each crust lightly with oil. Sprinkle with mozzarella, provolone and Asiago, dividing evenly.

7. Bake one sheet at a time for 10 to 12 minutes or until cheese is bubbling and crust is golden brown. Let cool slightly on pans, then slice and serve.

continued after photos…

Roasted Bell Pepper and
Kalamata Olive Bread (page 104)

The Miller's Cinnamon
and Raisin Bread (page 114)

Butternut Squash Rolls (page 207) and
Caraway Rye Horns (page 205)

Apricot Almond Loaf
(page 130)

Tips

As you roll out the dough, if it feels too springy and elastic, let it rest for 2 to 3 minutes, then try again.

To prevent the dough from rising too much and making a very thick crust, roll out and top 4 of the crusts and get them in the oven, then roll out the remaining 4.

Prepared pizza dough can be frozen for up to 3 months. Simply thaw and roll out the pizza crust.

For the most authentic crust, use a pizza or baking stone in your oven. Place it on the oven rack and heat it as you preheat the oven. Sprinkle a three-sided cookie sheet or a baker's peel with cornmeal, place the pizza on it, then slide it onto the stone with a quick forward jerk of your arms.

Pizza Quattro Formaggi

Reduce the mozzarella and provolone to 1 cup (250 mL) each and add 1 cup (250 mL) crumbled Gorgonzola cheese.

Pizza with Caramelized Onions and Brie

Prepare the dough through step 5. Brush dough rounds with olive oil and top each with $1/4$ cup (60 mL) Easy Caramelized Onions (page 282). Substitute 2 cups (500 mL) chopped Brie, with the rind on, for the shredded cheeses.

Gorgonzola and Fig Pizza

Prepare the dough through step 5. Brush dough rounds with olive oil and spread 2 tbsp (30 mL) prepared fig preserves over each. Substitute 2 cups (500 mL) crumbled Gorgonzola for the shredded cheeses.

Crispy Cornmeal Pizza with Goat Cheese, Kale and Black Olives

Equipment
- Bread machine with a 2-lb (1 kg) capacity
- Rolling pin
- Two 10-inch (25 cm) pizza pans, greased

This crispy yet robustly flavored pizza could become addictive — you're forewarned. If you like, add chopped smoked sausage, cooked bacon or pancetta for a meat-lover's version.

Tip
Ideally, the water should be between 86°F and 95°F (30°C and 35°C), the temperature range in which yeast is most active. Warm it in the microwave or in a saucepan on the stove, and check the temperature with an instant-read thermometer.

Dough

1¼ tsp	salt	6 mL
1 tsp	hot pepper flakes	5 mL
1½ cups	lukewarm water (see tip, at left)	375 mL
¼ cup	olive oil	60 mL
2 tsp	milk	10 mL
2½ cups	bread flour	625 mL
1½ cups	fine yellow cornmeal	375 mL
2¼ tsp	instant or bread machine yeast	11 mL

Topping

12 oz	kale, leaves torn from tougher stems and stems discarded	375 g
6 oz	goat cheese, softened	175 g
1 cup	pitted kalamata olives	250 mL
¼ cup	olive oil	60 mL
	Kosher salt or pretzel salt	

1. *Dough:* Add salt, hot pepper flakes, water, oil and milk to the bread pan. Spoon flour and cornmeal on top of liquid. Add yeast.

2. Select the Dough cycle and press Start.

3. When the cycle is finished, transfer dough to a floured surface and punch down gently. Preheat oven to 450°F (230°C).

4. Divide dough in half. Lightly dust top of dough with flour. Roll out each half into a 10-inch (25 cm) circle. Transfer to prepared pans.

5. *Topping:* Sprinkle kale over dough, dividing evenly. Dot with goat cheese, then olives. Drizzle with oil.

6. Bake one pizza at a time for 15 minutes or until crust is golden brown, cheese is bubbling and kale is scorched. Sprinkle with salt. Let cool slightly on pans, then slice and serve.

Tips

If your dough does not form a ball during the first few minutes of kneading, do one of two things: if the dough looks dry and crumbly, add 1 tbsp (15 mL) water at 1-minute intervals until the dough forms a ball; if the dough looks wet, add 1 tbsp (15 mL) bread flour at 1-minute intervals until the dough forms a ball.

As you roll out the dough, if it feels too springy and elastic, let it rest for 2 to 3 minutes, then try again.

To prevent the dough from rising too much and making a very thick crust, roll out and top one crust and get it in the oven, then roll out the remaining crust.

If you only want to make one pizza, you can freeze the prepared dough for up to 3 months, then thaw it and roll out the pizza crust. Or you can fully bake the crust and let it cool on a wire rack, then wrap and freeze it for up to 2 months.

Cornmeal Crust Pizza with Wild Mushrooms and Thyme Cream

Prepare the basic recipe through step 4. While dough is in machine, in a large skillet, heat 2 tbsp (30 mL) unsalted butter over medium-high heat. Sauté 1 lb (500 g) sliced mushrooms and 4 oz (125 g) sliced wild mushrooms for about 7 minutes or until they begin to release their juices. Add 1 cup (250 mL) heavy or whipping (35%) cream and 1 tsp (5 mL) dried thyme. Cook, stirring, until cream starts to bubble and mixture is thickened. Season to taste with salt and freshly ground white pepper. Transfer to a bowl and let cool to lukewarm. Spread this mixture over the dough in place of the topping opposite. Bake for 15 minutes or until crust is golden brown. Serve sprinkled with chopped fresh flat-leaf (Italian) parsley.

Cornmeal Crust Pizza with Peaches, Serrano Ham and Arugula

Equipment
- Bread machine with a 2-lb (1 kg) capacity
- Rolling pin
- Two 10-inch (25 cm) pizza pans, greased

Sweet, juicy peaches and thin Serrano or country ham complement each other perfectly. Serve this pizza as an appetizer with chilled sangria or craft beer.

Tips
Ideally, the water should be between 86°F and 95°F (30°C and 35°C), the temperature range in which yeast is most active. Warm it in the microwave or in a saucepan on the stove, and check the temperature with an instant-read thermometer.

If your dough does not form a ball during the first few minutes of kneading, do one of two things: if the dough looks dry and crumbly, add 1 tbsp (15 mL) water at 1-minute intervals until the dough forms a ball; if the dough looks wet, add 1 tbsp (15 mL) bread flour at 1-minute intervals until the dough forms a ball.

Dough

1¼ tsp	salt	6 mL
1 tsp	hot pepper flakes	5 mL
1½ cups	lukewarm water (see tip, at left)	375 mL
¼ cup	olive oil	60 mL
2 tsp	milk	10 mL
2½ cups	bread flour	625 mL
1½ cups	fine yellow cornmeal	375 mL
2¼ tsp	instant or bread machine yeast	11 mL

Topping

3	ripe peaches, peeled and cut into ½-inch (1 cm) slices	3
6 oz	Serrano or country ham, sliced paper thin	175 g
6 oz	goat cheese, softened	175 g
¼ cup	Marcona almonds, coarsely chopped	60 mL
¼ cup	olive oil	60 mL
	Coarse kosher salt or pretzel salt	
	Coarsely ground black pepper	
1 cup	baby arugula	250 mL

1. *Dough:* Add salt, hot pepper flakes, water, oil and milk to the bread pan. Spoon flour and cornmeal on top of liquid. Add yeast.

2. Select the Dough cycle and press Start.

3. When the cycle is finished, transfer dough to a floured surface and punch down gently. Preheat oven to 450°F (230°C).

4. Divide dough in half. Lightly dust top of dough with flour. Roll out each half into a 10-inch (25 cm) circle. Transfer to prepared pans.

5. *Topping:* Arrange peaches and ham over dough, dividing evenly. Dot with goat cheese and sprinkle with almonds. Drizzle with oil.

6. Bake one pizza at a time for 15 minutes or until crust is golden brown, cheese is bubbling and ham is scorched. Sprinkle with salt and pepper. Top with arugula, slice and serve.

Tips

As you roll out the dough, if it feels too springy and elastic, let it rest for 2 to 3 minutes, then try again.

To prevent the dough from rising too much and making a very thick crust, roll out one crust and get it in the oven, then roll out the remaining crust.

If you only want to make one pizza, you can freeze the prepared dough for up to 3 months, then thaw it and roll out the pizza crust. Or you can fully bake the crust and let it cool on a wire rack, then wrap and freeze it for up to 2 months.

Cornmeal Crust Pizza with Apples and Bacon

Prepare the basic recipe through step 4. Replace the peaches, ham, goat cheese and almonds with 2 large tart apples, peeled and thinly sliced, 8 oz (250 g) sliced bacon, crisply cooked and crumbled, 2 cups (500 mL) shredded Swiss cheese and $1/4$ cup (60 mL) chopped walnuts. Omit the olive oil. Bake as directed and top with arugula or baby spinach.

Savory Rolls

ROLLS AND BUNS are a snap to make using the bread machine. You let it do the mixing, kneading and rising, then you waltz in, form the dough, bake it and take all the credit. The secret to light and airy rolls is to let them rise for the specified amount of time, no matter how tempting it is to rush the process.

If you want to convert an oven-baked loaf recipe to rolls, know that rolls usually bake in about half as much time as a loaf, and at the same temperature. Check the rolls after 15 minutes of baking to make sure they don't overbake.

The recipes in the Flavored Breads chapter all make great rolls. To convert a bread machine loaf recipe to 12 rolls, simply make the 1½-lb (750 g) dough on the Dough cycle, then form the dough into rolls of the desired shape (see chart, opposite). For 18 rolls, use the 2-lb (1 kg) dough, and for 24 rolls, use the 3-lb (1.5 kg dough). Once the rolls are formed, cover them with a clean towel and let them rise in a warm, draft-free place for 30 minutes. Bake the rolls at 350°F (180°C) for 15 to 20 minutes or until they're lightly browned and an instant-read thermometer inserted in the center of a roll registers 190°F (90°C). Easy!

The Art of the Dinner Roll

Dinner rolls can be made in a variety of delectable shapes to show off the baker's artistry.

Shape	How to Form
Bowknot	Divide dough in half. Cut each half into 6 pieces. Using your hands, roll each piece into a 6-inch (15 cm) long rope. Tie each rope into a loose single knot and place at least 2 inches (5 cm) apart on a baking sheet lined with parchment paper.
Cloverleaf	Pinch off about 1 tbsp (15 mL) dough and roll it into a ball about 1 inch (2.5 cm) in diameter. Dip in melted butter and place in a muffin pan. Repeat the process, placing 3 balls of dough in each muffin cup to form a cloverleaf.
Crescent	Roll out dough to a 12-inch (30 cm) circle. Using an electric mixer or food processor, cream $\frac{1}{4}$ cup (60 mL) softened butter. Spread butter over dough. Using a pizza wheel or a sharp knife, cut circle into 12 triangles. Starting with the wide end, roll up each triangle. Place rolls, seam side down, at least 2 inches (5 cm) apart on prepared baking sheet and form into crescents.
Fantan	Roll out dough to a 12-inch (30 cm) square. Brush with $\frac{1}{4}$ cup (60 mL) melted butter, then cut into twelve 1-inch (2.5 cm) wide strips. Stack strips on top of each other so that you have two stacks of 6 strips each. Cut each stack into 2-inch (5 cm) pieces. Press each piece, cut side up, into a greased muffin cup.
Pull-aparts	Divide dough in half. Cut each half into 6 pieces. Roll each piece into a ball and dip in $\frac{1}{4}$ cup (60 mL) melted butter. Arrange dough balls in a greased 9-inch (23 cm) round metal baking pan so that each ball touches another.
Twists	Divide dough in half. Cut each half into 6 pieces. Using your hands, roll each piece into a 6-inch (15 cm) long rope. Twist each rope into a spiral and place at least 2 inches (5 cm) apart on a baking sheet lined with parchment paper. Brush twists with $\frac{1}{4}$ cup (60 mL) melted butter and sprinkle with dried herbs, chopped garlic, poppy seeds, sesame seeds or coarse salt.

Blue Ribbon Buns

Makes 8 buns

Equipment

- Bread machine with a 1½-lb (750 g) capacity
- Large baking sheet, lined with parchment paper
- Instant-read thermometer

If bread machine users gave out blue ribbons, this recipe would win. The method is a bit unusual — the yeast is mixed with sugar and warm water *before* the dry ingredients are added — but it works. For dinner rolls, hamburger buns or hot dog buns, this is as deliciously easy as it gets.

Tips

Warm the water in the microwave or in a saucepan on the stove, and check the temperature with an instant-read thermometer.

If your dough does not form a ball during the first few minutes of kneading, do one of two things: if the dough looks dry and crumbly, add 1 tbsp (15 mL) water at 1-minute intervals until the dough forms a ball; if the dough looks wet, add 1 tbsp (15 mL) bread flour at 1-minute intervals until the dough forms a ball.

Kitchen scales are very handy to help you make buns of an even size. Weigh the dough, then divide it into pieces, weighing each piece to make sure they're approximately the same weight. Then shape into buns.

2 tbsp	granulated sugar	30 mL
1½ tsp	instant or bread machine yeast	7 mL
1 cup	warm water (110°F/43°C)	250 mL
¼ cup	vegetable oil	60 mL
3 cups	bread flour	750 mL
1 tsp	salt	5 mL

1. Add sugar, yeast and water to the bread pan. Let stand for 10 minutes or until yeast starts to bubble.

2. Add oil. Spoon flour on top of liquid. Add salt.

3. Select the Dough cycle and press Start.

4. When the cycle is finished, transfer dough to a floured surface and punch down gently. Divide into 8 pieces. Form each piece into a bun. Place at least 2 inches (5 cm) apart on prepared baking sheet. Cover with a clean towel and let rise for 45 minutes. Meanwhile, preheat oven to 350°F (180°C).

5. Bake for 15 to 20 minutes or until risen and lightly browned and an instant-read thermometer inserted in the center of a roll registers 190°F (90°C). Remove from pan and let cool on a wire rack. Serve warm or let cool completely.

Hot Dog Buns

Form each piece of dough into a 6-inch (15 cm) cylinder. Bake at 400°F (200°C) for 10 to 12 minutes or until risen and lightly browned and an instant-read thermometer inserted in the center of a bun registers 190°F (90°C).

Featherweight Yeast Rolls

Equipment

- Bread machine with a 2-lb (1 kg) capacity
- Two 9-inch (23 cm) round or square metal baking pans, greased
- Instant-read thermometer

The dough for these light dinner rolls is looser and more batter-like than traditional roll dough, so it's easier to pinch it off and form it into rolls. While you're making dinner rolls, you might as well make a bunch: enjoy some, give some away and freeze the rest for when you want a little homemade comfort.

Tips

Ideally, the milk and water should be between 86°F and 95°F (30°C and 35°C), the temperature range in which yeast is most active. Warm them in the microwave or in a saucepan on the stove, and check the temperature with an instant-read thermometer.

If your dough does not form a ball during the first few minutes of kneading, do one of two things: if the dough looks dry and crumbly, add 1 tbsp (15 mL) water at 1-minute intervals until the dough forms a ball; if the dough looks wet, add 1 tbsp (15 mL) all-purpose flour at 1-minute intervals until the dough forms a ball.

½ cup	granulated sugar	125 mL
1 tsp	salt	5 mL
1	large egg, beaten	1
1 cup	lukewarm milk (see tip, at left)	250 mL
½ cup	unsalted butter, softened	125 mL
2 tbsp	lukewarm water	30 mL
3½ cups	all-purpose flour	875 mL
1¾ tsp	instant or bread machine yeast	8 mL

Topping

2 tbsp	unsalted butter, melted	30 mL

1. Add sugar, salt, egg, milk, butter and water to the bread pan. Spoon flour on top of liquid. Add yeast.

2. Select the Dough cycle and press Start.

3. When the cycle is finished, transfer the slack dough to a floured surface and punch down gently. Dust with flour and divide in half. Dust your hands with flour and pinch off 12 equal pieces of dough from each half. Form each piece into a ball. Place 12 balls in each prepared pan. Cover with clean towels and let rise for 45 minutes. Meanwhile, preheat oven to 425°F (220°C).

4. Bake for 15 to 20 minutes or until risen and lightly browned and an instant-read thermometer inserted in the center of a roll registers 190°F (90°C).

5. *Topping:* While still hot in the pans, brush tops of rolls with butter. Let cool in pans on a wire rack. Serve warm or let cool completely.

Ciabattini

Equipment

- Rolling pin
- 2 large baking sheets, lined with parchment paper and sprinkled with cornmeal
- Baking stone
- Broiler pan
- Instant-read thermometer

These square rolls with a crisp crust, a somewhat chewy crumb and a honeycomb texture are wonderful for small sandwiches. Ciabatta dough remains soft and batter-like, and it is mixed rather than kneaded. The combination of naturally leavened starter with a yeast dough adds a wonderful depth of flavor.

Tips

This is a soft, slightly sticky dough. You may need to scrape the corners of the bread machine pan to make sure all of the flour gets incorporated, since the ball of dough tends to stick in one corner at the start of kneading.

To scrape dough out of the bread pan, use a silicone spatula dipped in flour. Keep the work surface, your hands, the rolling pin and the pizza wheel floured to make shaping the buns easier and neater.

1 cup	active prepared sourdough starter (see page 141)	250 mL
2 tsp	fine sea salt	10 mL
1 cup + 2 tbsp	water, at room temperature (see tip, page 147)	280 mL
1 tbsp	milk	15 mL
1 tbsp	olive oil	15 mL
3¼ cups	bread flour	800 mL
2 tsp	instant or bread machine yeast	10 mL

1. Transfer starter to the bread pan. Add salt, water, milk and oil. Spoon flour on top of liquid. Add yeast.

2. Select the Artisan Dough or Dough cycle and press Start.

3. When the cycle is finished, transfer the slack dough to a floured surface and punch down gently. Dust with flour and roll out into a 10-inch (25 cm) square. Using a pizza wheel or a sharp knife, cut into 2-inch (5 cm) squares. As you cut each square, transfer it to the prepared baking sheets, as the dough reforms quickly. Place squares at least 2 inches (5 cm) apart. Cover with plastic wrap and let rise for 40 minutes.

4. Meanwhile, preheat oven to 450°F (230°C). Place baking stone on the middle rack and broiler pan on the bottom rack.

5. Remove the plastic wrap from buns. Add 2 cups (500 mL) hot water to the broiler pan. Place one baking sheet on baking stone. Bake for 12 to 15 minutes or until risen and deep brown and an instant-read thermometer inserted in the center of a roll registers 190°F (90°C). Remove from pan and let cool on a wire rack. Repeat with remaining baking sheet.

Brioche Buns

Equipment
- Bread machine with a 1½-lb (750 g) capacity
- 2 large baking sheets, lined with parchment paper

Gourmet burger restaurants treat this North American classic like the fabulous food it is: they use freshly ground steak to make the burger, top it with good cheese and homemade condiments, and serve it on a brioche bun. Have the butcher grind your steak, then go home and make this dough in your bread machine. Rosemary Brioche Buns are especially delicious with turkey, salmon or lobster "burgers."

Tips

If your dough does not form a ball during the first few minutes of kneading, do one of two things: if the dough looks dry and crumbly, add 1 tbsp (15 mL) water at 1-minute intervals until the dough forms a ball; if the dough looks wet, add 1 tbsp (15 mL) bread flour at 1-minute intervals until the dough forms a ball.

Kitchen scales are very handy to help you make buns of an even size. Weigh the dough, then divide it into pieces, weighing each piece to make sure they're approximately the same weight. Then shape into buns.

2 tbsp	granulated sugar	30 mL
1½ tsp	salt	7 mL
2	large eggs, beaten	2
½ cup	butter, softened	125 mL
⅓ cup	lukewarm buttermilk (see tip, page 238)	75 mL
3 tbsp	lukewarm water	45 mL
3 cups	bread flour	750 mL
1½ tsp	instant or bread machine yeast	7 mL

Egg Wash

1	large egg, beaten with 1 tbsp (15 mL) water	1

1. Add sugar, salt, eggs, butter, buttermilk and water to the bread pan. Spoon flour on top of liquid. Add yeast.

2. Select the Dough cycle and press Start.

3. When the cycle is finished, transfer dough to a floured surface and punch down gently. Divide dough in half. Dust your hands with flour and pinch off 6 equal pieces of dough from each half. Roll each piece into a ball, then flatten into a 4-inch (10 cm) round. Place at least 3 inches (7.5 cm) apart on prepared baking sheets. Cover with a clean towel and let rise for 30 minutes. Meanwhile, preheat oven to 350°F (180°C).

4. *Egg Wash:* Brush each bun with egg wash.

5. Bake one sheet at a time for 20 to 22 minutes or until risen and browned and an instant-read thermometer inserted in the center of a roll registers 190°F (90°C). Remove from pan and let cool on a wire rack. Serve warm or let cool completely.

Rosemary Brioche Buns
Add 1½ tsp (7 mL) dried rosemary with the flour.

Mexican Bolillos

Equipment

- Bread machine with a 1½-lb (750 g) capacity
- Large baking sheet, lined with parchment paper
- Instant-read thermometer

Bolillos — hard, crusty rolls with a chewy crumb — are wonderful for breakfast, with butter and homemade preserves, and make hearty sandwiches (*tortas*). Try them filled with chorizo sausage and cheese, pinto beans, taco-seasoned ground beef, strips of sautéed red and green bell pepper, cubes of fried potato or slow-roasted pork carnitas.

Tips

Ideally, the water should be between 86°F and 95°F (30°C and 35°C), the temperature range in which yeast is most active. Warm it in the microwave or in a saucepan on the stove, and check the temperature with an instant-read thermometer.

If your dough does not form a ball during the first few minutes of kneading, do one of two things: if the dough looks dry and crumbly, add 1 tbsp (15 mL) water at 1-minute intervals until the dough forms a ball; if the dough looks wet, add 1 tbsp (15 mL) all-purpose flour at 1-minute intervals until the dough forms a ball.

2 tsp	granulated sugar	10 mL
1 tsp	salt	5 mL
1 cup + 2 tbsp	lukewarm water (see tip, at left)	280 mL
3 cups	all-purpose flour	750 mL
2 tsp	instant or bread machine yeast	10 mL
	Vegetable oil	

1. Add sugar, salt and water to the bread pan. Spoon flour on top of liquid. Add yeast.

2. Select the Dough cycle and press Start.

3. When the cycle is finished, transfer dough to a floured surface and punch down gently. Dust with flour and divide in half. Cut each half into 4 pieces and roll each piece into an oval. Brush with oil, dust with flour and flatten into a 4-inch (10 cm) oblong or football shape. Place at least 3 inches (7.5 cm) apart on prepared baking sheet. Cover with a clean towel and let rise for 30 minutes. Meanwhile, preheat oven to 375°F (190°C).

4. Using a serrated knife, cut a 1-inch (2.5 cm) deep lengthwise slash down the top of each roll. Brush rolls with oil.

5. Bake for 25 to 35 minutes or until risen and golden brown and an instant-read thermometer inserted in the center of a roll registers 190°F (90°C). Remove from pan and let cool on a wire rack.

Caraway Rye Horns

Equipment

- Bread machine with a 1½-lb (750 g) capacity
- Rolling pin
- Large baking sheet, lined with parchment paper
- Instant-read thermometer

Serve these stylishly rustic rolls with a grilled steak or pork roast dinner, or as part of a selection in a roll basket.

Tips

Ideally, the water and buttermilk should be between 86°F and 95°F (30°C and 35°C), the temperature range in which yeast is most active. Warm them in the microwave or in a saucepan on the stove, and check the temperature with an instant-read thermometer.

As you roll out the dough, if it feels too springy and elastic, let it rest for 2 to 3 minutes, then try again.

1 tbsp	granulated sugar	15 mL
¾ tsp	salt	3 mL
1	large egg, beaten	1
½ cup	lukewarm water (see tip, at left)	125 mL
½ cup	lukewarm buttermilk	125 mL
1 tbsp	butter, softened	15 mL
2 cups	all-purpose flour	500 mL
1 cup	dark rye flour	250 mL
1 tbsp	caraway seeds	15 mL
2 tsp	instant or bread machine yeast	10 mL

Topping

2 tbsp	butter, melted	30 mL
1 tbsp	coarse sea salt, kosher salt or pretzel salt	15 mL

1. Add sugar, salt, egg, water, buttermilk and butter to the bread pan. Spoon all-purpose flour and rye flour on top of liquid. Add caraway seeds and yeast.

2. Select the Dough cycle and press Start.

3. When the cycle is finished, transfer dough to a floured surface and punch down gently. Divide dough in half. Dust rolling pin with flour and roll each half into a 10-inch (25 cm) circle. Using a pizza wheel or a sharp knife, cut each circle into 8 triangles. Starting with the wide end, roll up each triangle. Place rolls, seam side down, at least 1 inch (2.5 cm) apart on prepared baking sheet and form into crescents. Cover with a clean towel and let rise in a warm, draft-free place for 30 minutes. Meanwhile, preheat oven to 425°F (220°C).

4. *Topping:* Brush rolls with butter and sprinkle with salt.

5. Bake for 12 to 15 minutes or until risen and lightly browned and an instant-read thermometer inserted in the center of a roll registers 190°F (90°C). Remove from pan and let cool on a wire rack.

Whole Wheat, Onion and Dill Rolls

Equipment

- Bread machine with a 1½-lb (750 g) capacity
- Two 9-inch (23 cm) square or round metal baking pans, greased
- Instant-read thermometer

These hearty rolls are fabulous with just about any meal and also make delicious small sandwich buns for grilled sausage, chicken or cheese.

Tips

Three cups (750 mL) whole wheat berries (available in bulk at health food stores) will finely grind to make 7 cups (1.75 L) whole wheat flour. Use some for this recipe and freeze the rest in an airtight container for up to 12 months.

If your dough does not form a ball during the first few minutes of kneading, do one of two things: if the dough looks dry and crumbly, add 1 tbsp (15 mL) water at 1-minute intervals until the dough forms a ball; if the dough looks wet, add 1 tbsp (15 mL) whole wheat flour at 1-minute intervals until the dough forms a ball.

These whole-grain rolls will keep at room temperature for a maximum of 2 days. Freeze leftover rolls for up to 2 months.

½ cup	finely chopped green onion	125 mL
1 tbsp	dried dillweed	15 mL
¾ tsp	salt	3 mL
¾ cup	lukewarm water (see tip, page 204)	175 mL
2 tbsp	liquid honey	30 mL
1 tbsp	vegetable oil	15 mL
2⅔ cups	finely ground whole wheat flour (see tip, at left)	650 mL
2 tsp	vital wheat gluten	10 mL
1½ tsp	Artisan Dough Enhancer (page 278) or packaged dough enhancer	7 mL
1½ tsp	instant or bread machine yeast	7 mL

1. Add green onion, dill, salt, water, honey and oil to the bread pan. Spoon flour on top of liquid. Add wheat gluten, dough enhancer and yeast.

2. Select the Dough cycle and press Start.

3. When the cycle is finished, transfer dough to a floured surface and punch down gently. Divide dough in half. Cut each half into 9 pieces. Roll each piece into a ball. Place 9 balls in each prepared pan, spacing evenly. Cover with a clean towel and let rise in a warm, draft-free place for 30 minutes. Meanwhile, preheat oven to 350°F (180°C).

4. Bake for 12 to 15 minutes or until risen and golden brown and an instant-read thermometer inserted in the center of a roll registers 190°F (90°C). Let cool in pans on a wire rack. Serve warm or let cool completely.

Butternut Squash Rolls

Equipment
- Bread machine with a 1½-lb (750 g) capacity
- Large baking sheet, lined with parchment paper
- Instant-read thermometer

You'll want to eat these golden rolls, warm and savory with the scent of herbs, right out of the oven. They can go uptown if made into sophisticated sliders filled with poached chicken, tiny steamed green beans and aioli. Or they can be down home as part of an autumn dinner centered around roast duck, pheasant or chicken. They also make a fabulous turkey sandwich.

Tip
To make butternut squash purée, cut a 1½-lb (750 kg) squash in half lengthwise and scoop out seeds. Place cut side down in a baking dish and bake in a 350°F (180°C) oven for about 45 minutes or until soft. Let cool slightly, then scoop out flesh from skins, discarding skins. Transfer flesh to a food processor and purée until smooth. You will have about 1½ cups (375 mL) purée. Measure out ⅔ cup (150 mL) for this recipe. Refrigerate extra purée in an airtight container for up to 3 days or freeze for up to 3 months.

⅓ cup	milk	75 mL
⅓ cup	packed light brown sugar	75 mL
2 tbsp	unsalted butter	30 mL
½ tsp	salt	2 mL
1	large egg, beaten	1
⅔ cup	butternut squash purée (see tip, at left)	150 mL
2⅔ cups	all-purpose flour	650 mL
2 tsp	instant or bread machine yeast	10 mL

Herb Topping

½ tsp	freshly ground white pepper	2 mL
½ tsp	dried dillweed	2 mL
¼ tsp	dried chives	1 mL
¼ tsp	dried basil	1 mL
¼ tsp	dried tarragon	1 mL
¼ cup	butter, melted	60 mL

1. In a small saucepan, scald milk over medium-high heat until small bubbles form around the edges. Remove from heat and stir in brown sugar and butter. Transfer to the bread pan and let cool to lukewarm (between 86°F and 95°F/30°C and 35°C).

2. Add salt, egg and squash to the bread pan. Spoon flour on top of liquid. Add yeast.

3. Select the Dough cycle and press Start.

4. When the cycle is finished, transfer dough to a floured surface and punch down gently. Divide dough in half. Cut each half into 6 pieces. Roll each piece into a ball. Place at least 2 inches (5 cm) apart on prepared baking sheet. Cover with a clean towel and let rise in a warm, draft-free place for 30 minutes. Meanwhile, preheat oven to 375°F (190°C).

5. Bake for 15 to 20 minutes or until risen and browned and an instant-read thermometer inserted in the center of a roll registers 190°F (90°C).

6. *Topping:* In a small bowl, combine pepper, dill, chives, basil and tarragon. Brush hot rolls with melted butter and sprinkle with herb mixture. Serve warm.

> ### Herbed Sweet Potato Rolls
> Replace the squash purée with sweet potato purée.

Herbed Pumpkin Rolls

These soft rolls with wonderful color and flavor are perfect with turkey and cranberry sauce at Thanksgiving dinner or with leftovers the day after.

Tips

Be sure to use unsweetened canned pumpkin purée for this recipe and not pie filling, which contains added sugar and spices.

If your dough does not form a ball during the first few minutes of kneading, do one of two things: if the dough looks dry and crumbly, add 1 tbsp (15 mL) water at 1-minute intervals until the dough forms a ball; if the dough looks wet, add 1 tbsp (15 mL) all-purpose flour at 1-minute intervals until the dough forms a ball.

⅓ cup	milk	75 mL
⅓ cup	packed light brown sugar	75 mL
2 tbsp	unsalted butter	30 mL
½ tsp	salt	2 mL
½ tsp	dried basil	2 mL
¼ tsp	dried rosemary or thyme	1 mL
¼ tsp	freshly ground black pepper	1 mL
1	large egg, beaten	1
⅔ cup	pumpkin purée (not pie filling)	150 mL
2⅔ cups	all-purpose flour	650 mL
2 tsp	instant or bread machine yeast	10 mL

1. In a small saucepan, scald milk over medium-high heat until small bubbles form around the edges. Remove from heat and stir in brown sugar and butter. Transfer to the bread pan and let cool to lukewarm (between 86°F and 95°F/30°C and 35°C).

2. Add salt, basil, rosemary, pepper, egg and pumpkin to the bread pan. Spoon flour on top of liquid. Add yeast.

3. Select the Dough cycle and press Start.

4. When the cycle is finished, transfer dough to a floured surface and punch down gently. Divide dough in half. Cut each half into 6 pieces. Roll each piece into a ball. Place at least 2 inches (5 cm) apart on prepared baking sheet. Cover with a clean towel and let rise in a warm, draft-free place for 30 minutes. Meanwhile, preheat oven to 375°F (190°C).

5. Bake for 15 to 20 minutes or until risen and browned and an instant-read thermometer inserted in the center of a roll registers 190°F (90°C).

English Muffins

Equipment
- Bread machine with a 1½-lb (750 g) capacity
- Large nonstick griddle or skillet
- Instant-read thermometer

You'll be amazed by how much better these English muffins taste than store-bought. Because they are formed by hand, they won't be perfectly round, but that way your family and friends will know they really are homemade. Still, for you type A bakers — you know who you are —I've also included instructions for making perfect rings.

Tips

Ideally, the milk, buttermilk and water should be between 86°F and 95°F (30°C and 35°C), the temperature range in which yeast is most active. Warm them in the microwave or in a saucepan on the stove, and check the temperature with an instant-read thermometer.

If your dough does not form a ball during the first few minutes of kneading, do one of two things: if the dough looks dry and crumbly, add 1 tbsp (15 mL) water at 1-minute intervals until the dough forms a ball; if the dough looks wet, add 1 tbsp (15 mL) all-purpose flour at 1-minute intervals until the dough forms a ball.

2 tsp	granulated sugar	10 mL
1½ tsp	salt	7 mL
½ cup	lukewarm milk (see tip, at left)	125 mL
½ cup	lukewarm buttermilk	125 mL
¼ cup	lukewarm water	60 mL
3 cups	all-purpose flour	750 mL
2¼ tsp	instant or bread machine yeast	11 mL
⅛ tsp	baking soda	0.5 mL
	Cornmeal	

1. Add sugar, salt, milk, buttermilk and water to the bread pan. Spoon flour on top of liquid. Add yeast and baking soda.

2. Select the Dough cycle and press Start.

3. When the cycle is finished, transfer dough to a floured surface and punch down gently. Divide dough in half. Cut each half into 6 pieces. Form each piece into a ball, then flatten into a ½-inch (1 cm) thick round. Place rounds on a baking sheet, cover with a clean towel and let rise in a warm, draft-free place for 30 to 45 minutes or until puffy.

4. Heat griddle over medium-high heat. Sprinkle hot griddle with cornmeal. Griddle-bake muffins for 3 to 4 minutes or until browned on the bottom. Flip muffins over and griddle-bake for 3 minutes or until risen and browned and an instant-read thermometer inserted in the center of a muffin registers 190°F (90°C). Adjust heat as necessary to prevent burning. Serve warm.

Perfect English Muffins

Oil the inside of twelve 4-inch (10 cm) metal baking rings (or use clean tuna, jalapeño or pineapple cans with their tops and bottoms removed). In step 4, after sprinkling the griddle with cornmeal, press each piece of dough into a ring, scoop it up with a pancake turner and place it on the griddle. Griddle-bake as in step 4.

Whole Wheat English Muffins

Replace 1½ cups (375 mL) of the all-purpose flour with whole wheat or white whole wheat flour.

Bread Machine Bagels

Fresh-baked bagels, without preservatives, don't taste quite as good the next day, so set the delay timer so the dough is ready when you wake up in the morning. Then it just takes minutes to make your own bagels. Boiling bagels before baking gives them that characteristic shine and an authentic flavor and chewy texture. If you like chewier bagels, boil them for 1 minute longer before baking.

1 tbsp	granulated sugar	15 mL
1 tsp	salt	5 mL
¾ cup	lukewarm water (see tip, at right)	175 mL
1 tbsp	liquid honey	15 mL
2¼ cups	all-purpose flour	550 mL
1½ tsp	instant or bread machine yeast	7 mL

1. Add sugar, salt, water and honey to the bread pan. Spoon flour on top of liquid. Add yeast.

2. Select the Dough cycle and press Start.

3. When the cycle is finished, transfer dough to a lightly floured surface and punch down gently. Divide dough into 6 pieces. Roll each piece into a 10-inch (25 cm) rope. Pinch the ends of each rope together to form a circle. Place on prepared baking sheet at least 2 inches (5 cm) apart. Cover with a clean towel and let rise for 30 to 45 minutes or until doubled in bulk.

4. Meanwhile, bring a large pot of water to a boil over high heat and preheat oven to 350°F (180°C).

5. Using slotted spatula, lift each bagel and plunge into boiling water. Boil for 2 minutes, flipping over halfway through, then return to the baking sheet, placing bagels 2 inches (5 cm) apart.

6. Bake for 20 to 22 minutes or until golden brown and an instant-read thermometer inserted in the center of a bagel registers 190°F (90°C). Remove from pan and let cool on a wire rack.

Whole Wheat Bagels
Replace 1 cup (250 mL) of the all-purpose flour with whole wheat flour.

Cinnamon and Raisin Bagels
Increase the sugar to 2 tbsp (30 mL) and add ¼ cup (60 mL) raisins and 1 tsp (5 mL) ground cinnamon with the yeast.

Tips

Ideally, the water should be between 86°F and 95°F (30°C and 35°C), the temperature range in which yeast is most active. Warm it in the microwave or in a saucepan on the stove, and check the temperature with an instant-read thermometer.

If your dough does not form a ball during the first few minutes of kneading, do one of two things: if the dough looks dry and crumbly, add 1 tbsp (15 mL) water at 1-minute intervals until the dough forms a ball; if the dough looks wet, add 1 tbsp (15 mL) all-purpose flour at 1-minute intervals until the dough forms a ball.

Bagel Flavorings

Flavoring	How Used	Flavor
Caraway seeds	Mixed into dough with the yeast	Caraway
Dehydrated onion flakes	Sprinkled on boiled bagels before baking	Toasted onion
Dill seeds	Sprinkled on boiled bagels before baking	Dill
Fennel seeds	Sprinkled on boiled bagels before baking	Licorice
Ground cinnamon	Mixed with sugar and sprinkled on dough after baking	Cinnamon
Nigella seeds	Sprinkled on boiled bagels before baking	Onion
Poppy seeds	Sprinkled on boiled bagels before baking	Sweet
Sesame seeds	Sprinkled on boiled bagels before baking	Sesame

Black Pepper Taralli

These oval snack crackers are delicious with a glass of wine and a savory dip. They have an uneven, wrinkly charm, so you know they're homemade. As with bagels, you boil them first, then finish them in the oven. I've flavored the dough with black pepper, but you can try hot pepper flakes, white pepper, chopped fresh oregano, fennel seeds or garlic powder for your own house specialty.

Tips

Together, the hot water and wine create the optimum warm temperature for mixing the dough.

Doppio zero flour is available at Italian grocery stores and online. If you can't find doppio zero flour, substitute 1¾ cups (425 mL) all-purpose flour.

1 tsp	granulated sugar	5 mL
¾ tsp	salt	3 mL
¼ cup	hot water	60 mL
¼ cup	dry white wine	60 mL
2 tbsp	olive oil	30 mL
2 cups	doppio zero flour	500 mL
1½ tsp	coarsely ground black pepper	7 mL
1½ tsp	instant or bread machine yeast	7 mL

Egg Wash
1	large egg, beaten with 1 tbsp (15 mL) water	1

1. Add sugar, salt, water, wine and oil to the bread pan. Spoon flour on top of liquid. Add pepper and yeast.

2. Select the Dough cycle and press Start.

3. When the cycle is finished, transfer dough to a floured surface and punch down gently. Bring a large pot of water to a boil over high heat and preheat oven to 375°F (190°C).

4. Lightly dust dough with flour and divide into 4 portions. Roll each portion into a 24-inch (60 cm) long rope. Cut each rope into six 4-inch (10 cm) pieces. Roll each piece into a thin 5-inch (12.5 cm) long rope. Pinch the ends of each rope together to form an oval.

5. Drop several ovals at a time into boiling water. When they float to the top, in about 20 seconds, use a slotted spoon to transfer them to the prepared baking sheets, placing them about 1 inch (2.5 cm) apart.

6. *Egg Wash:* When all the taralli are on the baking sheets, brush them with egg wash.

7. Bake for 35 to 40 minutes, rotating baking sheets if necessary, until golden brown and crisp. Remove from pan and let cool on a wire rack.

Wild Rice Stalks

Equipment

- Bread machine with a 2-lb (1 kg) capacity
- 2 large baking sheets, lined with parchment paper
- Kitchen shears

These seeded breadsticks go well with soups and stews. Cook the wild rice ahead of time and freeze it in 1-cup (250 mL) portions for up to 1 year.

Tips

If your dough does not form a ball during the first few minutes of kneading, do one of two things: if the dough looks dry and crumbly, add 1 tbsp (15 mL) water at 1-minute intervals until the dough forms a ball; if the dough looks wet, add 1 tbsp (15 mL) bread flour at 1-minute intervals until the dough forms a ball.

As you roll out the dough into stalks, if it feels too springy and elastic, let it rest for 2 to 3 minutes, then try again.

1 cup	cooked wild rice	250 mL
1 tbsp	granulated sugar	15 mL
2 tsp	salt	10 mL
1½ tsp	fennel seeds	7 mL
1⅓ cups	lukewarm water (see tip, page 211)	325 mL
¼ cup	vegetable oil	60 mL
3½ cups	bread flour	875 mL
½ cup	dark rye or pumpernickel flour	125 mL
2 tsp	instant or bread machine yeast	10 mL

Topping

1	large egg, beaten	1
	Coarse kosher salt or pretzel salt	

1. Add wild rice, sugar, salt, fennel seeds, water and oil to the bread pan. Spoon bread flour and rye flour on top of liquid. Add yeast.

2. Select the Dough cycle and press Start.

3. When the cycle is finished, transfer dough to a floured surface and punch down gently. Preheat oven to 375°F (190°C).

4. Lightly dust dough with flour and divide in half. Dust your hands with flour and pinch off 8 pieces of dough from each half. Form each piece into a 12-inch (30 cm) stalk. Place 8 stalks on each prepared baking sheet. Using kitchen shears, snip diagonal slices at random intervals into the top third of each stalk until it resembles a grain head.

5. *Topping:* Brush stalks with egg and sprinkle with salt.

6. Bake for 27 to 30 minutes or until browned and crisp. Remove from pan and let cool on wire racks.

Sweet Rolls

TENDER, FLAKY SWEET dough can be a blank canvas for your creativity. Pair it with a wonderful filling, roll it into a special shape, then finish it with a flavored glaze. The Orange-Caramel Sticky Buns (page 220) are a great example. I had been reading about them for years in the fun escapist novels by Marne Davis Kellogg about jewel thief Kick Keswick. These fabulous rolls are worth their weight in precious gems — they're worth stealing. Thankfully, I didn't have to commit a crime in order to enjoy them and share them with you: Marne sent me the recipe, which I've adapted for the bread machine. Thank you, Marne!

You'll be using the Dough cycle for the rolls in this chapter, then baking them in the oven. To keep rolls very, very tender as they bake, place them close together in the pan so that they touch each other when they rise; this will keep the sides moist. To let rolls spread out and get even larger, place them 2 inches (5 cm) on a prepared baking sheet, then once baked and cooled, glaze them all over to keep them moist.

Rolling Right Along

Just as there are traditional shapes for savory dinner rolls, there are also special shapes for sweet rolls, especially delicious when made with Danish Pastry Dough (page 226). The rolls in this chapter can be made in any of these shapes. Follow the recipes for rising and baking instructions.

Shape	How to Form and Bake
Crescents	Roll dough into a 16- by 10-inch (40 by 25 cm) rectangle. Using a zigzag pattern, cut the rectangle into 5 triangles with approximately 6-inch (15 cm) sides and a 3-inch (7.5 cm) base. Place 1 tbsp (15 mL) filling or jam about 1 inch (2.5 cm) from each triangle's base. Starting at the base, roll up triangles. Place rolls at least 2 inches (5 cm) apart on a baking sheet lined with parchment paper, with the tip of the triangle facing down, and bend rolls to form crescents.
Bear claws	Roll dough into a 16- by 8-inch (40 by 20 cm) rectangle. Cut the rectangle into eight 4-inch (10 cm) squares. Spread 2 tsp (10 mL) filling in a strip along the center of each square. Brush one side of the square parallel to the filling with egg wash, then fold the opposite side over the filling, pressing the edges together to seal. Make 3 cuts on the folded side, almost but not quite to the seam side. Place pastries at least 2 inches (5 cm) apart on a baking sheet lined with parchment paper and gently fan out the "toes" slightly.
Pinwheels or snails	Roll dough into a 16- by 10-inch (40 by 25 cm) rectangle. Spread ½ cup (125 mL) filling over dough, leaving a ½-inch (1 cm) perimeter along each long edge. Starting with a long edge, roll dough into a tight cylinder. Using dental floss or a sharp knife, cut cylinder into 1-inch (2.5 cm) slices. Place slices, spiral side up, on a baking sheet lined with parchment paper.

Hot Cross Buns

Makes 24 small rolls

Equipment
- Bread machine with a 2½-lb (1.25 kg) capacity
- Large baking sheet, lined with parchment paper
- Instant-read thermometer

This centuries-old recipe is so popular we still sing about it in a nursery rhyme. The yeasty spice and dried fruit buns are eaten in England on Good Friday, a tradition that likely began when London law limited their sale to Good Friday, Christmas and funerals. This bread machine version offers a tasty nod to the past, with our feet firmly planted in the modern kitchen.

Tips

Ideally, the buttermilk should be between 86°F and 95°F (30°C and 35°C), the temperature range in which yeast is most active. Warm it in the microwave or in a saucepan on the stove, and check the temperature with an instant-read thermometer.

This recipe makes 24 small buns. If you prefer, make 12 larger ones and place them about 2 inches (5 cm) apart on the baking sheet. Increase the baking time to about 28 minutes.

½ cup	granulated sugar	125 mL
1½ tsp	ground cinnamon	7 mL
1¼ tsp	salt	6 mL
3	large eggs, beaten	3
¾ cup	lukewarm buttermilk (see tip, at left)	175 mL
6 tbsp	butter, softened	90 mL
4¼ cups	all-purpose flour	1.06 L
2¼ tsp	instant or bread machine yeast	11 mL
¼ cup	dried currants or raisins (optional)	60 mL

Egg Wash

1	large egg, beaten with 1 tsp (5 mL) water	1

Icing

1 cup	confectioners' (icing) sugar	250 mL
1½ tsp	milk	7 mL
1 tsp	vanilla extract	5 mL

1. Add sugar, cinnamon, salt, eggs, buttermilk and butter to the bread pan. Spoon flour on top of liquid. Add yeast. Place currants in the dispenser (or add at the "add ingredient" or "mix in" signal).

2. Select the Dough cycle and press Start.

3. When the cycle is finished, transfer dough to a floured surface and punch down gently. Divide dough in half. Cut each half into 12 equal pieces and form each into a ball. Place close together on prepared baking sheet. Cover with plastic wrap and let rise in a warm, draft-free place for 30 minutes. Meanwhile, preheat oven to 350°F (180°C).

4. *Egg Wash:* Remove plastic wrap and brush tops of rolls with egg wash.

5. Bake for 22 to 25 minutes or until risen and lightly browned and an instant-read thermometer inserted in the center of a roll registers 190°F (90°C). Remove from pan and let cool on a wire rack for 30 minutes.

6. *Icing:* In a small bowl, whisk together confectioners' sugar, milk and vanilla until smooth. Spoon into a sealable plastic bag. Snip a corner from the bag and squeeze an icing cross onto each bun.

Classic Cinnamon Rolls

Equipment

- Bread machine with a 2-lb (1 kg) capacity
- Rolling pin
- 13- by 9-inch (33 by 23 cm) metal baking pan, greased
- Instant-read thermometer

When you crave the comfort of cinnamon rolls, these are the ones to make. They rise high, have just the right touch of spice and have a tender, feathery crumb.

Tips

Ideally, the buttermilk should be between 86°F and 95°F (30°C and 35°C), the temperature range in which yeast is most active. Warm it in the microwave or in a saucepan on the stove, and check the temperature with an instant-read thermometer.

If your dough does not form a ball during the first few minutes of kneading, do one of two things: if the dough looks dry and crumbly, add 1 tbsp (15 mL) water at 1-minute intervals until the dough forms a ball; if the dough looks wet, add 1 tbsp (15 mL) all-purpose flour at 1-minute intervals until the dough forms a ball.

¼ cup	granulated sugar	60 mL
1¼ tsp	salt	6 mL
3	large eggs, beaten	3
¾ cup	lukewarm buttermilk (see tip, at left)	175 mL
6 tbsp	unsalted butter, softened	90 mL
4¼ cups	all-purpose flour	1.06 L
2¼ tsp	instant or bread machine yeast	11 mL
Filling		
1 cup	Cinnamon Filling (page 284)	250 mL
Glaze		
½ cup	Vanilla Glaze (page 291)	125 mL

1. Add sugar, salt, eggs, buttermilk and butter to the bread pan. Spoon flour on top of liquid. Add yeast.

2. Select the Dough cycle and press Start.

3. When the cycle is finished, transfer dough to a floured surface and punch down gently. Lightly dust with flour and roll out into an 18- by 12-inch (45 by 30 cm) rectangle, with a long edge closest to you.

4. *Filling:* Spread filling over dough, leaving a ½-inch (1 cm) perimeter along each long edge. Lightly brush the long edge farthest from you with water. Starting with the opposite long edge, roll dough into a tight cylinder and pinch seam to seal. Using dental floss or a sharp knife, cut cylinder into 1½-inch (4 cm) slices. Place slices, spiral side up, in prepared pan. Cover with plastic wrap and let rise in a warm, draft-free place for 1 hour. Meanwhile, preheat oven to 350°F (180°C).

5. Remove plastic wrap and bake for 20 to 25 minutes or until risen and lightly browned and an instant-read thermometer inserted in the center of a roll registers 190°F (90°C). Let cool in pan on a wire rack for 10 minutes.

6. *Glaze:* Drizzle warm rolls with glaze while they're still in the pan. To serve, cut rolls out of the pan.

White Whole Wheat Cinnamon Rolls

Ooey-gooey and better for you! Each type of flour has a role to play in this recipe: whole wheat for added nutrition, all-purpose for a soft crumb and bread flour for volume. These rolls get a zigzag of glaze at the end.

Tip

Ideally, the milk should be between 86°F and 95°F (30°C and 35°C), the temperature range in which yeast is most active. Warm it in the microwave or in a saucepan on the stove, and check the temperature with an instant-read thermometer.

¼ cup	granulated sugar	60 mL
1½ tsp	salt	7 mL
1	large egg, beaten	1
1 cup + 2 tbsp	lukewarm milk (see tip, at left)	280 mL
2 tbsp	unsalted butter, softened	30 mL
1⅔ cups	bread flour	400 mL
1 cup	all-purpose flour	250 mL
1 cup	white whole wheat or whole wheat flour	250 mL
2 tsp	instant or bread machine yeast	10 mL

Filling

1 cup	packed dark brown sugar	250 mL
1 tbsp	ground cinnamon	15 mL
¼ cup	unsalted butter, softened	60 mL

Glaze

¼ cup	Vanilla Glaze (page 291)	60 mL

1. Add sugar, salt, egg, milk and butter to the bread pan. Spoon bread flour, all-purpose flour and whole wheat flour on top of liquid. Add yeast.

2. Select the Dough cycle and press Start.

3. When the cycle is finished, transfer dough to a floured surface. Dust with flour and divide in half. Roll out each half into a 16- by 12-inch (40 by 30 cm) rectangle, with a short edge closest to you.

4. *Filling:* In a small bowl, using a fork, combine brown sugar, cinnamon and butter until smooth. Spread half the filling over each dough rectangle, leaving a 1-inch (2.5 cm) perimeter along each short edge. Lightly brush the short edge farthest from you with water. Starting with the short edge closest to you, roll each rectangle up into a tight cylinder and pinch seam to seal. Using dental floss or a sharp knife, cut each cylinder into 1-inch (2.5 cm) slices. Place slices, spiral side up, almost touching on prepared baking sheet. Cover with plastic wrap and let rise in a warm, draft-free place for 1 hour. Meanwhile, preheat oven to 375°F (190°C).

Tips

When you're trying to get your family to eat more whole-grain breads, start by using 1 cup (250 mL) whole wheat flour in this recipe. Over time, increase the amount of whole wheat flour — up to 2 cups (500 mL) total — and decrease the amount of all-purpose flour by the same amount.

If your dough does not form a ball during the first few minutes of kneading, do one of two things: if the dough looks dry and crumbly, add 1 tbsp (15 mL) water at 1-minute intervals until the dough forms a ball; if the dough looks wet, add 1 tbsp (15 mL) bread flour at 1-minute intervals until the dough forms a ball.

5. Remove plastic wrap and bake for 18 to 20 minutes or until risen, golden brown and an instant-read thermometer inserted in the center of a roll registers 190°F (90°C). Let cool on pan on a wire rack for 10 minutes.

6. *Glaze:* Dip the fingertips of one hand (or the tines of a fork) into the glaze and wave in a back-and-forth motion about 2 inches (5 cm) above the rolls, creating a zigzag pattern. Serve warm.

Whole Wheat Cinnamon Raisin Rolls
Soak 1 cup (250 mL) raisins in hot water for 15 minutes. Drain well and pat dry. Sprinkle raisins evenly over cinnamon filling.

Orange-Caramel Sticky Buns

Equipment

- Bread machine with a 1½-lb (750 g) capacity
- 8-inch (20 cm) square metal baking pan, greased
- Rolling pin

These decadent rolls are based on a recipe from a series of novels by Marne Davis Kellogg. Her reformed jewel thief heroine, Kick Keswick, nibbles on these whenever she's back at her former employer's office in London. The rolls have an irresistible "orange-caramel toffee-like glaze flecked with bits of orange," the author writes.

Tip

Ideally, the buttermilk should be between 86°F and 95°F (30°C and 35°C), the temperature range in which yeast is most active. Warm it in the microwave or in a saucepan on the stove, and check the temperature with an instant-read thermometer.

¼ cup	granulated sugar	60 mL
¾ tsp	salt	3 mL
2	large eggs, beaten	2
6 tbsp	lukewarm buttermilk (see tip, at left)	90 mL
3 tbsp	unsalted butter, softened	45 mL
2¼ cups	all-purpose flour	550 mL
1½ tsp	instant or bread machine yeast	7 mL

Sweet Orange Filling

¼ cup	granulated sugar	60 mL
2 tsp	grated orange zest	10 mL
⅛ tsp	salt	0.5 mL
¼ cup	unsalted butter, softened	60 mL

Orange Caramel

6 tbsp	packed light or dark brown sugar	90 mL
1 tsp	grated orange zest	5 mL
¼ cup	freshly squeezed orange juice	60 mL
2 tbsp	unsalted butter, melted	30 mL
½ cup	toffee candy bits (optional)	125 mL

1. Add sugar, salt, eggs, buttermilk and butter to the bread pan. Spoon flour on top of liquid. Add yeast.

2. Select the Dough cycle and press Start.

3. *Filling:* In a small bowl, using a fork, combine sugar, orange zest, salt and butter until smooth. Set aside.

4. *Caramel:* In another bowl, combine brown sugar, orange zest, orange juice and butter until smooth. Spread in prepared baking pan. Top with toffee bits (if using).

5. When the cycle is finished, transfer dough to a floured surface and punch down gently. Roll into a 12- by 10-inch (30 by 25 cm) rectangle, with a long edge closest to you. Spread filling over dough, leaving a ½-inch (1 cm) perimeter along each long edge. Lightly brush the long edge farthest from you with water. Starting with the long edge closest to you, roll dough into a tight cylinder and pinch seam to seal. Using dental floss or a sharp knife, cut cylinder into 1-inch (2.5 cm) slices. Place slices, spiral side up, on the caramel in the pan. Cover with plastic wrap and let rise while the oven is preheating. Preheat oven to 350°F (180°C).

Tips

You'll need about 1 large orange for the zest and juice. Try using a blood orange.

If your dough does not form a ball during the first few minutes of kneading, do one of two things: if the dough looks dry and crumbly, add 1 tbsp (15 mL) water at 1-minute intervals until the dough forms a ball; if the dough looks wet, add 1 tbsp (15 mL) all-purpose flour at 1-minute intervals until the dough forms a ball.

6. Bake for 25 to 30 minutes or until risen and lightly browned and an instant-read thermometer inserted in the center of a roll registers 190°F (90°C). Let cool in pan on a wire rack for 15 minutes. Loosen rolls from sides of pan and invert onto a serving platter. Serve warm.

Lemon Ginger Caramel Sticky Buns

Substitute lemon zest for the orange zest in both the filling and the caramel. Substitute ⅓ cup (75 mL) lemon juice for the orange juice in the caramel. Add ½ tsp (2 mL) ground ginger to the caramel.

Apricot Kolachke

Equipment

- Bread machine with a 1½-lb (750 g) capacity
- Large baking sheet, lined with parchment paper
- Instant-read thermometer

Made with a sweetened, sour cream–enriched yeast dough, kolachke are enjoyed throughout Slovakia, Poland, the Czech Republic, Serbia and Croatia. They're also beloved in the Great Plains region of North America, from Texas to Saskatchewan. Each soft little bun has a small depression filled with a dollop of apricot, cottage cheese or poppy seed filling, then a sprinkling of buttery streusel.

Tips

Ideally, the water should be between 86°F and 95°F (30°C and 35°C), the temperature range in which yeast is most active. Warm it in the microwave or in a saucepan on the stove, and check the temperature with an instant-read thermometer.

Full-fat sour cream works best in this recipe, adding richness, moisture and golden color. For the best results, let the sour cream warm to room temperature before adding it to the bread pan. Cold ingredients will decrease the activity of the yeast.

¼ cup	granulated sugar	60 mL
1 tsp	salt	5 mL
1 cup	sour cream	250 mL
2 tbsp	lukewarm water (see tip, at left)	30 mL
2½ cups	all-purpose flour	625 mL
2¼ tsp	instant or bread machine yeast	11 mL
½ tsp	baking soda	2 mL

Streusel Topping

2 tbsp	granulated sugar	30 mL
1½ tbsp	all-purpose flour	22 mL
1 tbsp	butter, melted	15 mL

Filling

½ cup	Apricot Filling (page 287)	125 mL

1. Add sugar, salt, sour cream and water to the bread pan. Spoon flour on top of liquid. Add yeast and baking soda.

2. Select the Dough cycle and press Start.

3. *Topping:* In a bowl, combine sugar, flour and butter until crumbly.

4. When the cycle is finished, transfer dough to a floured surface and punch down gently. Divide dough in half. Cut each half into 6 pieces. Roll each piece into a ball. Place 2 inches (5 cm) apart on prepared baking sheet. Cover with plastic wrap and let rise in a warm, draft-free place for 30 minutes. Meanwhile, preheat oven to 350°F (180°C).

6. *Filling:* With your knuckle, make a depression in the middle of each ball. Fill each depression with 2 tsp (10 mL) filling. Sprinkle evenly with topping.

7. Bake for 15 to 18 minutes or until risen and golden brown and an instant-read thermometer inserted in the center of a pastry registers 190°F (90°C). Let cool on pan on a wire rack for 15 minutes. Serve warm or transfer to rack and let cool completely.

Cottage Cheese Kolachke
Use ½ cup (125 mL) Cottage Cheese Filling (page 289) in place of the Apricot Filling.

Poppy Seed Kolachke
Use ½ cup (125 mL) Poppy Seed Filling (page 285) in place of the Apricot Filling.

Pumpkin Pull-Aparts

Makes 9 rolls

Equipment
- Bread machine with a 1½-lb (750 kg) capacity
- Rolling pin
- 9-inch (23 cm) square metal baking pan, greased

These golden rolls will be the highlight of an autumn breakfast table, but they're good any time of year, providing a boost of beta carotene and vitamin A.

Tips

You could also use cooked and puréed pumpkin, squash or sweet potatoes in place of the canned pumpkin purée.

If your dough does not form a ball during the first few minutes of kneading, do one of two things: if the dough looks dry and crumbly, add 1 tbsp (15 mL) water at 1-minute intervals until the dough forms a ball; if the dough looks wet, add 1 tbsp (15 mL) all-purpose flour at 1-minute intervals until the dough forms a ball.

⅓ cup	granulated sugar	75 mL
½ tsp	salt	2 mL
1	large egg, beaten	1
⅔ cup	canned pumpkin purée (not pie filling)	150 mL
⅓ cup	lukewarm buttermilk (see tip, page 220)	75 mL
2 tbsp	unsalted butter, softened	30 mL
2⅔ cups	all-purpose flour	650 mL
2 tsp	instant or bread machine yeast	10 mL

Filling

½ cup	pumpkin or apple butter	125 mL

Topping

2 tbsp	Cinnamon Sugar (page 290)	60 mL

1. Add sugar, salt, egg, pumpkin, buttermilk and butter to the bread pan. Spoon flour on top of liquid. Add yeast.

2. Select the Dough cycle and press Start.

3. When the cycle is finished, transfer to a floured surface and punch down gently. Lightly dust with flour and roll out into a 12- by 10-inch (30 by 25 cm) rectangle, with a long side closest to you.

4. *Filling:* Spread pumpkin butter over dough, leaving a ½-inch (1 cm) perimeter along both long sides. Lightly brush the long edge farthest from you with water. Starting with the opposite long side, roll dough into a tight cylinder and pinch seam to seal. Using dental floss or a sharp knife, cut cylinder into 9 slices.

5. *Topping:* Dip both spiral sides of rolls in cinnamon sugar. Place spiral side up in prepared pan. Cover with plastic wrap and let rise in a warm, draft-free place for 30 minutes. Set remaining cinnamon sugar aside. Meanwhile, preheat oven to 350°F (180°C).

6. Remove plastic wrap and sprinkle reserved cinnamon sugar over rolls. Bake for about 30 minutes or until risen and lightly browned and an instant-read thermometer inserted in the center of a roll registers 190°F (90°C). Let cool in pan on a wire rack for 15 minutes. Serve warm.

Saffron Buns for St. Lucia Day

These pastries are served on December 13, St. Lucia Day, celebrated in Scandinavian countries. The S shape is the most traditional, but you can also form the dough into other shapes (see box, opposite). To turn this dough into a Lucia Crown, complete with small candles, see page 234.

1 cup	light (5%) or half-and-half (10%) cream	250 mL
1/4 cup	water	60 mL
1/2 cup	granulated sugar	125 mL
1/2 cup	butter, softened	125 mL
3/4 tsp	salt	3 mL
1/2 tsp	powdered saffron	2 mL
1	large egg, beaten	1
4 1/4 cups	all-purpose flour	1.06 L
2 1/4 tsp	instant or bread machine yeast	11 mL

Topping

1	large egg, beaten	1
	Pearl sugar or coarse sugar	
2 tbsp	dried currants or raisins	30 mL

1. In a small saucepan, scald cream and water over medium-high heat until small bubbles form around the edges. Remove from heat and stir in sugar and butter. Transfer to the bread pan and let cool to lukewarm (between 86°F and 95°F/30°C and 35°C).

2. Add salt, saffron and egg to the bread pan. Spoon flour on top of liquid. Add yeast.

3. Select the Dough cycle and press Start.

4. When the cycle is finished, transfer dough to a floured surface and punch down gently. Divide dough in half. Cut each half into 10 pieces. Roll out each piece into a 6- by 1/2-inch (15 by 1 cm) strip. Shape each strip into an S figure. Place well apart on prepared baking sheets. Cover with a clean towel and let rise in a warm, draft-free place for 30 minutes. Meanwhile, preheat oven to 400°F (200°C).

5. *Topping:* Brush buns with beaten egg and sprinkle with sugar. Place a currant in each curve of the S.

6. Bake one sheet at a time for 10 to 12 minutes or until risen and golden and an instant-read thermometer inserted in the center of a bun registers 190°F (90°C).

Tips

If your dough does not form a ball during the first few minutes of kneading, do one of two things: if the dough looks dry and crumbly, add 1 tbsp (15 mL) water at 1-minute intervals until the dough forms a ball; if the dough looks wet, add 1 tbsp (15 mL) all-purpose flour at 1-minute intervals until the dough forms a ball.

Pearl sugar is available at baking supply shops or online.

Fun with Saffron Buns

Have fun experimenting with these traditional shapes.

Lily: Lay a strip out lengthwise and coil each end to form a flattened C. Rotate the strip a quarter turn to the right so that the coiled ends face down. Press your finger in the middle of the strip and draw up the ends to form a V, or lily with the curly ends out. Place a dried currant or raisin in the center of each coil.

Lucia Cat: Lay two strips out lengthwise and coil the ends of each strip so that it forms a flattened C. Place the two strips so that their backs are joined together, with the coils of one strip facing right and the coils of the other facing left. Place a dried currant or raisin in the center of where the backs join. Makes 10 cats.

Danish Pastry Dough

Equipment

- Bread machine with a 1½-lb (750 g) capacity
- Pastry blender or food processor
- Rolling pin
- Dough scraper

True Danish pastry is heartbreakingly tender, buttery and slightly sweet. The dough starts with what's known as the *detrempe* (a sweet yeast dough), to which you add a butter layer, or *beurrage*, to create a laminated dough, or one in which layers of butter create rich flakiness during baking. Traditional recipes have you pound cold butter into rectangles, a tricky proposition. This streamlined method cuts the butter in with some of the flour. The beurrage is then rolled into the dough. A little orange juice in the detrempe adds a nuanced flavor note and helps cut some of the richness.

Detrempe

⅓ cup	granulated sugar	75 mL
1 tsp	kosher salt	5 mL
2	large eggs, beaten	2
½ cup	lukewarm whole or 2% milk (see tip, at right)	125 mL
2 tbsp	freshly squeezed orange juice	30 mL
2½ cups	all-purpose flour	625 mL
1 tbsp	instant or bread machine yeast	15 mL

Beurrage

¾ cup	all-purpose flour	175 mL
12 tbsp	cold unsalted butter, cut into 12 pieces	180 mL

1. *Detrempe:* Add sugar, salt, eggs, milk and orange juice to the bread pan. Spoon flour on top of liquid. Add yeast.

2. Select the Dough cycle and press Start.

3. *Beurrage:* Place flour in a bowl. Using the pastry blender, cut in butter until butter is the size of small peas or smaller. (Or place flour and butter in the food processor and pulse until butter is the size of small peas or smaller.) Do not overwork; you want the butter to stay cold and solid. Cover and refrigerate for at least 1 hour or for up to 1 day.

4. When the cycle is finished, transfer dough to a floured surface and punch down gently. Dust very lightly with flour. Lightly flour your hands and the rolling pin. Working dough as little as possible and adding just enough flour as necessary to prevent sticking, roll out into an 18- by 12-inch (45 by 30 cm) rectangle, using a dough scraper and your hands to lift and help form dough into an even rectangle with the long sides on your right and left.

5. Sprinkle half the beurrage on top two-thirds of dough, leaving a 1½-inch (4 cm) border on the right and left sides. With your hands, lightly press the beurrage into the dough so it will stick. Fold the bottom third of the dough up and over some of the filling, like you're folding a business letter. Fold the top third of the dough down so the filling is completely covered and you have a 12- by 6-inch (30 by 15 cm) rectangle. Use your hands to scoop up stray beurrage and tuck it back under the dough, and to help form the dough into an even rectangle.

Tips

Ideally, the milk should be between 86°F and 95°F (30°C and 35°C), the temperature range in which yeast is most active. Warm it in the microwave or in a saucepan on the stove, and check the temperature with an instant-read thermometer.

It's very important to keep laminated dough cold so the butter layers stay intact. Use a marble pastry work surface, if possible, and work in a cool room. If the dough starts to feel warm and look shiny, cover and refrigerate it for 15 minutes.

Plan on at least 2 days to make Danish pastry: one day to make the silken dough and let it rest and chill, the next day to form and bake the pastries.

6. Turn dough a quarter turn, lightly flouring under and on top of dough as necessary, and roll out into an 18- by 12-inch (45 by 30 cm) rectangle with the long sides on your right and left. Repeat the process with the remaining beurrage. Wrap with plastic wrap and refrigerate for 30 minutes.

7. Roll out dough into a rectangle and fold like a business letter two more times. Use your hands to help form dough into an even 12- by 6-inch (30 by 15 cm) rectangle of laminated dough. Lightly flour any sticky places on the dough. The dough should feel firm all over, with flattened pieces of butter visible within the dough, but not at all sticky.

8. Wrap the dough with plastic wrap and refrigerate for at least 30 minutes, until well chilled, or for up to 24 hours before using.

Almond-Filled Bear Claws

Makes 16 bear claws

Equipment
- Rolling pin
- 2 large baking sheets, lined with parchment paper

Bear claws start out as squares. Then they're filled, folded and cut so that the edge of the pastry resembles stubby toes, which separate and spread out during baking. With a drizzle of glaze at the end, they're irresistible.

Tips

It's very important to keep laminated dough cold so the butter layers stay intact. Use a marble pastry work surface, if possible, and work in a cool room. The dough should be at a warm room temperature only during the final rise.

Bear claws can be stored in the freezer for up to 3 months. Let them cool completely, then layer with parchment paper in an airtight container and freeze.

1	recipe prepared Danish Pastry Dough (page 226)	1
	All-purpose flour	
½ cup	Danish Almond Filling (page 286) or apricot, cherry or plum preserves	125 mL
1	large egg, lightly beaten with 1 tbsp (15 mL) water	1
¼ cup	Almond Glaze (variation, page 291)	60 mL

1. Cut dough in half. Rewrap one half and return it to the refrigerator. Transfer the other half to a lightly floured surface and dust very lightly with flour. Lightly flour your hands and the rolling pin. Roll out dough into a 16- by 8-inch (40 by 20 cm) rectangle. The dough should feel cold, firm and smooth all over, but not at all sticky. Using a pizza wheel or a sharp knife, cut dough into 4-inch (10 cm) squares.

2. Spread 2 tsp (10 mL) almond filling in a strip along the center of each square. Brush one side of the square parallel to the filling with egg wash, then fold the opposite side over the filling, pressing the edges together to seal. Make 3 cuts on the folded side, almost but not quite to the seam side. Place bear claws at least 2 inches (5 cm) apart on prepared baking sheets and gently fan out the "toes" slightly. Repeat the process with the remaining dough.

3. Cover baking sheets with plastic wrap and refrigerate for up to 24 hours, or let rise in a warm, draft-free place for 2 hours or until about doubled in size. (If chilling first, let bear claws come to room temperature, then let rise.) Cover and refrigerate egg wash. Preheat oven to 400°F (200°C).

4. Brush bear claws with egg wash.

5. Bake one sheet at a time for 10 to 12 minutes or until golden brown. Remove from pan and let cool on a wire rack set over a baking sheet for 15 minutes, then drizzle with glaze.

> ### Chocolate Almond Bear Claws
> Use 1 tsp (5 mL) almond filling and 1 tsp (5 mL) chocolate chips per square.

Apricot and Pistachio Galettes

These pastries are like sweet, buttery, yeasty freeform tarts, and they're favorites at French *pâtisseries* and *boulangeries*. Once you've got your dough, they're easy to make.

Tips

It's very important to keep laminated dough cold so the butter layers stay intact. Use a marble pastry work surface, if possible, and work in a cool room. The dough should be at a warm room temperature only during the final rise.

Pearl sugar is available at baking supply shops or online.

1	recipe prepared Danish Pastry Dough (page 226)	1
	All-purpose flour	
12	fresh apricots, halved (or 24 canned apricot halves, drained)	12
½ cup	amaretto	125 mL
1	egg, lightly beaten with 1 tbsp (15 mL) water	1
¼ cup	heavy or whipping (35%) cream	60 mL
¼ cup	raw or turbinado sugar crystals or pearl sugar	60 mL
¼ cup	chopped roasted shelled pistachios	60 mL

1. Cut dough in half. Rewrap one half and return it to the refrigerator. Transfer the other half to a generously floured surface and dust very lightly with flour. Flour your hands and the rolling pin. Roll out dough into a 16-inch (40 cm) square. The dough should feel cold, firm and smooth all over, but not at all sticky. Using a pizza wheel or a sharp knife, cut dough into 4-inch (10 cm) squares. Place 2 inches (5 cm) apart on prepared baking sheet. Repeat the process with the remaining dough.

2. Cover baking sheet with plastic wrap and refrigerate for up to 24 hours, or let rise in a warm (72°F/22°C) place for 2 hours or until about doubled in height. (If chilling first, let galettes come to room temperature, then let rise.) Preheat oven to 400°F (200°C).

3. Meanwhile, in a bowl, combine apricots and amaretto; let stand for 30 minutes. Drain and pat apricots dry. Reserve amaretto for another use.

4. Brush each square with egg wash. Place 3 apricot halves, cut side down, in the center of each square. Brush apricots with cream and sprinkle with sugar and pistachios.

5. Bake for 8 minutes, then reduce the temperature to 350°F (180°C). Bake for 10 to 15 minutes or until golden brown. Remove from pan and let cool on a wire rack. Serve warm or at room temperature.

Flaky, Buttery Croissants

1	recipe prepared Danish Pastry Dough (page 226)	1
	All-purpose flour	
1	large egg, lightly beaten with 1 tbsp (15 mL) water	1

1. Cut dough in half. Rewrap one half and return to the refrigerator. Transfer the other half to a lightly floured surface and dust very lightly with flour. Lightly flour your hands and the rolling pin. Roll out dough into a 12-inch (30 cm) square. The dough should feel cold, firm and smooth all over, but not at all sticky. Using a pizza wheel or a sharp knife, cut dough into 3-inch (7.5 cm) squares.

2. Lift each square and gently press all around to stretch it to 3½ inches (8.5 cm). Starting at a corner, tightly roll each square into a crescent, stretching and pulling it as you go. Place croissants 2 inches (5 cm) apart on a prepared baking sheet, arranging them so that the pointed tip is visible. Repeat the process with the remaining dough.

3. Cover baking sheets with plastic wrap and refrigerate for up to 24 hours, or let rise in a warm (72°F/22°C) place for 2 hours or until about doubled in size. (If chilling first, let croissants come to room temperature, then let rise.) Preheat oven to 400°F (200°C).

4. Brush croissants with egg wash, being sure to seal tip of triangle down.

5. Bake one sheet at a time for 8 to 10 minutes or until golden brown. Remove from pan and let cool on a wire rack. Serve warm or let cool completely.

Tips

It's very important to keep laminated dough cold so the butter layers stay intact. Use a marble pastry work surface, if possible, and work in a cool room. The dough should be at a warm room temperature only during the final rise.

You can freeze formed but unbaked croissants for up to 3 months, layered with parchment paper in an airtight container. Transfer to baking sheets lined with parchment paper and let thaw overnight in the refrigerator before baking.

Almond Croissants

Place 1 tsp (5 mL) of Danish Almond Filling (page 286) in the center of each square and roll up, then proceed with the recipe.

Chocolate Croissants

Place 2 tsp (10 mL) chopped bittersweet or dark chocolate in the center of each square and roll up, then proceed with the recipe.

Ham and Cheese Croissants

Place 1 tsp (5 mL) each chopped ham and shredded Gruyère or Cheddar cheese in the center of each square and roll up, then proceed with the recipe.

Festive Breads

CELEBRATIONS CALL FOR special breads, and the holiday menus of cultures around the world feature traditional festive loafs, which are usually labor-intensive and filled with rich ingredients saved for special occasions. The bread machine can, at least, cut down on some of the labor as you prepare one of these classic recipes for your next holiday gathering:

- **Babka:** Polish and Russian immigrants to North America gloried in their Easter babkas, enriched yeast breads studded with dried fruit and nuts. Russian Mennonites in wheat farming communities still make a plainer babka, baked in a coffee can and drizzled with icing.

- **Limpa:** At Christmas, traditional Swedish households make "Dip-in-the-Pot-Soup." Hungry family members furtively dip pieces of limpa — a fennel-flavored rye bread — into the brothy soup while the lady of the house attends to the finishing touches on the smorgasbord, which will also feature this bread.

- **Lucia Crown:** This braided sweet bread, redolent with saffron, is shaped like the crown worn by the oldest daughter in the family on St. Lucia Day in Sweden.

- **Pan de los Muertos:** This Mexican bread, made for the Day of the Dead, November 2, has a soft, airy texture and a sweet flavor accented by anise and orange.

- **Pan Dolce or Pan d'Oro:** This Italian Christmas bread resembling a giant brioche is traditionally made in special paper molds. The rich dough, flavored with dried fruits plumped in fortified wine or brandy, rises high to a golden finish.

- **Povitica:** Commonly served at weddings and for Easter and Christmas, povitica is an Eastern European bread made of thin, strudel-like dough spread with a walnut or cream cheese filling, rolled up into a long cylinder, folded over itself and baked in a loaf pan.

Festive breads sometimes call for special decorative techniques, such as braiding the dough over a filling, as in the savory Sausage, Apple and Cheddar Braid (page 240) or the sweet Festive Almond Braid (page 248). The Lucia Crown (page 234) takes braiding a step further, as you join the ends of the braid together to form a circle, or crown, which you can accent with jewel-like candied cherries and small candles after the crown is baked.

Making the rich Classic Brioche (page 238) involves creating the traditional topknot before baking. The unique look of Saucisson en Brioche (page 241) comes from wrapping a savory sausage in the brioche dough before baking it.

The ingredients, the rich culinary heritage and the care involved in making these breads dictate that they should also be beautifully presented. Cake supply shops often carry decorative paper or cardboard containers, labels you can customize and other signature touches to make these gifts from your kitchen look as special as they taste.

Lucia Crown

This braided tea ring is
served in Swedish households
on December 13 — St. Lucia
Day — and decorated with
small candles, a symbol of
light on one of the darkest
days of the year.

1 cup	light (5%) or half-and-half (10%) cream	250 mL
¼ cup	water	60 mL
½ cup	granulated sugar	125 mL
½ cup	butter, softened	125 mL
½ tsp	salt	2 mL
½ tsp	powdered saffron	2 mL
1	large egg, beaten	1
4 cups	all-purpose flour	1 L
2 tsp	instant or bread machine yeast	10 mL

Egg Wash

1	large egg, beaten	1

Glaze

¼ cup	Vanilla Glaze (page 291) or Orange Glaze (variation, page 291)	60 mL

Decoration

	Red and green candied cherries	
6	small candles	6

1. In a small saucepan, scald cream and water over medium-high heat until small bubbles form around the edges. Remove from heat and stir in sugar and butter. Transfer to the bread pan and let cool to lukewarm (between 86°F and 95°F/30°C and 35°C).

2. Add salt, saffron and egg to the bread pan. Spoon flour on top of liquid. Add yeast.

3. Select the Dough cycle and press Start.

4. When the cycle is finished, transfer dough to a floured surface and punch down gently. Divide dough into thirds. Roll each third into a 24-inch (60 cm) rope. Lay the three ropes out parallel to each other on a floured surface so that they are very close but not touching. Braid ropes together snugly. Form braid into a circle, pinching the ends together. Place on prepared baking sheet. Cover with a clean towel and let rise in a warm, draft-free place for 45 minutes. Meanwhile, preheat oven to 375°F (190°C).

Tip

If your dough does not form a ball during the first few minutes of kneading, do one of two things: if the dough looks dry and crumbly, add 1 tbsp (15 mL) water at 1-minute intervals until the dough forms a ball; if the dough looks wet, add 1 tbsp (15 mL) bread flour at 1-minute intervals until the dough forms a ball.

5. *Egg Wash:* Brush the crown with egg wash.

6. Bake for 35 to 40 minutes or until risen and golden and an instant-read thermometer inserted in the center registers 190°F (90°C). Remove from pan and let cool on a wire rack set over a baking sheet for 1 hour.

7. *Glaze and Decoration:* Brush or drizzle with glaze and decorate with cherries. Let set for 30 minutes before serving. Make 6 holes in the braid and insert the candles. To serve, light the candles, then blow them out before slicing and serving.

Iced Almond and Cherry Babka

1½ lb (750 g)

¾ cup	milk	175 mL
¼ cup	granulated sugar	60 mL
3 tbsp	unsalted butter, softened	45 mL
1¼ tsp	salt	6 mL
1	large egg, beaten	1
1	large egg yolk, beaten	1
1 tsp	almond extract	5 mL
2½ cups	all-purpose flour	625 mL
1½ tsp	instant or bread machine yeast	7 mL
½ cup	dried cherries	125 mL
½ cup	candied cherries, cut in half	125 mL
3 tbsp	slivered almonds	45 mL
Glaze		
¼ cup	Almond Glaze (variation, page 291)	60 mL

2 lb (1 kg)

¾ cup	milk	175 mL
⅓ cup	granulated sugar	75 mL
¼ cup	unsalted butter, softened	60 mL
1½ tsp	salt	7 mL
2	large eggs, beaten	2
2 tsp	almond extract	10 mL
3 cups	all-purpose flour	750 mL
1½ tsp	instant or bread machine yeast	7 mL
¾ cup	dried cherries	175 mL
¾ cup	candied cherries, cut in half	175 mL
¼ cup	slivered almonds	60 mL
Glaze		
½ cup	Almond Glaze (variation, page 291)	125 mL

1. In a small saucepan, scald milk over medium-high heat until small bubbles form around the edges. Remove from heat and stir in sugar and butter. Transfer to the bread pan and let cool to lukewarm (between 86°F and 95°F/30°C and 35°C).

2. Add salt, eggs and almond extract to the bread pan. Spoon flour on top of liquid. Add yeast.

3. Select the Dough cycle and press Start.

If your dough does not form a ball during the first few minutes of kneading, do one of two things: if the dough looks dry and crumbly, add 1 tbsp (15 mL) water at 1-minute intervals until the dough forms a ball; if the dough looks wet, add 1 tbsp (15 mL) all-purpose flour at 1-minute intervals until the dough forms a ball.

If desired, you can dust the glazed babka with sanding sugar, available at cake supply stores, for a glistening effect.

4. When the cycle is finished, transfer dough to a floured surface and punch down gently. Flatten dough and sprinkle half each of the dried cherries, candied cherries and almonds over one side. Fold opposite half over and sprinkle with remaining dried cherries, candied cherries and almonds. Knead gently to evenly distribute through the dough. Let rest for 5 minutes. Form dough into a round (for the coffee can or brioche mold) or ring (for the Bundt or kugelhopf pan). Place in prepared pan. Cover with plastic wrap and let rise in a warm, draft-free place for 45 minutes. Meanwhile, preheat oven to 350°F (180°C).

5. Remove plastic wrap. Bake (see chart, below) until risen and browned and an instant-read thermometer inserted in the center registers 190°F (90°C). Let cool in pan on a wire rack set over a baking sheet for 5 minutes, then transfer to the rack and let cool for 30 to 60 minutes or until cool to the touch.

6. *Glaze:* Pour glaze over the surface of the babka so that the top is coated and the glaze drips down the sides. Let set for 30 minutes before slicing.

Dough Size	Pan	Baking Time
1½ lb (750 g)	Can or fluted brioche pan	40 to 45 minutes
	Bundt or kugelhopf pan	30 to 35 minutes
2 lb (1 kg)	Can or fluted brioche pan	45 to 50 minutes
	Bundt or kugelhopf pan	35 to 40 minutes

Classic Brioche

With this classic recipe,
your brioche will rival that
of a fine Parisian patisserie.
The egg wash gives the
finished loaf a dark,
glossy sheen.

Tip

Ideally, the buttermilk and
water should be between
86°F and 95°F (30°C and
35°C), the temperature
range in which yeast is most
active. Warm them in the
microwave or in a saucepan
on the stove, and check the
temperature with an instant-
read thermometer.

1 lb (500 g)

4 tsp	granulated sugar	20 mL
1 tsp	salt	5 mL
2	large eggs, beaten	2
1/3 cup	unsalted butter, softened	75 mL
1/4 cup	lukewarm buttermilk (see tip, at left)	60 mL
2 tbsp	lukewarm water	30 mL
2 cups	bread flour	500 mL
3/4 tsp	instant or bread machine yeast	3 mL

Egg Wash

1	large egg, beaten with 1 tbsp (15 mL) water	1

1 1/2 lb (750 g)

2 tbsp	granulated sugar	30 mL
1 1/2 tsp	salt	7 mL
2	large eggs, beaten	2
1/2 cup	unsalted butter, softened	125 mL
1/3 cup	lukewarm buttermilk (see tip, at left)	75 mL
3 tbsp	lukewarm water	45 mL
3 cups	bread flour	750 mL
1 1/2 tsp	instant or bread machine yeast	7 mL

Egg Wash

1	large egg, beaten with 1 tbsp (15 mL) water	1

2 lb (1 kg)

3 tbsp	granulated sugar	45 mL
2 tsp	salt	10 mL
3	large eggs, beaten	3
2/3 cup	unsalted butter, softened	150 mL
1/2 cup	lukewarm buttermilk (see tip, at left)	125 mL
1/4 cup	lukewarm water	60 mL
4 cups	bread flour	1 L
1 1/2 tsp	instant or bread machine yeast	7 mL

Egg Wash

1	large egg, beaten with 1 tbsp (15 mL) water	1

When making the smallest loaf allowed by your machine, check the dough a few minutes after kneading starts to make sure the ingredients are incorporated. You may need to help the machine along by using a rubber spatula to scrape the corners of the pan.

Rich, eggy breads like this one make great French toast and airy bread puddings.

3 lb (1.5 kg)

¼ cup	granulated sugar	60 mL
1½ tsp	salt	7 mL
4	large eggs, beaten	4
½ cup	unsalted butter, softened	125 mL
⅔ cup	lukewarm buttermilk (see tip, page 238)	150 mL
⅓ cup	lukewarm water	75 mL
4½ cups	bread flour	1.125 L
1¾ tsp	instant or bread machine yeast	8 mL

Egg Wash

1	large egg, beaten with 1 tbsp (15 mL) water	1

1. Add sugar, salt, eggs, butter, buttermilk and water to the bread pan. Spoon flour on top of liquid. Add yeast.

2. Select the Dough cycle and press Start.

3. When the cycle is finished, transfer dough to a floured surface and punch down gently. Cut off about ¼ cup (60 mL) of the dough for the 1-lb (500 g) and 1½-lb (750 g) loaves and ½ cup (125 mL) for the 2-lb (1 kg) and 3-lb (1.5 kg) loaves. Roll it into a ball and set aside. Form the remaining dough into a large ball, pinching seams tightly at the bottom. Place seam side down in prepared pan. Dust your thumb with flour and make a 1-inch (2.5 cm) indentation in the top of the large ball. Place the small ball in the indentation. Cover with plastic wrap and let rise in a warm, draft-free place for 30 minutes. Meanwhile, preheat oven to 350°F (180°C).

4. *Egg Wash:* Brush brioche with egg wash, being careful not to dislodge the crown.

5. Bake (see chart, below) until browned and risen and an instant-read thermometer inserted in the center registers 190°F (90°C). Let cool in pan on a wire rack for 15 minutes, then transfer to the rack to cool completely.

Dough Size	Fluted Brioche Pan	Baking Time
1 lb (500 g)	7-inch (18 cm)	30 to 35 minutes
1½ lb (750 g)	8-inch (20 cm)	35 to 40 minutes
2 lb (1 kg)	9-inch (23 cm)	40 to 50 minutes
	Two 7-inch (18 cm)	30 to 35 minutes
3 lb (1.5 kg)	10-inch (25 cm)	50 to 60 minutes
	Two 8-inch (20 cm)	35 to 40 minutes

Sausage, Apple and Cheddar Braid

Makes 2 braids, to serve 12

Equipment
- Rolling pin
- Large baking sheet, lined with parchment paper

Whether you make it for a buffet, a festive brunch or a casual supper, this braid looks like you went to a lot more trouble than you did.

Tip

If you don't have dried herb stuffing mix, substitute toasted coarse bread crumbs and 1½ tsp (7 mL) of your favorite dried herb (or a mixture).

1 lb	breakfast-style or Italian pork or turkey sausage (bulk or casings removed)	500 g
1	large onion, chopped	1
2	large Granny Smith apples, peeled and chopped	2
1	large egg, beaten	1
1 lb	sharp (old) Cheddar cheese, cut into 1-inch (2.5 cm) cubes	500 g
¾ cup	dried herb stuffing mix	175 mL
	Salt and freshly ground black pepper	
1½ lb	recipe Classic Brioche dough (page 238)	750 g

Egg Wash

| 1 | large egg, beaten with 1 tbsp (15 mL) water | 1 |

1. In a large skillet over medium-high heat, cook sausage and onion, breaking sausage up with a spoon, for 8 minutes or until sausage is no longer pink. Remove from heat and drain off fat. Transfer to a bowl and stir in apples, egg, cheese and herb stuffing until well combined. Season to taste with salt and pepper. Let cool to room temperature.

2. Place dough on a floured surface and punch down gently. Divide dough in half. Dust lightly with flour and roll out each half into a 14- by 10-inch (35 by 25 cm) rectangle, with a short edge facing you.

3. Spoon half the sausage mixture down the center of each rectangle. Fold top and bottom edges of pastry over filling. Using a paring knife, cut the pastry on each side of the filling into ½-inch (1 cm) wide diagonal strips angled to the top of the rectangle. Starting at the top, fold the strips over the filling, alternating sides, to create a braided effect. Place braids at least 4 inches (10 cm) apart on prepared baking sheet. Cover with clean towels and let rise in a warm, draft-free place for 15 to 20 minutes or until slightly risen. Meanwhile, preheat oven to 350°F (180°C).

4. *Egg Wash:* Brush braids with egg wash.

5. Bake for about 30 minutes or until dough is risen and browned and filling is hot. Let cool on pan on a wire rack for 5 minutes, then slice and serve warm.

Saucisson en Brioche

This classic French appetizer usually features garlic sausage or sausage flavored with truffles and pistachios. Hearty winter fare, it's wonderful for a holiday buffet table or when you have friends over to watch the big game. Serve slices of it with Dijon mustard or whatever condiment fits the sausage you choose.

2 lbs	cooked or smoked garlic sausage or other sausage (about 2 inches/5 cm in diameter)	1 kg
1½ lb	recipe Classic Brioche dough (page 238)	750 g
1	large egg, beaten	1

Egg Wash

1	large egg, beaten with 1 tbsp (15 mL) water	1

1. Trim ends of sausage and remove any skin. Cut into two 10-inch (25 cm) lengths.

2. Place dough on a floured surface and punch down gently. Divide dough in half. Dust lightly with flour and roll out each half into a 12- by 10-inch (30 by 25 cm) rectangle, with a short edge facing you.

3. Brush egg down the center of each rectangle. Brush sausage with egg. Place one length of sausage down the center of each rectangle. Fold top and bottom edges of pastry over sausage. Fold sides over and pinch together. Place brioches, seam side down, at least 3 inches (7.5 cm) apart on prepared baking sheet. Cover with clean towels and let rise in a warm, draft-free place for 20 minutes. Meanwhile, preheat oven to 350°F (180°C).

4. *Egg Wash:* Brush brioches with egg wash.

5. Bake for about 25 minutes or until risen and browned and sausage is hot. Remove from pan and let cool on a wire rack. Serve warm or let cool completely. Cut into thick slices.

Pan Dolce

Makes 1 large loaf, to serve 12

If you like Italian panettone, that domed bread in the red package usually available at Christmastime, you'll love homemade pan dolce, or "sweet bread," from Liguria. Bejeweled with dried fruits soaked in heady spirits, this festive bread with a feathery crumb can be baked in a large, clean coffee can or a large brioche pan, or on coated panettone baking paper. If you can find a metal *pan d'oro* pan, which is narrower and more sharply fluted than a brioche pan, go for it.

½ cup	brandy, cognac, sherry or other fortified wine	125 mL
2 cups	mixed dried fruit (see tip, at right), snipped into ½-inch (1 cm) pieces	500 mL
1½ lb	recipe Classic Brioche dough (page 238)	750 g
2 cups	hot water	500 mL
Glaze		
¼ cup	Almond Glaze (variation, page 291)	60 mL
	Colored sprinkles	

1. In a small saucepan over low heat, heat brandy until just warm, about 100°F (38°C). Remove from heat and add dried fruit; let stand for 30 minutes or until fruit is plump. Drain, reserving brandy for another use, if desired, and pat fruit dry.

2. Place dough on a floured surface and dust very lightly with flour. Lightly flour your hands and the rolling pin. Working the dough as little as possible and adding just enough flour as necessary to prevent sticking, roll out into a 12- by 6-inch (30 by 15 cm) oval. Lightly flour any sticky places on the dough. The dough should feel soft and smooth all over, like a baby's skin, but not at all sticky.

3. Arrange one-quarter of the fruit filling on the upper half of the dough oval and press into the dough with your hands. Fold the other half over the filling. Turn the dough a quarter turn. Working the dough as little as possible and adding flour as necessary, roll out the dough into an oval. Arrange another quarter of the fruit on the upper half of the oval and press into the dough with your hands. Fold the other half over the filling. Turn the dough a quarter turn. Working the dough as little as possible and adding flour as necessary, roll out the dough into an oval. Repeat this process twice more, sprinkling with flour as necessary, until all of the fruit has been incorporated into the dough. Form the dough into a ball, pinching seams tightly at the bottom. Place seam side down in the prepared can or pan, or on the paper. Cover with a clean towel and let rise in a warm, draft-free place for 40 minutes.

For the mixed dried fruit, you can use apricots, apples, cherries, cranberries, dates, figs and/or raisins. Use kitchen shears to snip larger fruit into small pieces.

4. Meanwhile, preheat oven to 425°F (220°C). Place baking stone on the middle rack and broiler pan on the bottom rack.

5. Add hot water to the broiler pan. Place can, pan or paper on baking stone. Bake for 10 minutes, then reduce the temperature to 350°F (180°C). Bake for 35 to 40 minutes or until risen and browned and an instant-read thermometer inserted in the center registers at least 190°F (90°C). Let cool in pan on a wire rack set over a baking sheet.

6. *Glaze:* When cool, remove loaf from the can or pan (but leave on the paper) and place on the rack. Drizzle the top of the loaf with glaze so that it drips down the sides. Sprinkle with colored sprinkles. Let set for 30 minutes before slicing.

Pan de los Muertos

Although this fragrant bread is usually served on the Day of the Dead in Mexico, you don't have to wait until November 2 to enjoy it. It's delicious on its own, as part of a festive brunch buffet or for an elegant tea. You can bake it completely in the machine, though for the traditional shape, it's best to bake it in the oven (see box, opposite).

¼ cup	milk	60 mL
¼ cup	water	60 mL
¼ cup	granulated sugar	60 mL
¼ cup	unsalted butter	60 mL
1 tbsp	grated orange zest	15 mL
2 tsp	anise seeds	10 mL
½ tsp	salt	2 mL
2	large eggs, beaten	2
3 cups	all-purpose flour	750 mL
1½ tsp	instant or bread machine yeast	7 mL

Orange Glaze

¼ cup	granulated sugar	60 mL
1 tbsp	grated orange zest	15 mL
¼ cup	freshly squeezed orange juice	60 mL
	Pearl sugar	

1. In a small saucepan, scald milk and water over medium-high heat until small bubbles form around the edges. Remove from heat and stir in sugar and butter. Transfer to the bread pan and let cool to lukewarm (between 86°F and 95°F/30°C and 35°C).

2. Add orange zest, anise seeds, salt and eggs to the bread pan. Spoon flour on top of eggs. Add yeast.

3. Select the Basic/White cycle and press Start. When the cycle is finished, transfer the loaf to a wire rack set over a baking sheet and let cool for 1 hour.

4. *Glaze:* In a small saucepan, combine sugar, orange zest and orange juice. Bring to a boil over medium heat; boil for 2 minutes. Remove from heat and let cool.

5. Lightly brush loaf with glaze and sprinkle with pearl sugar. Let set for 30 minutes before slicing.

Tips

Pearl sugar is available at baking supply shops or online.

If your dough does not form a ball during the first few minutes of kneading, do one of two things: if the dough looks dry and crumbly, add 1 tbsp (15 mL) water at 1-minute intervals until the dough forms a ball; if the dough looks wet, add 1 tbsp (15 mL) all-purpose flour at 1-minute intervals until the dough forms a ball.

Oven-Baked Pan de los Muertos

Prepare the recipe through step 2, then select the Dough cycle and press Start. Line a large baking sheet with parchment paper. When the cycle is finished, transfer dough to a floured surface and punch down gently. Cut off about 1/4 cup (60 mL) of the dough, roll it into a ball and set aside. Form the remaining dough into a round. Place on prepared baking sheet. Dust your thumb with flour and make a 1-inch (2 cm) indentation in the top of the round. Place the ball of dough in the indentation. Cover with a clean towel and let rise for 15 minutes. Meanwhile, preheat oven to 350°F (180°C). Bake for 35 to 40 minutes or until risen and browned and an instant-read thermometer inserted in the center registers 190°F (90°C). Remove from pan and let cool on a wire rack set over a baking sheet for 1 hour. Prepare the glaze as in step 4. Lightly brush loaf with glaze and sprinkle with pearl sugar. Let cool completely.

Swedish Limpa Bread

Makes 1 loaf

Tekla Erikson emigrated from Vastmanland, Sweden, to the wheat country of Lindsborg, Kansas, in 1907, bringing with her a heritage of family recipes. Her recipe for limpa bread, which I've adapted for the bread machine, was a fixture of her Christmas smorgasbord. I've added the orange zest. Soft-textured and fragrant, with notes of dark caramel, this medium-dark bread slices well for open-faced sandwiches, perfect for a buffet gathering. You can bake it in the bread machine, but for the traditional shape, make the dough in the machine, then bake it in the oven (see box, opposite).

Tip

Ideally, the water should be between 86°F and 95°F (30°C and 35°C), the temperature range in which yeast is most active. Warm it in the microwave or in a saucepan on the stove, and check the temperature with an instant-read thermometer.

1 lb (500 g)

2 tsp	grated orange zest	10 mL
1 tsp	packed brown sugar	5 mL
1/2 tsp	salt	2 mL
3/4 cup	lukewarm water (see tip, at left)	175 mL
2 tbsp	light (fancy) molasses	30 mL
2 tbsp	sorghum or dark corn syrup	30 mL
2 tsp	vegetable oil	10 mL
2 cups	all-purpose flour	500 mL
1/4 cup	rye flour	60 mL
1/2 tsp	fennel seeds	2 mL
1 1/2 tsp	instant or bread machine yeast	7 mL

Topping

1 tbsp	unsalted butter, melted	15 mL

1 1/2 lb (750 g

1 tbsp	grated orange zest	15 mL
1 1/2 tsp	packed brown sugar	7 mL
2 tsp	salt	10 mL
3/4 cup + 2 tbsp	lukewarm water (see tip, at left)	205 mL
3 tbsp	light (fancy) molasses	45 mL
3 tbsp	sorghum or dark corn syrup	45 mL
1 tbsp	vegetable oil	15 mL
2 2/3 cups	all-purpose flour	650 mL
1/3 cup	rye flour	75 mL
3/4 tsp	fennel seeds	3 mL
2 tsp	instant or bread machine yeast	10 mL

Topping

1 tbsp	unsalted butter, melted	15 mL

2 lb (1 kg)

1 1/2 tbsp	grated orange zest	22 mL
2 tsp	packed brown sugar	10 mL
2 1/2 tsp	salt	12 mL
1 cup + 3 tbsp	lukewarm water (see tip, at left)	295 mL
1/4 cup	light (fancy) molasses	60 mL
1/4 cup	sorghum or dark corn syrup	60 mL
1 1/2 tbsp	vegetable oil	22 mL
3 1/2 cups	all-purpose flour	875 mL
1/2 cup	rye flour	125 mL
2 tsp	fennel seeds	10 mL
2 tsp	instant or bread machine yeast	10 mL

Sorghum syrup is available in well-stocked supermarkets and health food stores.

If your dough does not form a ball during the first few minutes of kneading, do one of two things: if the dough looks dry and crumbly, add 1 tbsp (15 mL) water at 1-minute intervals until the dough forms a ball; if the dough looks wet, add 1 tbsp (15 mL) all-purpose flour at 1-minute intervals until the dough forms a ball.

Topping

1 tbsp	unsalted butter, melted	15 mL

3 lb (1.5 kg)

2 tbsp	grated orange zest	30 mL
1 tbsp	packed brown sugar	15 mL
1 tbsp	salt	15 mL
1²⁄₃ cups	lukewarm water (see tip, page 246)	400 mL
¹⁄₃ cup	light (fancy) molasses	75 mL
¹⁄₃ cup	sorghum or dark corn syrup	75 mL
2 tbsp	vegetable oil	30 mL
4¹⁄₂ cups	all-purpose flour	1.125 L
1 cup	rye flour	250 mL
1 tbsp	fennel seeds	15 mL
1³⁄₄ tsp	instant or bread machine yeast	8 mL

Topping

2 tbsp	unsalted butter, melted	30 mL

1. Add orange zest, brown sugar, salt, water, molasses, sorghum syrup and oil to the bread pan. Spoon all-purpose flour and rye flour on top of liquid. Add fennel seeds and yeast.

2. Select the Sweet cycle and the Light Crust setting and press Start.

3. *Topping:* When the cycle is finished, let bread cool in pan on a wire rack for 5 minutes. Transfer loaf to rack and let cool completely. Brush top with melted butter.

Oven-Baked Swedish Limpa Bread

Prepare the recipe through step 1, then select the Dough cycle and press Start. Line a large baking sheet with parchment paper. When the cycle is finished, transfer dough to a floured surface and punch down gently. Form dough into an oblong loaf (see chart, below) and place on prepared baking sheet. Cover with a clean towel and let rise for 30 minutes. Meanwhile, preheat oven to 350°F (180°C). Using a serrated knife, cut 5 deep diagonal slashes across top of loaf. Bake until risen and browned and an instant-read thermometer inserted in the center registers 190°F (90°C). Remove from pan and let cool on a wire rack. Brush top of loaf with melted butter.

Dough	Loaf Size	Baking Time
1 lb (500 g)	10 inches (25 cm) long	35 to 40 minutes
1¹⁄₂ lb (750 g)	12 inches (30 cm) long	40 to 45 minutes
2 lb (1 kg)	14 inches (35 cm) long	45 to 50 minutes
3 lb (1.5 kg)	16 inches (40 cm) long	50 to 55 minutes

Festive Almond Braid

These pastries look like
you apprenticed in a
fancy bakery, but they're
relatively simple. With
dark roast coffee and fresh
fruit, they make a breakfast
worth getting up for.

Tip
Ideally, the water and milk
should be between 86°F and
95°F (30°C and 35°C), the
temperature range in which
yeast is most active. Warm
them in the microwave or in
a saucepan on the stove, and
check the temperature with
an instant-read thermometer.

¼ cup	granulated sugar	60 mL
1 tsp	salt	5 mL
1	large egg, beaten	1
½ cup	lukewarm water (see tip, at left)	125 mL
¼ cup	lukewarm milk	60 mL
¼ cup	unsalted butter, softened	60 mL
3 cups	all-purpose flour	750 mL
2½ tsp	instant or bread machine yeast	12 mL

Filling
1¾ cups	Danish Almond Filling (page 286)	425 mL

Topping
¼ cup	Almond Glaze (variation, page 291)	60 mL
½ cup	toasted sliced almonds	125 mL

1. Add sugar, salt, egg, water, milk and butter to the bread pan. Spoon flour on top of liquid. Add yeast.

2. Select the Dough cycle and press Start.

3. When the cycle is finished, transfer dough to a floured surface and punch down gently. Divide dough in half. Dust lightly with flour and roll out each half into a 14- by 10-inch (35 by 25 cm) rectangle, with a short edge facing you.

4. *Filling:* Spoon half the filling down the center of each rectangle. Fold top and bottom edges of pastry over filling. Using a paring knife, cut the pastry on each side of the filling into ½-inch (1 cm) wide diagonal strips angled to the top of the rectangle. Starting at the top, fold the strips over the filling, alternating sides, to create a braided effect. Place braids at least 4 inches (10 cm) apart on prepared baking sheet. Cover with clean towels and let rise in a warm, draft-free place for 30 minutes. Meanwhile, preheat oven to 350°F (180°C).

Tips

If your dough does not form a ball during the first few minutes of kneading, do one of two things: if the dough looks dry and crumbly, add 1 tbsp (15 mL) water at 1-minute intervals until the dough forms a ball; if the dough looks wet, add 1 tbsp (15 mL) all-purpose flour at 1-minute intervals until the dough forms a ball.

You can also use the 1½-lb (750 g) recipe for Classic Brioche dough (page 238) to make these braids.

Instead of the Danish Almond Filling, you can use a 1-lb (500 g) container of good-quality prepared almond paste, pulsed in the food processor.

5. Bake for 25 to 30 minutes or until risen and browned. Remove from pan and let cool on a wire rack set over a baking sheet for 30 to 60 minutes or until cool to the touch.

6. *Topping:* Lightly brush braids with glaze and sprinkle with almonds. Let set for 30 minutes before slicing.

> ### Polish Poppy Seed Braid
> Use 1⅓ cups (325 mL) Poppy Seed Filling (page 285) in place of the Danish Almond Filling and use Lemon Glaze (variation, page 291) instead of the Almond Glaze. Sprinkle glazed braids with poppy seeds instead of almonds.

Slavic Nut Roll

Equipment
- Bread machine with a 2-lb (1 kg) capacity
- Rolling pin
- 2 large baking sheets, lined with parchment paper

Also known as povitica, meaning "swaddled" in Croatian, this festive pastry is like a soft strudel, and it's the star in an Eastern European breakfast that includes eggs and sausage. In the old days, families made a large batch of dough, covered a large round table with a clean bed sheet and dumped the dough in the center of the sheet. Several people at a time reached their arms under the dough and gently stretched it until it was paper thin. This easier, more streamlined method still produces a sumptuous strudel.

1½ tbsp	granulated sugar	22 mL
1 tsp	salt	5 mL
2	large eggs, beaten	2
½ cup	unsalted butter, softened	125 mL
½ cup	lukewarm sour cream (see tip, at right)	125 mL
¼ cup	lukewarm milk	60 mL
3¼ cups	all-purpose flour	800 mL
2½ tsp	instant or bread machine yeast	12 mL

Walnut Filling

2 cups	finely ground walnuts	500 mL
½ cup	granulated sugar	125 mL
1 tsp	vanilla extract or vanilla, butter and nut extract	5 mL

Egg Wash

1	large egg white, beaten with 1 tbsp (15 mL) water	1

1. Add sugar, salt, eggs, butter, sour cream and milk to the bread pan. Spoon flour on top of liquid. Add yeast.

2. Select the Dough cycle and press Start.

3. When the cycle is finished, transfer dough to a floured surface and punch down gently. Divide in half. Dust lightly with flour and roll out each half into a 16- by 8-inch (40 by 20 cm) rectangle, with a long edge closest to you.

4. *Filling:* In a bowl, combine walnuts, sugar and vanilla. Sprinkle half the filling over each rectangle, leaving a 1-inch (2.5 cm) perimeter. Lightly brush the long edge farthest from you with water. Starting with the long edge closest to you, roll up like a jelly roll. Pinch the seam to seal. Pinch ends and tuck them under. Bend into a horseshoe shape and transfer to prepared baking sheets (or place straight, if desired). Cover with clean towels and let rise in a warm, draft-free place for 30 minutes. Meanwhile, preheat oven to 350°F (180°C).

5. *Egg Wash:* Brush nut rolls with egg wash.

6. Bake one sheet at a time for 30 to 35 minutes or until risen and browned and filling is hot. Remove from pan and let cool on a wire rack.

Tips

Ideally, the sour cream and milk should be between 86°F and 95°F (30°C and 35°C), the temperature range in which yeast is most active. Warm them in the microwave or in a saucepan on the stove, and check the temperature with an instant-read thermometer.

If your dough does not form a ball during the first few minutes of kneading, do one of two things: if the dough looks dry and crumbly, add 1 tbsp (15 mL) water at 1-minute intervals until the dough forms a ball; if the dough looks wet, add 1 tbsp (15 mL) all-purpose flour at 1-minute intervals until the dough forms a ball.

Sweet Cheese Povitica

Use 2½ cups (625 mL) Cottage Cheese Filling (page 289) instead of the walnut filling.

Hungarian Apple Strudel

For the filling, combine 2 cups (500 mL) finely chopped apple and ⅔ cup (150 mL) Honey Spice Applesauce (page 283); use in place of the walnut filling. Do not form rolls into a horseshoe shape.

Savory Sweet Potato and Red Onion Strudel

1½ tbsp	granulated sugar	22 mL
1 tsp	salt	5 mL
2	large eggs, beaten	2
½ cup	unsalted butter, softened	125 mL
½ cup	lukewarm sour cream (see tip, at right)	125 mL
¼ cup	lukewarm milk	60 mL
3¼ cups	all-purpose flour	800 mL
2½ tsp	instant or bread machine yeast	12 mL

Sweet Potato and Red Onion Filling

2	large sweet potatoes, peeled and cut into ½-inch (1 cm) pieces	2
1	large red onion, cut into ½-inch (1 cm) pieces	1
2 tbsp	olive oil	30 mL
⅔ cup	freshly grated Parmesan cheese	150 mL
	Salt and freshly ground black pepper	

Topping

1	large egg yolk	1
2 tbsp	heavy or whipping (35%) cream	30 mL
¼ cup	freshly grated Parmesan cheese	60 mL

1. Add sugar, salt, eggs, butter, sour cream and milk to the bread pan. Spoon flour on top of liquid. Add yeast.

2. Select the Dough cycle and press Start.

3. *Filling:* Preheat oven to 350°F (180°C). In a bowl, combine sweet potatoes and red onion. Add oil and toss to coat. Spread in a single layer on a large baking sheet. Bake for about 35 minutes or until sweet potatoes are fork-tender. Return to the bowl, toss with cheese and season to taste with salt and pepper. Let cool.

4. When the cycle is finished, transfer dough to a floured surface and punch down gently. Divide in half. Dust lightly with flour and roll out each half into a 16- by 8-inch (40 by 20 cm) rectangle, with a long edge closest to you.

5. Sprinkle half the filling over each rectangle, leaving a 1-inch (2.5 cm) perimeter. Lightly brush the long edge farthest from you with water. Starting with the long edge closest to you, roll up like a jelly roll. Pinch the seam to seal. Pinch ends and tuck them under. Bend into a horseshoe shape and transfer to prepared baking sheets (or place straight, if desired). Cover with clean towels and let rise in a warm, draft-free place for 45 minutes. Meanwhile, preheat oven to 350°F (180°C).

6. *Topping*: In a small bowl, beat together egg yolk and cream. Brush over strudel. Sprinkle with cheese.

7. Bake one sheet at a time for 40 to 45 minutes or until risen and browned and filling is hot. Let cool for 10 minutes on pan on a wire rack before slicing.

Gluten-Free
Breads

GLUTEN, THE PROTEIN in wheat and other cereal grains, can be a problem for those with celiac disease or food allergies. Gluten forms the strong structure that traps the gases released by yeast, allowing bread to rise. So trying to approximate the crust, crumb and interior structure of wheat bread without the gluten inherent in wheat flour takes some doing. But family and friends who are gluten-intolerant will be glad you made the effort.

Wheat, rye and oat flours also have a reliably mellow flavor and pale color. For a successful gluten-free dough, you need an assortment of gluten-free flours, which will work together to approximate the taste, color and texture of wheat bread. Most gluten-free yeast breads use rice flour as a base and add potato starch, tapioca flour, corn flour and/or cornstarch for softness. Other flours, such as buckwheat, chickpea (garbanzo bean), millet and sorghum, add flavor, color and texture. Xanthan gum, which is made from the fermentation of corn sugar, provides a structure similar to that of dough made with gluten. Eggs, vinegar, sugar and applesauce or pumpkin purée soften and round out the flavor of the dough.

You can find gluten-free flours and xanthan gum in the specialty baking section of the grocery or health food store, or online at www.bobsredmill.com or www.kingarthurflour.com.

For some people who are gluten-intolerant, even the tiniest speck of gluten can be a problem, so make sure all ingredients you put in the dough are gluten-free. Read the labels of manufactured products to make sure nothing has been processed in a facility that also processes gluten. If you also make wheat-based doughs, run your bowls, measuring cups, whisk and so on through the dishwasher again before making a gluten-free dough. Wash the bread machine pan and paddle very thoroughly, being sure to clean all gluten traces from the creases. Because some people with gluten intolerance are also allergic to dairy products, eggs, soy and/or nuts, each of the recipes in this chapter offers alternatives for these ingredients.

Gluten-free flours and xanthan gum mix better in the bread machine if they're whisked together in a bowl before they're added to the bread pan. You should also be aware that the dough is unique — at first, it resembles a very wet batter, then it thickens to the consistency of brownie batter. The raw dough doesn't taste like a yeast bread dough, but magically, during baking, it develops into bread with a moist and tender crumb, a browned crust and a mellow, yeasty flavor.

Because gluten-free doughs do not require kneading to develop structure, they do best with a shorter time in the bread machine — about $1\frac{1}{2}$ hours for a full mixing and baking cycle (compared to 3 hours or more for wheat bread). Newer bread machines, such as the Breadman Ultimate and Cuisinart Convection, have a Gluten-Free cycle, which produces fabulously light and airy bread. If your machine does not have a gluten-free cycle, consult your manual and choose the shortest cycle, perhaps a Rapid or Express cycle that takes $1\frac{1}{2}$ hours or less from start to finish.

Gluten-Free Flours

Flour	Color	Flavor
Amaranth flour	Pale yellow	Mild
Buckwheat flour	Medium brown	Strong
Chickpea (garbanzo bean) flour	Tan	Strong
Chestnut flour	Pale brown	Strong
Corn flour	White	Very mild
Fava bean flour	Very pale green	Mild
Millet flour	Pale yellow	Mild
Quinoa flour	Beige	Medium
Rice flour (glutinous or brown)	Beige	Very mild
Sorghum (milo) flour	Beige	Mild
Soy flour	Pale yellow	Bean sprouts
Tapioca flour	White	Very mild
Teff flour	Medium brown	Earthy

Gluten-free breads generally taste best the day they're made. If you're not going to eat it right away, it's best to freeze the bread as soon as it's cooled. Wrap slices or a whole loaf in plastic wrap, then place in a freezer bag or airtight container and freeze for up to 1 month.

Grinding Your Own Gluten-Free Flour

Flours made from dried beans or tiny grains such as millet taste best when freshly ground. You don't need a grain mill to grind small amounts of these flours — although you can use one — just a clean, sturdy coffee grinder. Buy the beans or grains in bulk at a health food store, then add them to the coffee grinder in small batches, about 2 tbsp (30 mL) at a time.

Try grinding your own flour from these beans and grains:

- Dried amaranth
- Dried fava beans
- Dried millet
- Dried quinoa
- Dried soy beans
- Dried white or dark teff

An electric coffee grinder or grain mill will grind 2 tbsp (30 mL) of whole grains or beans into a generous ¼ cup (60 mL) of fine flour. Use it right away or freeze it in an airtight container for up to 3 months.

Gluten-Free All-Purpose Baking Mix

Although companies such as Bob's Red Mill and King Arthur Flour sell gluten-free all-purpose baking mixes, there's something to be said for making your own. You get to decide what goes into it, so you know it only includes ingredients you like. And it's so handy to have it ready to go in your freezer whenever the urge to bake strikes you. Here's a sample baking mix to get you started, but by all means experiment with gluten-free flours to create your own signature mix.

2 cups	finely ground white or brown rice flour (preferably stabilized)	500 mL
2 cups	chickpea (garbanzo bean), soy, amaranth, millet, quinoa, sorghum or bean flour, or a combination	500 mL
2 cups	potato starch	500 mL
1 cup	tapioca flour	250 mL

1. In a large sealable plastic bag, combine rice flour, chickpea flour, potato starch and tapioca flour. Store in the freezer for up to 6 months. Shake well before use.

Pumpkin Pull-Aparts
(page 223)

Pan de los Muertos
(page 244)

Cornmeal Pepper Bread (page 260)

Counterclockwise from top: Apricot Filling (page 287), Honey Spice Applesauce (page 283) and Luscious Peach Chutney (page 295)

White Bread

Equipment
- Bread machine with a 2-lb (1 kg) capacity

Made with a combination of gluten-free flours that contribute color, flavor and texture, this classic bread rises high, has a mellow flavor and a tender crumb, and is great for toast or sandwiches.

Tips

You can use an equivalent amount of ready-made gluten-free all-purpose baking mix, such as the one on page 256, in place of the flours.

If you are allergic to eggs, use an equivalent amount of liquid egg substitute in place of the eggs.

If you have an older bread machine, you might need to help the mixing along a little bit by scraping down the sides of the bread pan with a spatula every so often.

¾ cup	stone-ground brown rice flour	175 mL
¾ cup	tapioca flour or potato starch	175 mL
¾ cup	chickpea (garbanzo bean) flour	175 mL
½ cup	cornstarch or corn flour	125 mL
1 tbsp	xanthan gum	15 mL
2½ tbsp	packed light brown sugar	37 mL
1 tsp	salt	5 mL
2	large eggs, lightly beaten, or equivalent substitute (see tip, at left)	2
1 cup	lukewarm water (see tip, page 258)	250 mL
½ cup	unsweetened applesauce	125 mL
2½ tbsp	vegetable oil	37 mL
1 tsp	cider vinegar	5 mL
2 tsp	instant or bread machine yeast	10 mL

1. In a large bowl, whisk together rice flour, tapioca flour, chickpea flour, cornstarch and xanthan gum until well combined.

2. Add brown sugar, salt, eggs, water, applesauce, oil and vinegar to the bread pan. Spoon flour mixture on top of liquid. Add yeast.

3. Select the Gluten-Free, Rapid or Express cycle and press Start.

Soy Bread

Makes 1 loaf

Equipment
- Bread machine with a 2-lb (1 kg) capacity

Although the raw dough for this bread tastes a bit like bean sprouts, thanks to the soy flour, that taste dissipates on baking. What you get is a high, golden loaf with a tender crumb and a mellow flavor. If soy is a dietary concern, you can use sorghum, fava bean or quinoa flour instead.

Tips

If you are allergic to eggs, use an equivalent amount of liquid egg substitute in place of the eggs.

Ideally, the water should be between 86°F and 95°F (30°C and 35°C), the temperature range in which yeast is most active. Warm it in the microwave or in a saucepan on the stove, and check the temperature with an instant-read thermometer.

¾ cup	stone-ground brown rice flour	175 mL
¾ cup	tapioca flour or potato starch	175 mL
¾ cup	soy flour	175 mL
½ cup	cornstarch or corn flour	125 mL
1 tbsp	xanthan gum	15 mL
2½ tbsp	packed light brown sugar	37 mL
1 tsp	salt	5 mL
2	large eggs, lightly beaten, or equivalent substitute (see tip, at left)	2
1 cup	lukewarm water (see tip, at left)	250 mL
½ cup	unsweetened applesauce	125 mL
2½ tbsp	vegetable oil	37 mL
1 tsp	cider vinegar	5 mL
2 tsp	instant or bread machine yeast	10 mL

1. In a large bowl, whisk together rice flour, tapioca flour, soy flour, cornstarch and xanthan gum until well combined.

2. Add brown sugar, salt, eggs, water, applesauce, oil and vinegar to the bread pan. Spoon flour mixture on top of liquid. Add yeast.

3. Select the Gluten-Free, Rapid or Express cycle and press Start.

Sorghum Bread

Both sorghum syrup and sorghum flour are featured in this bread. Sorghum syrup is a pure food, similar to maple syrup, that is usually processed in a mill that produces only sorghum syrup, so it's great for anyone with a food allergy. Sorghum flour and sorghum syrup are available at health food stores.

Tips

If you are allergic to eggs, use an equivalent amount of liquid egg substitute in place of the eggs.

Ideally, the water should be between 86°F and 95°F (30°C and 35°C), the temperature range in which yeast is most active. Warm it in the microwave or in a saucepan on the stove, and check the temperature with an instant-read thermometer.

¾ cup	stone-ground brown rice flour	175 mL
¾ cup	tapioca flour or potato starch	175 mL
¾ cup	sorghum flour	175 mL
½ cup	cornstarch or corn flour	125 mL
1 tbsp	xanthan gum	15 mL
1 tsp	salt	5 mL
2	large eggs, lightly beaten, or equivalent substitute (see tip, at left)	2
1 cup	lukewarm water (see tip, at left)	250 mL
½ cup	unsweetened applesauce	125 mL
2½ tbsp	sorghum syrup or liquid honey	37 mL
2½ tbsp	vegetable oil	37 mL
1 tsp	cider vinegar	5 mL
2 tsp	instant or bread machine yeast	10 mL

1. In a large bowl, whisk together rice flour, tapioca flour, sorghum flour, cornstarch and xanthan gum until well combined.

2. Add salt, eggs, water, applesauce, sorghum syrup, oil and vinegar to the bread pan. Spoon flour mixture on top of liquid. Add yeast.

3. Select the Gluten-Free, Rapid or Express cycle and press Start.

Cornmeal Pepper Bread

Equipment
- Bread machine with a 2-lb (1 kg) capacity

The sophisticated flavor of this savory bread is addictive. Gluten-free eating can, indeed, be very, very enjoyable.

Tips

If you are allergic to eggs, use an equivalent amount of liquid egg substitute in place of the eggs.

Ideally, the water should be between 86°F and 95°F (30°C and 35°C), the temperature range in which yeast is most active. Warm it in the microwave or in a saucepan on the stove, and check the temperature with an instant-read thermometer.

³/₄ cup	stone-ground brown rice flour	175 mL
³/₄ cup	tapioca flour or potato starch	175 mL
³/₄ cup	fine yellow cornmeal	175 mL
¹/₂ cup	cornstarch or corn flour	125 mL
1 tbsp	xanthan gum	15 mL
2 tsp	granulated sugar	10 mL
¹/₂ tsp	salt	2 mL
2	large eggs, lightly beaten, or equivalent substitute (see tip, at left)	2
1 cup	lukewarm water (see tip, at left)	250 mL
¹/₂ cup	canned pumpkin purée (not pie filling)	125 mL
2¹/₂ tbsp	sorghum syrup or liquid honey	37 mL
2¹/₂ tbsp	vegetable oil	37 mL
1 tsp	cider vinegar	5 mL
1 tsp	freshly ground white pepper	5 mL
1 tsp	freshly ground black pepper	5 mL
2 tsp	instant or bread machine yeast	10 mL

1. In a large bowl, whisk together rice flour, tapioca flour, cornmeal, cornstarch and xanthan gum until well combined.

2. Add sugar, salt, eggs, water, pumpkin, sorghum syrup, oil and vinegar to the bread pan. Spoon flour mixture on top of liquid. Add white pepper, black pepper and yeast.

3. Select the Gluten-Free, Rapid or Express cycle and press Start.

> ### Cornmeal Pepper Dinner Rolls
>
> Prepare the recipe through step 2, then select the Dough cycle and press Start. Oil a 12-cup muffin pan. When the cycle is finished, use a dough scraper to transfer dough to an oiled surface. Divide dough equally among prepared muffin cups. Let rest, uncovered, for 30 minutes. Meanwhile, preheat oven to 350°F (180°C). Bake for 22 to 25 minutes or until risen and golden and an instant-read thermometer inserted in the center of a roll registers 190°F (90°C).

Caraway "Rye" Bread

Equipment
- Bread machine with a 2-lb (1 kg) capacity

Since rye flour has more texture than flavor and rye bread gets most of its flavor and color from other ingredients, you can make gluten-free rye-style bread without the rye. Use caraway seeds and molasses for the rye bread flavor and gluten-free cocoa powder (make sure to read the label) to achieve the color.

Tips

If you are allergic to eggs, use an equivalent amount of liquid egg substitute in place of the eggs.

Ideally, the water should be between 86°F and 95°F (30°C and 35°C), the temperature range in which yeast is most active. Warm it in the microwave or in a saucepan on the stove, and check the temperature with an instant-read thermometer.

³/₄ cup	stone-ground brown rice flour	175 mL
³/₄ cup	tapioca flour or potato starch	175 mL
³/₄ cup	chickpea (garbanzo bean), millet, quinoa or teff flour, or a combination	175 mL
¹/₂ cup	cornstarch or corn flour	125 mL
¹/₄ cup	gluten-free unsweetened cocoa powder	60 mL
1 tbsp	xanthan gum	15 mL
2 tsp	granulated sugar	10 mL
¹/₂ tsp	salt	2 mL
2	large eggs, lightly beaten, or equivalent substitute (see tip, at left)	2
1 cup	lukewarm water (see tip, at left)	250 mL
¹/₄ cup	light (fancy) molasses	60 mL
2 tbsp	vegetable oil	30 mL
1 tsp	cider vinegar	5 mL
2 tsp	caraway seeds	10 mL
2 tsp	instant or bread machine yeast	10 mL

1. In a large bowl, whisk together rice flour, tapioca flour, chickpea flour, cornstarch, cocoa and xanthan gum until well combined.

2. Add sugar, salt, eggs, water, molasses, oil and vinegar to the bread pan. Spoon flour mixture on top of liquid. Add caraway seeds and yeast.

3. Select the Gluten-Free, Rapid or Express cycle and press Start.

> ### Caraway "Rye" Dinner Rolls
> Prepare the recipe through step 2, then select the Dough cycle and press Start. Oil a 12-cup muffin pan. When the cycle is finished, use a dough scraper to transfer dough to an oiled surface. Divide dough equally among prepared muffin cups. Let rest, uncovered, for 30 minutes. Meanwhile, preheat oven to 350°F (180°C). Bake for 22 to 25 minutes or until risen and an instant-read thermometer inserted in the center of a roll registers 190°F (90°C).

Seeded Bread

With a golden color, a mellow flavor and a seeded texture, this bread makes delicious toast or sandwiches. The dough also makes an interesting flatbread that can be served as an appetizer or as the main course of a casual meal (see box, at right).

Tips

If you are allergic to eggs, use an equivalent amount of liquid egg substitute in place of the eggs.

Ideally, the water should be between 86°F and 95°F (30°C and 35°C), the temperature range in which yeast is most active. Warm it in the microwave or in a saucepan on the stove, and check the temperature with an instant-read thermometer.

If you like the flavor of fennel seeds, you can add 1 to 2 tsp (5 to 10 mL) with the other seeds.

You can use this dough to make dinner rolls. Follow steps 3 to 5 on page 272.

¾ cup	stone-ground brown rice flour	175 mL
¾ cup	tapioca flour or potato starch	175 mL
¾ cup	soy, sorghum, fava bean, millet or quinoa flour, or a combination	175 mL
½ cup	cornstarch or corn flour	125 mL
1 tbsp	xanthan gum	15 mL
2½ tbsp	packed light brown sugar	37 mL
½ tsp	salt	2 mL
2	large eggs, lightly beaten, or equivalent substitute (see tip, at left)	2
1 cup	lukewarm water (see tip, at left)	250 mL
½ cup	canned pumpkin purée (not pie filling)	125 mL
2½ tbsp	vegetable oil	37 mL
1 tsp	cider vinegar	5 mL
⅓ cup	poppy, millet, toasted green pumpkin or sunflower seeds, or a combination	75 mL
2 tsp	instant or bread machine yeast	10 mL

1. In a large bowl, whisk together rice flour, tapioca flour, soy flour, cornstarch and xanthan gum until well combined.

2. Add brown sugar, salt, eggs, water, pumpkin, oil and vinegar to the bread pan. Spoon flour mixture on top of liquid. Add seeds and yeast.

3. Select the Gluten-Free, Rapid or Express cycle and press Start.

Butternut Squash, Caramelized Onion and Sage Flatbread

Prepare the recipe through step 2, then select the Dough cycle and press Start. Oil a large rimmed baking sheet. When the cycle is finished, use a dough scraper to transfer dough to prepared baking sheet. Oil your hands and press dough out to make a thin crust. Let rest, uncovered, for 30 minutes. Meanwhile, preheat oven to 400°F (200°C). Spoon Easy Caramelized Onions (page 282), made with vegetable oil, over dough. Top with 2 cups (500 mL) cubed cooked butternut squash and ¼ cup (60 mL) fresh sage leaves. Drizzle with ¼ cup (60 mL) olive oil. Bake for 20 to 22 minutes or until browned and bubbling.

Cinnamon Apple Bread

¾ cup	stone-ground brown rice flour	175 mL
¾ cup	tapioca flour or potato starch	175 mL
¾ cup	chickpea (garbanzo bean) flour	175 mL
½ cup	cornstarch or corn flour	125 mL
1 tbsp	xanthan gum	15 mL
2 tsp	ground cinnamon	10 mL
1 cup	grated Granny Smith or other tart apple	250 mL
3 tbsp	packed light brown sugar	45 mL
1 tsp	salt	5 mL
2	large eggs, lightly beaten, or equivalent substitute (see tip, at left)	2
½ cup	lukewarm water (see tip, at left)	125 mL
3 tbsp	vegetable oil	45 mL
1 tsp	cider vinegar	5 mL
2 tsp	instant or bread machine yeast	10 mL
Glaze		
¼ cup	Cider Glaze with Rum (variation, page 291)	60 mL

1. In a large bowl, whisk together rice flour, tapioca flour, chickpea flour, cornstarch, xanthan gum and cinnamon until well combined.

2. Add apple, brown sugar, salt, eggs, water, oil and vinegar to the bread pan. Spoon flour mixture on top of liquid. Add yeast.

3. Select the Gluten-Free, Rapid or Express cycle and press Start. When the cycle is finished, transfer the loaf to a wire rack set over a baking sheet and let cool for 1 hour.

4. *Glaze:* Brush or drizzle bread with glaze. Let set for 30 minutes before slicing.

Banana Chocolate Chip Bread with Chocolate Glaze

Equipment
• Bread machine with a 2-lb (1 kg) capacity

Oooohhhh. Fresh banana adds texture and flavor, while chocolate adds deep, dark interest. Just make sure the chocolate chips you use are gluten-free.

Tips

If you are allergic to eggs, use an equivalent amount of liquid egg substitute in place of the eggs.

Ideally, the water should be between 86°F and 95°F (30°C and 35°C), the temperature range in which yeast is most active. Warm it in the microwave or in a saucepan on the stove, and check the temperature with an instant-read thermometer.

For a dairy-free glaze, use soy or rice milk in place of the cream.

¾ cup	stone-ground brown rice flour	175 mL
¾ cup	tapioca flour or potato starch	175 mL
¾ cup	chickpea (garbanzo bean) or amaranth flour	175 mL
½ cup	cornstarch or corn flour	125 mL
1 tbsp	xanthan gum	15 mL
1 tsp	ground cinnamon	5 mL
2½ tbsp	packed light brown sugar	37 mL
1 tsp	salt	5 mL
2	large eggs, lightly beaten, or equivalent substitute (see tip, at left)	2
1 cup	mashed ripe bananas	250 mL
½ cup	lukewarm water (see tip, at left)	125 mL
2½ tbsp	vegetable oil	37 mL
1 tsp	cider vinegar	5 mL
1 cup	gluten-free semisweet chocolate chips	250 mL
2 tsp	instant or bread machine yeast	10 mL

Glaze

½ cup	Chocolate Glaze (page 292)	125 mL

1. In a large bowl, whisk together rice flour, tapioca flour, chickpea flour, cornstarch, xanthan gum and cinnamon until well combined.

2. Add brown sugar, salt, eggs, bananas, water, oil and vinegar to the bread pan. Spoon flour mixture on top of liquid. Add chocolate chips and yeast.

3. Select the Gluten-Free, Rapid or Express cycle and press Start. When the cycle is finished, transfer the loaf to a wire rack set over a baking sheet and let cool for 1 hour.

4. *Glaze:* Brush or drizzle bread with glaze. Let set for 30 minutes before slicing.

> **Banana Coconut Chocolate Chip Bread with Chocolate Glaze**
> Add ⅔ cup (150 mL) gluten-free sweetened flaked or desiccated coconut with the bananas.

Blueberry Lemon Bread

¾ cup	stone-ground brown rice flour	175 mL
¾ cup	tapioca flour or potato starch	175 mL
¾ cup	chickpea (garbanzo bean) or amaranth flour	175 mL
½ cup	cornstarch or corn flour	125 mL
1 tbsp	xanthan gum	15 mL
3 tbsp	packed light brown sugar	45 mL
2 tsp	grated lemon zest	10 mL
1 tsp	salt	5 mL
2	large eggs, lightly beaten, or equivalent substitute (see tip, at left)	2
1 cup	lukewarm water (see tip, at left)	250 mL
½ cup	unsweetened applesauce	125 mL
2½ tbsp	vegetable oil	37 mL
1 tsp	freshly squeezed lemon juice or cider vinegar	5 mL
2 tsp	instant or bread machine yeast	10 mL
¾ cup	gluten-free dried blueberries	175 mL

Glaze

¼ cup	Lemon Glaze (variation, page 291)	60 mL

1. In a large bowl, whisk together rice flour, tapioca flour, chickpea flour, cornstarch and xanthan gum until well combined.

2. Add brown sugar, lemon zest, salt, eggs, water, applesauce, oil and lemon juice to the bread pan. Spoon flour mixture on top of liquid. Add yeast. Place blueberries in the dispenser (or add at the "add ingredient" or "mix in" signal).

3. Select the Gluten-Free, Rapid or Express cycle and the Light Crust setting and press Start. When the cycle is finished, transfer the loaf to a wire rack set over a baking sheet and let cool for 1 hour.

4. *Glaze:* Brush or drizzle bread with glaze. Let set for 30 minutes before slicing.

Pumpkin Swirl Bread

Equipment

- Bread machine with a 2-lb (1 kg) capacity
- 20-inch (50 cm) long piece of parchment paper
- Large baking sheet
- Instant-read thermometer

Glazed with sweet orange, this golden bread will be a welcome addition to a holiday breakfast table. Look for gluten-free pumpkin or apple butter for the filling.

Tips

If you are allergic to eggs, use an amount of liquid egg substitute equivalent to 2 large eggs.

Ideally, the water should be between 86°F and 95°F (30°C and 35°C), the temperature range in which yeast is most active. Warm it in the microwave or in a saucepan on the stove, and check the temperature with an instant-read thermometer.

¾ cup	stone-ground brown rice flour	175 mL
¾ cup	tapioca flour or potato starch	175 mL
¾ cup	sorghum, millet, quinoa or amaranth flour	175 mL
½ cup	cornstarch or corn flour	125 mL
1 tbsp	xanthan gum	15 mL
2 tsp	pumpkin pie spice	10 mL
2½ tbsp	packed light brown sugar	37 mL
½ tsp	salt	2 mL
2	large eggs, lightly beaten, or equivalent substitute (see tip, at left)	2
¾ cup	lukewarm water (see tip, at left)	175 mL
½ cup	canned pumpkin purée (not pie filling)	125 mL
2½ tbsp	vegetable oil	37 mL
1 tsp	cider vinegar	5 mL
2 tsp	instant or bread machine yeast	10 mL
	Nonstick cooking spray	

Filling

¾ cup	pumpkin or apple butter	175 mL

Glaze

¼ cup	Orange Glaze (variation, page 291)	60 mL
	Toasted green pumpkin seeds (optional)	

1. In a large bowl, whisk together rice flour, tapioca flour, sorghum flour, cornstarch, xanthan gum and pumpkin pie spice until well combined.

2. Add brown sugar, salt, eggs, water, pumpkin, oil and vinegar to the bread pan. Spoon flour mixture on top of liquid. Add yeast.

3. Select the Dough cycle and press Start.

4. When the cycle is finished, spray the parchment paper with cooking spray and place, sprayed side up, on a flat surface. Use a dough scraper or plastic spatula to transfer dough to prepared paper. Using a water-moistened plastic spatula or your hands, spread dough into a 14- by 10-inch (35 by 25 cm) rectangle.

5. *Filling:* Spread pumpkin butter over dough, leaving a ½-inch (1 cm) perimeter. Starting with a long end, gently lift the paper and nudge or scrape the dough so it rolls over on itself. Keep nudging and rolling until you have a loose cylinder. Slide cylinder into center of paper and slide paper onto baking sheet. Spread dough across ends to cover filling. Let rest, uncovered, for 30 minutes. Meanwhile, preheat oven to 350°F (180°C).

Tips

Make sure to use gluten-free confectioners' sugar in the glaze. For a dairy-free glaze, use soy or rice milk in place of the milk.

Gluten-free breads generally taste best the day they're made. If you're not going to eat it right away, it's best to freeze the bread as soon as it's cooled. Wrap slices or a whole loaf in plastic wrap, then place in a freezer bag or airtight container and freeze for up to 1 month.

6. Bake for about 40 minutes or until slightly risen and browned and an instant-read thermometer inserted in the center registers 190°F (90°C). Remove from pan and let cool on a wire rack set over a baking sheet for 1 hour.

7. *Glaze:* Brush or drizzle bread with glaze and sprinkle with toasted pumpkin seeds, if desired. Let set for 30 minutes before slicing.

Pumpkin Swirl Rolls

Prepare the recipe through step 5, but after rolling the dough into a cylinder, use the dough scraper to gently cut the cylinder into 12 slices. Oil a 12-cup muffin pan. Place one slice, spiral side up, in each prepared muffin cup. Cover with a clean towel and let rest for 30 minutes. Meanwhile, preheat oven to 350°F (180°C). Bake for 15 to 18 minutes or until risen and lightly browned and an instant-read thermometer inserted in the center registers 190°F (90°C). Let cool in pan on a wire rack for 5 minutes. Remove from pan and transfer to rack to cool. Brush or drizzle rolls with glaze.

Cinnamon Apple Kuchen

Equipment
- Bread machine with a
  2-lb (1 kg) capacity
- 9-inch (23 cm) square or
  round metal baking pan,
  oiled
- Instant-read thermometer

Apple in the dough, apple
in the filling, apple in the
glaze — this gluten-free
coffee cake is certainly
worth getting up for!

Tips

If you are allergic to eggs,
use an amount of liquid egg
substitute equivalent to
2 large eggs.

Ideally, the water should be
between 86°F and 95°F (30°C
and 35°C), the temperature
range in which yeast is
most active. Warm it in the
microwave or in a saucepan
on the stove, and check the
temperature with an instant-
read thermometer.

Make sure to use gluten-free
confectioners' sugar in the
glaze. Also make sure the
vanilla you use is labeled
"gluten-free." Even the
tiniest speck of gluten from
a manufacturing plant that
processes many different
foods can prompt a reaction
in a sensitive person.

¾ cup	stone-ground brown rice flour	175 mL
¾ cup	tapioca flour or potato starch	175 mL
¾ cup	chickpea (garbanzo bean) or amaranth flour	175 mL
½ cup	cornstarch or corn flour	125 mL
1 tbsp	xanthan gum	15 mL
1 tsp	ground cinnamon	5 mL
1 cup	grated Granny Smith or other tart apple (see tip, page 263)	250 mL
2½ tbsp	packed light brown sugar	37 mL
1 tsp	salt	5 mL
2	large eggs, lightly beaten, or equivalent substitute (see tip, at left)	2
½ cup	lukewarm water (see tip, at left)	125 mL
2½ tbsp	vegetable oil	37 mL
1 tsp	cider vinegar	5 mL
2 tsp	instant or bread machine yeast	10 mL

Filling

1 cup	Honey Spice Applesauce (page 283)	250 mL

Glaze

¼ cup	Cider Glaze with Rum (variation, page 291)	60 mL

1. In a large bowl, whisk together rice flour, tapioca flour, chickpea flour, cornstarch, xanthan gum and cinnamon until well combined.

2. Add apple, brown sugar, salt, eggs, water, oil and vinegar to the bread pan. Spoon flour mixture on top of liquid. Add yeast.

3. Select the Dough cycle and press Start.

4. When the cycle is finished, use a dough scraper or plastic spatula to transfer dough to prepared baking pan. Using a water-moistened spatula, spread dough to cover bottom of pan.

5. *Filling:* Spoon applesauce on top. Let rest, uncovered, for 30 minutes. Meanwhile, preheat oven to 350°F (180°C).

6. Bake for 25 to 30 minutes or until edges are golden brown and an instant-read thermometer inserted in the center registers 190°F (90°C). Let cool in pan on a wire rack for 1 hour.

7. *Glaze:* Drizzle kuchen with glaze. Let set for 30 minutes before slicing.

Focaccia

Equipment

- Bread machine with a 1½-lb (750 g) capacity
- 9-inch (23 cm) square or round metal baking pan, oiled

Light and airy in texture but bold in flavor, focaccia gets its signature taste from the slurry of olive oil and salt that is brushed on the dough. Add other gluten-free toppings as you see fit.

Tips

Ideally, the water should be between 86°F and 95°F (30°C and 35°C), the temperature range in which yeast is most active. Warm it in the microwave or in a saucepan on the stove, and check the temperature with an instant-read thermometer.

If you haven't made your own gluten-free all-purpose baking mix, look for one made by Bob's Red Mill or King Arthur Flour. Make sure to shake the container (while it's still securely closed) to distribute the flours before measuring.

1 tsp	fine kosher or sea salt	5 mL
1¾ cups	lukewarm water (see tip, at left)	425 mL
2½ cups	Gluten-Free All-Purpose Baking Mix (page 256)	625 mL
1 tbsp	xanthan gum	15 mL
2 tsp	instant or bread machine yeast	10 mL

Topping

½ tsp	fine kosher or sea salt	2 mL
1 tbsp	water	15 mL
1 tbsp	olive oil	15 mL
1 tbsp	fresh rosemary leaves	15 mL

1. Add salt and water to the bread pan. Spoon baking mix on top of liquid. Add xanthan gum and yeast.

2. Select the Dough cycle and press Start.

3. When the cycle is finished, use a dough scraper or plastic spatula to transfer dough to prepared pan. Oil your hands and spread dough to fit pan. Press the surface of the dough with your fingertip or knuckle to make random dimples. Let rest, uncovered, for 30 minutes. Meanwhile, preheat oven to 350°F (180°C).

4. *Topping:* In a bowl, combine salt, water and oil. Brush over dough. Sprinkle dough with rosemary.

5. Bake for 27 to 30 minutes or until top is light golden and an instant-read thermometer inserted in the center registers 190°F (90°C). Let cool in pan on a wire rack for 10 minutes, then cut into pieces and serve.

Focaccia with Heirloom Tomatoes and Basil

Prepare the recipe through step 4, but in place of rosemary, arrange ¼ cup (60 mL) fresh basil leaves on the dough. Top with 1 cup (250 mL) sliced fresh heirloom tomatoes and ½ cup (125 mL) freshly grated Parmesan cheese or dairy-free Parmesan cheese product. Drizzle with 1 tbsp (15 mL) additional olive oil. Bake as directed in step 5.

Thin-Crust Pepperoni and Mushroom Pizza

Equipment

- Bread machine with a 1-lb (500 g) capacity
- 12-inch (30 cm) pizza pan, lined with parchment paper

Gluten-free doughs look and feel different than wheat-based ones, but miraculously end up tasting much the same. Now you can enjoy pizza again!

¾ tsp	salt	3 mL
1 cup	lukewarm milk or rice milk (see tip, at right)	250 mL
2 tbsp	olive oil	30 mL
1 tbsp	liquid honey	15 mL
1½ cups	Gluten-Free All-Purpose Baking Mix (page 256)	375 mL
2 tsp	instant or bread machine yeast	10 mL
1 tsp	gluten-free baking powder	5 mL
1 tsp	xanthan gum	5 mL
1 tsp	dried Italian seasoning	5 mL

Topping

1 cup	gluten-free pizza sauce	250 mL
2 cups	thinly sliced mushrooms	500 mL
2 cups	sliced pepperoni or cooked gluten-free Italian sausage or ham	500 mL
2 cups	shredded mozzarella or provolone cheese or dairy-free cheese product	500 mL

1. Add salt, milk, oil and honey to the bread pan. Spoon baking mix on top of liquid. Add yeast, baking powder, xanthan gum and Italian seasoning.

2. Select the Dough cycle and press Start.

3. When the cycle is finished, use a dough scraper or plastic spatula to transfer the thick, sticky dough to the center of the prepared pizza pan. Oil your hands and press dough to form a 12-inch (30 cm) circle. Let rest, uncovered, for 15 minutes. Meanwhile, preheat oven to 400°F (200°C).

4. *Topping:* Spoon pizza sauce onto dough and smooth over the surface. Top with mushrooms, pepperoni and cheese.

5. Bake for 20 to 22 minutes or until browned and bubbling.

Tips

Ideally, the milk should be between 86°F and 95°F (30°C and 35°C), the temperature range in which yeast is most active. Warm it in the microwave or in a saucepan on the stove, and check the temperature with an instant-read thermometer.

If you haven't made your own gluten-free all-purpose baking mix, look for one made by Bob's Red Mill or King Arthur Flour. Make sure to shake the container (while it's still securely closed) to distribute the flours before measuring.

Grilled Chicken and Vegetable Pizza

Prepare the recipe through step 3. In a bowl, combine 1 minced clove garlic and 1/4 cup (60 mL) olive oil; brush over dough. Arrange 2 cups (500 mL) chopped grilled chicken and a 2-cup (500 mL) combination of chopped grilled red onion, zucchini and yellow summer squash on top. Top with sliced smoked mozzarella cheese or dairy-free mozzarella cheese product. Sprinkle with 1/4 cup (60 mL) chopped fresh herbs, such as flat-leaf (Italian) parsley, oregano, rosemary and thyme.

Dinner Rolls

The looser gluten-free dough will not form intricate shapes, but it makes a fine-tasting, mellow, round roll with a tender crumb.

Tips

If you are allergic to eggs, use an amount of liquid egg substitute equivalent to 2 large eggs.

Ideally, the water should be between 86°F and 95°F (30°C and 35°C), the temperature range in which yeast is most active. Warm it in the microwave or in a saucepan on the stove, and check the temperature with an instant-read thermometer.

¾ cup	stone-ground brown rice flour	175 mL
¾ cup	tapioca flour or potato starch	175 mL
¾ cup	chickpea (garbanzo bean) flour	175 mL
½ cup	cornstarch or corn flour	250 mL
4 tsp	xanthan gum	20 mL
2½ tbsp	packed light brown sugar	37 mL
1 tsp	salt	5 mL
2	large eggs, lightly beaten, or equivalent substitute (see tip, at left)	2
1 cup	lukewarm water (see tip, at left)	250 mL
½ cup	unsweetened applesauce	125 mL
2½ tbsp	vegetable oil	37 mL
1 tsp	cider vinegar	5 mL
2 tsp	instant or bread machine yeast	10 mL

1. In a large bowl, whisk together rice flour, tapioca flour, chickpea flour, cornstarch and xanthan gum until well combined.

2. Add brown sugar, salt, eggs, water, applesauce, oil and vinegar to the bread pan. Spoon flour mixture on top of liquid. Add yeast.

3. Select the Dough cycle and press Start.

4. When the cycle is finished, use a dough scraper or plastic spatula to transfer dough to an oiled surface. Divide dough equally among prepared muffin cups. Let rest, uncovered, for 30 minutes. Meanwhile, preheat oven to 350°F (180°C).

5. Bake for 22 to 25 minutes or until an instant-read thermometer inserted in the center of a roll registers 190°F (90°C).

Sandwich Buns

Equipment
- Bread machine with a 2-lb (1 kg) capacity
- Twelve 4-inch (10 cm) mini pie pans, oiled
- Instant-read thermometer

When you want a gluten-free bun for your sizzling burger, this is it. Make this large batch and freeze extras for up to 3 months. Because the dough is so batter-like, use 4-inch (10 cm) mini pie pans (available at kitchen shops) to form the buns.

Tips

If you are allergic to eggs, use an equivalent amount of liquid egg substitute in place of the eggs and egg white.

Ideally, the milk and water should be between 86°F and 95°F (30°C and 35°C), the temperature range in which yeast is most active. Warm them in the microwave or in a saucepan on the stove, and check the temperature with an instant-read thermometer.

1⅓ cups	stone-ground brown rice flour	325 mL
1⅓ cups	tapioca flour or potato starch	325 mL
1 tbsp	xanthan gum	15 mL
2½ tbsp	granulated sugar	37 mL
1½ tsp	salt	7 mL
2	large eggs, lightly beaten, or equivalent substitute (see tip, at left)	2
1 cup	lukewarm milk, rice milk or soy milk (see tip, at left)	250 mL
⅓ cup	lukewarm water	75 mL
2½ tbsp	vegetable oil (preferably canola)	37 mL
1 tsp	cider vinegar	5 mL
4 tsp	instant or bread machine yeast	20 mL

Topping

1	large egg white, beaten, or equivalent substitute	1
	Poppy or sesame seeds	

1. In a large bowl, whisk together rice flour, tapioca flour and xanthan gum until well combined.

2. Add sugar, salt, eggs, milk, water, oil and vinegar to the bread pan. Spoon flour mixture on top of liquid. Add yeast.

3. Select the Dough cycle and press Start.

4. When the cycle is finished, use a dough scraper or plastic spatula to transfer dough to an oiled bowl. Divide dough equally among prepared pie pans. Using a water-moistened spatula, smooth tops. Place pans on a baking sheet. Let rest, uncovered, for 30 minutes. Meanwhile, preheat oven to 350°F (180°C).

5. *Topping:* Brush tops of buns with egg white and sprinkle with poppy seeds.

6. Bake for 18 to 22 minutes or until risen and golden and an instant-read thermometer inserted in the center of a bun registers 190°F (90°C). Let cool in pans on a wire rack for 15 minutes, then remove from pans and transfer to rack to cool.

Cinnamon Rolls

Equipment
- Bread machine with a 2-lb (1 kg) capacity
- 12-cup muffin pan, oiled

With a more batter-like dough, these rolls are assembled differently than cinnamon rolls made with a wheat dough. But they taste very similar, so no one will mind the nontraditional shape.

Tips
If you are allergic to eggs, use an amount of liquid egg substitute equivalent to 2 large eggs.

Ideally, the milk should be between 86°F and 95°F (30°C and 35°C), the temperature range in which yeast is most active. Warm it in the microwave or in a saucepan on the stove, and check the temperature with an instant-read thermometer.

1⅓ cups	stone-ground brown rice flour	325 mL
1⅓ cups	tapioca flour or potato starch	325 mL
1 tbsp	xanthan gum	15 mL
3 tbsp	granulated sugar	45 mL
1 tsp	salt	5 mL
2	large eggs, lightly beaten, or equivalent substitute (see tip, at left)	2
⅔ cup	lukewarm milk or soy milk (see tip, at left)	150 mL
⅓ cup	unsweetened applesauce	75 mL
3 tbsp	vegetable oil	45 mL
1 tsp	cider vinegar	5 mL
2 tsp	instant or bread machine yeast	10 mL
Filling		
½ cup	Cinnamon Filling (page 284)	125 mL
Glaze		
¼ cup	Vanilla Glaze (page 291)	60 mL

1. In a large bowl, whisk together rice flour, tapioca flour and xanthan gum until well combined.

2. Add sugar, salt, eggs, milk, applesauce, oil and vinegar to the bread pan. Spoon flour mixture on top of liquid. Add yeast.

3. Select the Dough cycle and press Start.

4. When the cycle is finished, use a dough scraper or plastic spatula to transfer dough to an oiled bowl. Scoop a heaping tablespoon (15 mL) of the dough into each prepared muffin cup. Using water-moistened fingers, smooth batter in cups.

5. *Filling:* Spread 1 tsp (5 mL) of the filling over each cup of dough, leaving a ½-inch (1 cm) perimeter. Spoon remaining dough equally on top of filling and, using a toothpick, swirl batter slightly to incorporate filling into batter. Gently smooth tops with moistened fingers. Let rest, uncovered, for 30 minutes. Meanwhile, preheat oven to 350°F (180°C).

If dairy is a concern, make the filling with dairy-free margarine and the glaze with soy or rice milk.

Be sure to use gluten-free confectioners' sugar in the glaze. Also make sure the vanilla you use is labeled "gluten-free." Even the tiniest speck of gluten from a manufacturing plant that processes many different foods can prompt a reaction in a sensitive person.

6. Bake for 15 to 18 minutes or until risen and lightly browned and an instant-read thermometer inserted in the center of a roll registers 190°F (90°C). Let cool in pan on a wire rack for 5 minutes. Remove from pan and transfer to a wire rack. Spread remaining filling on top of hot rolls. Let cool.

7. *Glaze:* Drizzle rolls with glaze.

Lemon Poppy Seed Rolls

Replace the Cinnamon Filling with Poppy Seed Filling (page 285), using soy or rice milk if dairy is a concern. Bake as above, then glaze with Lemon Glaze (variation, page 291), taking care to use gluten-free almond extract and soy or rice milk if dairy is a concern.

Gluten-Free Apricot Almond Rolls

Replace the Cinnamon Filling with Apricot Filling (page 287), made with gluten-free vanilla extract. Bake as above, then glaze with Almond Glaze (variation, page 291), taking care to use gluten-free almond extract and soy milk or rice milk if dairy is a concern. Sprinkle with toasted, flaked almonds or slivered pistachios; if nuts are a concern, sprinkle instead with pearl sugar.

The Artisan Bread Machine Pantry

THE ARTISAN BREAD Machine Pantry includes recipes that enhance both sweet and savory breads — either in the dough itself, as a filling, topping or glaze or as something delicious to serve with your breads. These recipes have their own chapter because they can be used in so many ways with so many different breads throughout the book.

One of the not-so-secret ways to have consistently good results in the bread machine is to use a dough enhancer, which helps the yeast work better, the dough rise well and the crumb in the finished loaf become more tender. You can buy powdered dough enhancer at some grocery stores and online, but if you bake bread a lot, having your own homemade dough enhancer on hand makes better sense, so I've given you a recipe for one on page 278.

Just as the bread machine is an excellent kitchen assistant when you're making bread, other kitchen appliances make short work of preparing butter, fillings and glazes. For example, a food processor will help you make Artisan Butter in minutes, as well as whip up all kinds of fillings and glazes. A slow cooker is a fabulous way to make Easy Caramelized Onions, a delicious topping for pizzas or flatbreads.

Your bread machine can also make darn good preserves and chutneys. They're a little looser than those you boil on the stove, but they have wonderful flavor, with very little work on your part. The trick is to finely chop or mash the fruit, combine it with sugar and lemon juice, then put it all in the bread pan. The Jam cycle — which takes 1 to 2 hours on most machines — mixes and cooks the fruit to a jam-like consistency that thickens as it cools. Once you taste Sour Cherry Preserves or Fresh Strawberry Preserves, you'll never go back to store-bought preserves. Your artisan breads, fresh from your bread machine, deserve the best!

Artisan Dough Enhancer

Dough enhancer contains ingredients that help heavy doughs made with whole-grain flour rise better and help all-purpose flour do the heavy lifting of bread flour. So, if you make whole-grain breads, or bread flour is not always available in your area, make a batch of dough enhancer and keep it in a tightly closed jar in your refrigerator. To increase the level of protein in all-purpose flour so you can use it in place of bread flour, add 1 tsp (5 mL) Artisan Dough Enhancer to each cup (250 mL) of all-purpose flour.

Tip

You can also buy ready-made powdered dough enhancer in the baking aisle of better grocery stores.

1 cup	vital wheat gluten	250 mL
½ cup	instant skim milk powder	125 mL
2 tbsp	soy lecithin granules	30 mL
2 tbsp	pectin crystals	30 mL
2 tbsp	unflavored gelatin powder	30 mL
1 tsp	ground ginger	5 mL
1 tsp	ascorbic acid crystals	5 mL

1. In a glass jar, combine gluten, milk powder, soy lecithin granules, pectin, gelatin, ginger and ascorbic acid crystals. Close the lid and shake to blend. Store in the refrigerator for up to 1 year.

Where to Find Dough Enhancer Ingredients

Vital wheat gluten, instant skim milk powder and ground ginger are available in the baking aisle.

Unflavored gelatin powder can be found with pudding and gelatin mixes.

Pectin crystals and ascorbic acid crystals are shelved with canning and preserving items. (Ascorbic acid is sometimes also shelved with Jewish foods.)

Soy lecithin granules (Bob's Red Mill is one brand) can be found in the baking or health foods aisle.

Basil and Garlic Oil

Equipment
• Food processor

As a bread machine
ingredient or as a dipping
oil for fresh bread, this
aromatic mixture is sure
to please. Use this recipe
as a template to make
other flavored oils to use
in doughs or as dipping
sauces.

Tip
This recipe can easily be
doubled to make 1 cup
(250 mL).

1 cup	packed fresh basil leaves	250 mL
6	cloves garlic, peeled	6
¼ cup	olive oil	60 mL

1. In food processor, process basil and garlic for 30 seconds or until very finely chopped but not puréed. With the motor running, slowly drizzle oil through the feed tube; process until well combined.

2. Transfer to a bowl, cover and let stand for at least 1 hour to blend the flavors.

Artisan Butter

Equipment
• Food processor

Farm wives used to make their spending money by churning butter by hand to sell at the market. We can count ourselves fortunate that the food processor now takes the place of the old wooden churn in the home kitchen. If you're making artisan bread, you should also serve equally artisan butter, and this is it. This recipe makes unsalted butter; if you like, add sea salt to taste.

2 cups	heavy or whipping (35%) cream	500 mL

1. Line a sieve with a single layer of cheesecloth or a clean terrycloth tea towel and place the sieve over a bowl. Pour the cream into the food processor and process for about 5 minutes. The cream will go, in stages, from liquid to whipped cream to thick whipped cream to a solid mass of butter that separates from the milky liquid, or whey.

2. Transfer the butter to the lined sieve and press the butter with a wooden spoon or spatula to release more of the whey. When the butter does not release any more whey, scoop it from the sieve and cover with plastic wrap.

3. Use right away, keep covered in the refrigerator for up to 1 month or freeze indefinitely.

Tip

Ultra-pasteurized cream will take a little longer to process, but still makes delicious butter.

Garlic Herb Butter

In a bowl, combine 1 cup (250 mL) softened butter with 1 large clove garlic, minced, and 2 tbsp (30 mL) mixed chopped fresh herbs, such as flat-leaf (Italian) parsley, dill, tarragon, chives, oregano and/or rosemary, or to taste. Store in the refrigerator for up to 3 days.

Savory Whipped Onion Butter

In a food processor, combine 1 cup (250 mL) softened butter, 1/4 cup (60 mL) minced onion, 1/4 cup (60 mL) minced flat-leaf (Italian) parsley, 2 tsp (10 mL) Worcestershire sauce, 1/2 tsp (2 mL) dry mustard and 1/2 tsp (2 mL) cracked black pepper; process until light and fluffy. Store in the refrigerator for up to 3 days.

Honey Butter

In a bowl, combine 1 cup (250 mL) softened butter with 1 tbsp (15 mL) medium-colored liquid clover or wildflower honey, or to taste.

Raspberry Butter

In a bowl, combine 1 cup (250 mL) softened butter with 1 cup (250 mL) mashed fresh or thawed frozen raspberries. (Or use strawberries for Strawberry Butter.) Use immediately.

Spiced Pumpkin Butter

In a bowl, combine 1 cup (250 mL) softened butter with 1/3 cup (75 mL) canned pumpkin purée (not pie filling), 1 tsp (5 mL) grated orange zest and 1 tsp (5 mL) pumpkin pie spice. Store in the refrigerator for up to 3 days.

Pomegranate Orange Butter

In a bowl, combine 1 cup (250 mL) softened butter with 1/4 cup (60 mL) pomegranate molasses and 1 tbsp (15 mL) grated orange zest. Store in the refrigerator for up to 3 days.

Easy Caramelized Onions

Makes about 2 cups (500 mL)		

Equipment
- Small (2- to 4-quart) slow cooker

Who doesn't like caramelized onions? They're so adaptable as pizza and flatbread toppings, and savory roll and sandwich fillings, that you just have to have a batch on hand in the refrigerator or freezer. This recipe is adapted from one by Kathryn Moore and Roxanne Wyss (www. pluggedintocooking.com), and it's fabulous.

Tip

For caramelized onions on the stovetop, heat the oil and butter in a large saucepan over medium-low heat. Stir in the onions and cook, stirring occasionally, for 20 to 30 minutes or until the onions have caramelized. Season to taste with salt and pepper.

4	large onions, thinly sliced	4
2 tbsp	olive oil	30 mL
2 tbsp	unsalted butter or vegetable oil	30 mL
	Salt and freshly ground black pepper	

1. In slow cooker stoneware, combine onions, oil and butter. Cover and cook on High for 6 to 8 hours or until onions are medium brown and wilted. Season to taste with salt and pepper. Let cool.

2. Use right away or transfer to an airtight container and refrigerate for up to 1 week or freeze for up to 3 months.

Honey Spice Applesauce

Dark with spices, this
applesauce is wonderful
served warm or as a
flavorful ingredient in
gourmet bread machine
loaves such as Spiced
Applesauce Bread
(page 120).

4 cups	unsweetened applesauce	1 L
1 cup	clover or other mild honey	250 mL
2 tsp	ground cinnamon	10 mL
¼ tsp	freshly grated nutmeg	1 mL
¼ tsp	kosher salt, or to taste	1 mL
1 tsp	freshly squeezed lemon juice, or to taste	5 mL

1. In a large saucepan, heat applesauce, honey, cinnamon and nutmeg over medium-high heat until bubbling. Reduce heat and simmer, stirring often, for 5 minutes or until thickened. Taste, then add salt and lemon juice as needed.

2. Use right away or let cool, transfer to 1- or 2-cup (250 or 500 mL) airtight containers and refrigerate for up to 5 days or freeze for up to 6 months.

Cinnamon Filling

This is the classic filling for cinnamon rolls, Swedish tea rings and other pastries. This mild version uses granulated sugar and regular grocery-store cinnamon (usually from Indonesia).

Tip

For a stronger-flavored cinnamon filling, use packed light or dark brown sugar in place of granulated and Vietnamese or Chinese cassia cinnamon.

6 tbsp	granulated sugar	90 mL
2 tbsp	ground cinnamon	30 mL
¾ cup	unsalted butter, softened	175 mL

1. In a bowl, combine sugar and cinnamon. Using a fork, mash in butter until smooth and well blended. Use right away.

Poppy Seed Filling

Artisan bakers of Polish
and Slavic descent love
the combination of sweet,
crunchy poppy seeds and
tart lemon in festive breads
and pastries. Polish bakeries
often sell bags of poppy
seeds already ground, but
it's easy to do at home.

1 cup	poppy seeds	250 mL
2 tbsp	granulated sugar	30 mL
1 tsp	ground allspice	5 mL
½ cup	milk	125 mL
1 tbsp	honey	15 mL

1. Grind the poppy seeds, in batches if necessary, in a clean coffee grinder, spice grinder or small food processor, or by hand using a mortar and pestle.

2. In a saucepan, combine ground poppy seeds, sugar, allspice, milk and honey; bring to a boil over medium-high heat. Reduce heat and simmer, stirring frequently, for 10 minutes or until sugar and honey are well dissolved and the mixture has thickened slightly. Remove from heat and let cool.

3. Use right away or transfer to an airtight container and refrigerate for up to 1 week.

Danish Almond Filling

Equipment
- Food processor or blender

Midwesterners of
Scandinavian descent love
a vanilla-scented almond
filling. If you prefer a
stronger almond flavoring,
use the almond extract.
This filling tastes best if it
has a few days to mature.

Tips

Toasting the nuts first gives
this filling a better flavor.

For wonderful ready-made
fillings, check out American
Almond Products Company
(1-800-825-6663 or
www.americanalmond.com).

- Preheat oven to 300°F (150°C)

8 oz	sliced almonds	250 g
	(about 2½ cups/625 mL)	
1 cup	granulated sugar	250 mL
2	egg whites	2
1 tsp	almond or vanilla extract	5 mL

1. Spread almonds in a single layer on a baking sheet. Toast
in preheated oven for 10 to 15 minutes or until nuts are
golden and have a toasty aroma. (Check after 10 minutes,
and do not let brown.) Let cool, then discard any nuts that
have turned dark brown.

2. In food processor or blender, grind cooled almonds to
a fine paste. Add sugar and process until the mixture
resembles coarse flour. Add egg whites and almond
extract; process for 2 to 3 minutes or until a stiff paste
forms.

3. Transfer to an airtight container and refrigerate until ready
to use, for up to 3 days.

Toasted Hazelnut Filling
Substitute hazelnuts for the almonds and rub off the
skins after toasting. Omit the extract.

Pistachio Filling
Substitute unsalted roasted pistachios for the almonds
and skip the toasting step. Use almond extract.

Apricot Filling

Makes about ¾ cup (175 mL)

Equipment
• Food processor

Dried apricots have the fullest apricot flavor, so use them to make this filling for kolachke, Danish pastries, kuchen, coffee cakes, swirled loaves or sweet rolls.

Tip
You can double or triple this recipe if you want more filling.

6 oz	dried apricots, finely snipped	175 g
⅓ cup	granulated sugar	75 mL
½ tsp	vanilla extract	2 mL
	Freshly squeezed lemon juice, to taste	

1. Place apricots in a saucepan and add enough water to just cover. Bring to a boil over medium-high heat. Reduce heat and simmer, stirring often, for 12 to 15 minutes or until fruit is tender.

2. Transfer apricot mixture to food processor and purée until smooth. Transfer to a bowl and stir in sugar and vanilla. Taste, then add lemon juice if necessary.

3. Use right away or cover and refrigerate for up to 3 days.

Sweet Cream Cheese Filling

**Makes about
1⅓ cups (325 mL)**

Equipment
• Food processor

Delicious as a filling for pull-aparts, crescent rolls, Danish pastries, coffee cake or swirled loafs, this cream cheese mixture can be flavored in many different ways (**see variations, at right**).

¼ cup	granulated sugar	60 mL
2 tbsp	all-purpose flour	30 mL
1	egg yolk	1
8 oz	cream cheese, softened	250 g
1 tsp	vanilla extract	5 mL

1. In food processor, combine sugar, flour, egg yolk, cream cheese and vanilla; process until smooth.

2. Use right away or transfer to an airtight container and refrigerate for up to 3 days.

Almond Cream Cheese Filling
Use 1 tsp (5 mL) almond extract in place of the vanilla.

Lemon Cream Cheese Filling
Use 1 tsp (5 mL) lemon extract or grated lemon zest in place of the vanilla.

Orange Cream Cheese Filling
Use 1 tsp (5 mL) orange extract or grated orange zest in place of the vanilla.

Sweet Spice Cream Cheese Filling
Add 1 tsp (5 mL) apple pie spice.

Coconut Cream Cheese Filling
Add ½ cup (125 mL) sweetened flaked coconut.

Coconut Lime Cream Cheese Filling
Add ½ cup (125 mL) sweetened flaked coconut and use 1 tsp (5 mL) grated lime zest in place of the vanilla.

Cottage Cheese Filling

Equipment
• Food processor

**Delicious as a filling for
kolachke, schmierkuchen,
coffee cakes or swirled
loafs, this cottage cheese
mixture has a wonderful
homemade flavor.**

Tip
Dry-pressed cottage cheese
is available in low-fat and
full-fat versions. The full-fat
version is best for this recipe.

½ cup	granulated sugar	125 mL
1 tbsp	all-purpose flour	15 mL
½ tsp	salt	2 mL
2	large eggs, beaten	2
12 oz	dry-pressed cottage or farmer's cheese	375 g
¼ cup	heavy or whipping (35%) cream	60 mL
1 tsp	vanilla extract	5 mL

1. In food processor, combine sugar, flour, salt, eggs, cottage cheese, cream and vanilla; process until smooth.

2. Use right away or transfer to an airtight container and refrigerate for up to 3 days.

Cinnamon Sugar

**Makes about
½ cup (125 mL)**

Like everything else,
there is a difference
between ready-made and
homemade cinnamon
sugar — and it's the degree
of cinnamoniness. I prefer
to use the strongest type
of cinnamon, that which
is grown in Vietnam and
labeled either Vietnamese
or Saigon cinnamon.
Use this mixture to make
cinnamon rolls, to sprinkle
on balls of sweet roll
dough to make Sugar
and Spice Monkey Bread
(page 139) or to make
great cinnamon toast.

| ½ cup | granulated sugar | 125 mL |
| 1 tbsp | ground cinnamon | 15 mL |

1. In a small bowl, combine sugar and cinnamon until well blended. Store in an airtight container in a cool, dark place for up to 1 year.

Vanilla Glaze

Add a final sweet touch to your baked goods with a homemade glaze, thinner than either a frosting or an icing. A glaze is meant to give baked goods a sweet sheen and an initial flavor. Make glaze right before you're ready to use it; otherwise, it can harden and get lumpy.

Tip
You can double or triple this recipe if you need more glaze.

½ cup	confectioners' (icing) sugar	125 mL
1 to 2 tbsp	whole milk, half-and-half (10%) cream or heavy or whipping (35%) cream	15 to 30 mL
½ tsp	vanilla extract	2 mL

1. In a small bowl, whisk together confectioners' sugar and milk until smooth. Whisk in vanilla. Use right away.

Almond Glaze
Use almond extract in place of the vanilla.

Coffee Glaze
Use coffee extract in place of the vanilla or freshly brewed dark coffee in place of the milk.

Lemon Glaze
Use lemon extract or grated lemon zest in place of the vanilla.

Orange Glaze
Use freshly squeezed orange juice in place of the milk and orange extract or grated orange zest in place of the vanilla.

Lime Glaze
Use grated lime zest in place of the vanilla.

Cider Glaze with Rum
Use 1 to 2 tbsp (15 to 30 mL) unsweetened apple cider and 1½ to 2 tsp (7 to 10 mL) light or dark rum in place of the milk.

Cherry Glaze
Use cherry juice in place of the milk and almond extract in place of the vanilla.

Cranberry Orange Glaze
Use cranberry juice in place of the milk and orange extract or grated orange zest in place of the vanilla.

Chocolate Glaze

Sometimes a pastry just
calls out for a drizzle
of chocolate. This easy
method also results in
easy cleanup.

Tip

If you use larger, button-size
chocolate chips, it might be
necessary to microwave on
High for 15 to 30 seconds
longer, until the chocolate
has melted enough to knead
smooth.

| ½ cup | small semisweet chocolate chips | 125 mL |
| 2 tbsp | heavy or whipping (35%) cream | 30 mL |

1. In a small microwave-safe sealable plastic bag, combine
   chocolate chips and cream. Seal and microwave on High
   for 30 seconds. Remove the bag and knead the mixture
   until smooth and well blended.

2. Cut a tiny corner from the bottom of the bag and squeeze
   glaze over a cooled loaf in a decorative pattern.

Sour Cherry Preserves

Equipment

- Food processor
- Bread machine with a Jam cycle
- Sterilized jars with lids

Your trusty bread machine is also a dab hand at making preserves. Just put the fruit mixture in the bread pan, select the Jam cycle and let the machine do the rest. At the end, I like to add a signature flavoring — in this case, almond to complement the cherry.

Tips

To sterilize a glass jar, submerge it in a pot of boiling water. Use tongs to remove the jar and place it upside down on clean kitchen towels to dry.

Without pectin, this recipe makes softly set preserves, more for spooning over bread than for spreading.

3 cups	pitted sour cherries (fresh or thawed frozen)	750 mL
1½ cups	granulated sugar	375 mL
½	box (1.75 to 2 oz/49 to 60 g) powdered fruit pectin (optional)	½
1 tbsp	freshly squeezed lemon juice	15 mL
½ tsp	almond extract	2 mL

1. In food processor, combine cherries, sugar, pectin (if using) and lemon juice; pulse to roughly chop cherries.

2. Transfer cherry mixture to the bread pan. Select the Jam setting and press Start.

3. When the cycle is finished, carefully stir in almond extract. Spoon preserves into sterilized jars and let cool, then secure the lids. Store in the refrigerator for up to 3 months.

Fresh Strawberry Preserves

Equipment
- Bread machine with a Jam cycle
- Sterilized jars with lids

Mashing the strawberries first is the key to luscious preserves. The tiny bit of rose water enhances the berry flavor.

Tips

To sterilize a glass jar, submerge it in a pot of boiling water. Use tongs to remove the jar and place it upside down on clean kitchen towels to dry.

Without pectin, these preserves will be softly set and spoonable. With pectin, they'll be spreadable.

2 cups	mashed fresh strawberries (fresh or thawed frozen)	500 mL
¾ cup	granulated sugar	175 mL
½	box (1.75 to 2 oz/49 to 60 g) powdered fruit pectin (optional)	½
2 tbsp	freshly squeezed lemon juice	30 mL
¼ tsp	rose water	1 mL

1. Place strawberries, sugar, pectin (if using) and lemon juice in the bread pan. Select the Jam cycle and press Start.

2. When the cycle is finished, carefully stir in rose water. Spoon preserves into sterilized jars and let cool, then secure the lids. Store in the refrigerator for up to 3 months.

Luscious Peach Chutney

Equipment
- Bread machine with a Jam cycle
- Sterilized jars with lids

Delicious on bread, with pork or chicken, over a soft cheese for an appetizer or straight out of the jar, this chutney can be kept in the refrigerator for up to 3 months. It's slow to set up, so allow 3 to 4 days before you use it — if you can wait that long. The apple provides natural pectin, but the chutney will still be spoonable rather than spreadable.

Tip
To sterilize a glass jar, submerge it in a pot of boiling water. Use tongs to remove the jar and place it upside down on clean kitchen towels to dry.

2 cups	finely chopped peeled ripe peaches (about 1½ lbs/750 g)	500 mL
1 cup	chopped peeled tart apple (such as Granny Smith)	250 mL
2 tbsp	chopped onion	30 mL
½ tsp	grated gingerroot	2 mL
½ cup	dried cherries or cranberries	125 mL
2 tbsp	finely chopped crystallized ginger	30 mL
2 cups	granulated sugar	500 mL
½ cup	packed light or dark brown sugar	125 mL
1½ tsp	fine kosher or sea salt	7 mL
½ tsp	ground cinnamon	2 mL
¼ tsp	ground allspice	1 mL
¼ cup	cider vinegar	60 mL
2 tbsp	freshly squeezed lemon juice	30 mL

1. Place peaches, apple, onion, gingerroot, dried cherries, crystallized ginger, granulated sugar, brown sugar, salt, cinnamon, allspice, vinegar and lemon juice in the bread pan. Select the Jam cycle and press Start.

2. When the cycle is finished, spoon chutney into sterilized jars and let cool, then secure the lids. Store in the refrigerator for up to 3 months.

Bread Machine Ingredients, A to Z

Agave syrup. Made from a type of cactus, this syrup can be used in place of liquid honey.

All-purpose flour. With a protein content of 10% to 12%, all-purpose flour is ground from winter wheat from which the exterior bran and interior germ have been removed. It adds a soft crumb and tender texture to breads. Bleached all-purpose flour has a whiter color than unbleached.

Amaranth. This tiny pale yellow grain, grown by the Aztecs, can be ground into flour for gluten-free breads. It contains lysine, an essential amino acid for building protein in the body, which most flours lack.

Apple cider. Unsweetened apple cider can take the place of water in some bread machine recipes, for a fuller apple flavor. Whisked with confectioners' (icing) sugar, apple cider also makes a tartly sweet glaze or icing for cinnamon rolls or other sweet breads.

Applesauce. Applesauce adds body and a touch of apple flavor, usually in whole grain doughs. Spices such as cinnamon and nutmeg accentuate the flavor further.

Ascorbic acid. Also known as vitamin C, this ingredient is usually found in powdered dough enhancer (see page 297), which helps yeast activate.

Beer. *See* Lager beer.

Blood orange. This variety of orange, with a brindled red-orange rind and a darker red-orange interior, is in season during the winter months. Blood orange zest can be used in sweet doughs, and the zest and juice can flavor glazes and fillings for rolls and pastries.

Bran. The outer covering of grain kernels, the bran is retained in 100% whole-grain and stone-ground flour, but is removed from more refined flours, such as all-purpose and bread flour.

Bread flour. With a protein content of 12% to 14%, bread flour adds "muscle," body and a chewier texture to breads. It is a refined flour, which means the outer bran and inner germ have been removed during milling. Bleached bread flour has a whiter color than unbleached.

Brown sugar. Whether dark or light, brown sugar adds deeper, spicier flavor to fillings and doughs and is especially good paired with cinnamon. This moist processed sugar must be packed in the cup when you're measuring it.

Buckwheat flour. Buckwheat seed, grown in cool and damp climates, must be hulled before being ground into flour. Also used to make pancakes and crêpes, buckwheat flour can be combined with a higher-gluten flour to make yeast bread or with other gluten-free flours to make a gluten-free bread.

Butter. Added with the liquid ingredients, butter lends richness to doughs. Brushed on a loaf before or after baking, it adds a rich sheen to the crust. If you use unsalted butter when salted is called for, add a pinch more salt to the dough. Because salted butters have different amounts of salt, using unsalted butter and adding your own salt gives you better results in breads.

Buttermilk. This thick, cultured dairy product adds a pleasant tang, as well as moisture, to doughs, while helping the yeast work very efficiently. A little buttermilk added to doughs rich with butter and eggs helps round out the flavor.

Caraway seeds. The signature flavoring of rye breads, caraway seeds are usually added to the dough with the flour. They can also be sprinkled on risen dough that has first been brushed with a beaten egg, egg yolk or egg white wash.

Cardamom. Native to India, this distinctively flavored spice is usually combined with cinnamon in Swedish baked goods. Cardamom pods contain tiny seeds, which are ground to powder for use in baking.

Cheese. Crumbled, shredded or cubed, cheese adds flavor and depth to bread machine breads. It is usually added after the flour or during the final knead.

Chestnut flour. This fine flour, made by grinding dried chestnuts, can be used to make gluten-free breads.

Chickpea (garbanzo bean) flour. Ground from dried chickpeas (also known as garbanzo beans), this tan flour has a medium flavor and is used in gluten-free doughs.

Chocolate chips. Semisweet chocolate chips add flavor, color and texture to sweet breads and rolls. They're added via a dispenser (if your bread machine has that feature) or at the "add ingredient" or "mix in" signal so that they don't overmix into the dough. Breads with chocolate chips should bake at a lower temperature, such as on the Sweet cycle or the Fruit & Nut cycle, so they don't scorch during baking. If you prefer, use milk chocolate chips for a milder flavor or dark chocolate for a deeper flavor.

Cider vinegar. In gluten-free doughs, cider vinegar helps round out the flavor of the ingredients.

Cinnamon. This common baking ingredient differs in flavor depending on its origin. Vietnamese or Saigon cinnamon has the boldest, spiciest flavor and darkest color. Chinese cassia has a medium flavor and color. Ceylon cinnamon, usually an unmarked grocery store brand, has a slightly citrus flavor and the palest color of the three.

Cocoa powder. Unsweetened cocoa powder allows the home baker to deepen the color of a naturally medium brown rye dough. Caraway seeds then add the characteristic "rye bread" flavor.

Confectioners' (icing) sugar. This powdery sugar is made from very finely ground granulated sugar and a little bit of cornstarch. It's also called powdered sugar and *sucre glace*.

Corn flour. This flour is ground from a starchy, soft variety of corn and is used in gluten-free doughs.

Cornmeal. Not so finely ground as corn flour, fine cornmeal adds wonderful texture and flavor to yeast breads. Coarse or stone-ground cornmeal is better for cornmeal mush (porridge), polenta or cornbread not leavened by yeast, but can be added sparingly to bread machine breads to give them added texture, flavor and color.

Cracked wheat. In bulk or packaged, this dry wheat cereal can be used in whole-grain breads.

Dough enhancer. A powdered mixture that contains ingredients that help the yeast work (ascorbic acid, powdered ginger), the dough rise (vital wheat gluten), the crumb soften (non-diastatic malt powder), and the bread stay fresher, longer (soy lecithin). See my recipe for Artisan Dough Enhancer on page 278.

Dried fruits. Small dried fruits, such as blueberries, cherries, cranberries, currants or raisins, work well in bread machine doughs. Larger dried fruits, such as apricots, dates or figs, should be cut with kitchen shears into small pieces before they are added to the bread pan.

Dried herbs. Added after the flour, dried herbs add flavor to bread machine breads. They can also be sprinkled on doughs as a topping before or after baking.

Dried vegetables. Dehydrated vegetables in a soup/recipe mix or in bulk can be added to bread machine doughs as long as the pieces are small. Use kitchen shears to cut any large pieces.

Dry sauce or soup mixes. An easy way to flavor a bread is to add a dry sauce, soup or recipe mix to the flour. Packaged ranch dressing, pesto, béarnaise sauce, pasta sauce and vegetable soup mixes can add a new spin to bread machine doughs.

Durum and semolina flour. Ground from spring wheat and with a high protein content of 14%, finely ground durum and the more coarsely ground semolina flour add body and texture to bread machine breads.

Eggs. Eggs add color and richness when used whole in doughs. Beaten egg or egg yolk can be brushed on risen dough before baking to create a golden hue; beaten egg white creates a clear sheen while helping toppings stick to the crust.

Endosperm. The starchy inner bulk of wheat and rye kernels; when dried, the endosperm can be ground into flour.

Fava (broad bean) flour. Ground from pale green dried fava beans, this fine flour is used in gluten-free bread recipes.

Flour. Ground from dried kernels, seeds or beans, flour adds body and flavor to breads. *See different types of flours for more description.*

Fruits. *See* Dried fruits.

Germ. The germ is the tiny innermost part of the grain kernel, which would germinate if it were planted and watered. The germ contains some oil, which can turn rancid after exposure to the air, so flours ground from 100% whole grains (wheat, rye, oats, rice or barley) need to be used right away or frozen. When left in flour, the ground germ adds vitamins B and E, as well as other nutrients.

Ginger. A small amount of ground ginger is often added to dough enhancers (such as my recipe on page 278), which help yeast work more efficiently. Ground ginger has a strong spicy flavor, so a little goes a long way. Add a small pinch to a dough or include it with cinnamon to make a gingerbread-flavored filling for a cinnamon roll.

Gluten. This protein in wheat and other flours forms bands that trap carbon dioxide released by the activating yeast to make the dough rise. In bread machine doughs, gluten is activated by the kneading cycle.

Gluten-free. Gluten-free ingredients contain no gluten. In gluten-free breads, which use gluten-free flours, xanthan gum simulates the structure that gluten usually supplies. Gluten-free breads do not require kneading, and are made using the Gluten-Free cycle, if your bread machine has one, or on the Rapid or Express cycle.

Granola. This dry breakfast cereal or snack made from flaked cereal, dried fruits and nuts can be pulsed in a food processor to "grind" it, then added as a "flour" to whole-grain doughs.

Granulated sugar. A little bit of this refined sugar enhances the action of the yeast and adds a slight sweetness to doughs. Granulated sugar can also be used in fillings for sweet breads and rolls.

Herbs. *See* Dried herbs.

Honey. Liquid honey adds sweetness and contributes to a moist crumb. If possible, look for a locally produced medium-colored honey, such as clover or wildflower. Dark honeys, like sunflower, have a somewhat sulfurous flavor that is not desirable in bread, while the delicate flavor of pale honeys, like orange blossom, will be overwhelmed by other ingredients.

Icing sugar. *See* Confectioners' (icing) sugar.

Instant skim milk powder. This packaged product, which usually comes in a box or bag, is great when you want to make bread using the delay timer. Like regular milk, skim milk powder adds body and flavor to doughs and contributes to a browner crust. When you use instant skim milk powder, you also need to add water to reconstitute the powder.

Lager beer. Medium-flavored lager beers, not as bitter as ales or dark beer, can be used in flavored or slow-rise breads.

Malted milk powder. Found in the hot beverage aisle of the grocery store, malted milk powder combines dried milk powder and malt flavoring.

Malt syrup. Traditionally used to flavor the water for boiling bagels, malt syrup, made from sprouted, roasted barley, also adds a deep flavor to whole-grain breads.

Maple syrup. Boiled down from maple tree sap in late winter and early spring, maple syrup adds color, a touch of sweetness and a distinctive flavor to bread machine breads.

Milk. Used fresh or dried, milk adds body and flavor to breads while contributing to a crisper crust and a moist crumb. Whole milk adds more flavor and moisture than skim or 2%. Dried milk powder can be stored in your kitchen cabinet; it reconstitutes with liquid in bread machine recipes.

Millet. Tiny round, pale yellow millet grains are ground to a mild-tasting, gluten-free flour.

Milo. *See* Sorghum.

Molasses. This dark syrup, made from sugar cane, is used to add color and deep flavor to rye or anadama breads. Light (fancy) molasses is the type most often used in baking.

Pearl sugar. This decorative sugar, shaped like tiny, irregular pearls, is used as a topping on traditional Scandinavian baked goods.

Pesto. Made from fresh basil, garlic, salt, olive oil, pine nuts and grated hard cheese, pesto can be used to flavor bread machine breads. Add a dried pesto sauce mixture with the flour or add prepared pesto during the second knead.

Potato flour. This fine flour is made from dehydrated potatoes and is mainly used in Eastern European yeast breads.

Potato starch. The dried and powdered starch released by crushed potatoes is used in gluten-free breads for its smooth texture and binding properties.

Pumpkin purée. Made from mashed cooked pumpkin, this smooth paste adds color, flavor and vitamin A to bread. You can cook it yourself from a fresh pumpkin or use canned; just be sure to buy pumpkin purée that is not sweetened and spiced (avoid canned pumpkin pie filling).

Quinoa. This tall, tasseled, grass-like plant from the Andes Mountains in South America produces tiny brown seeds that can be ground into a gluten-free flour.

Raw sugar. With larger medium brown crystals, raw sugar is less processed than granulated sugar.

Rice flour. Brown or glutinous rice flour is the most common base flour used to make gluten-free breads.

Rye flour. Small rye grains, or "berries," are ground to a coarse-textured flour that is lower in protein and gluten than wheat flour, but is not gluten-free. Rye flour is often combined with bread flour to make rye breads in the bread machine.

Saffron. These dark red-orange threads are the stigma from a type of crocus. The ground threads taste something like cardamom. In bread machine baking, saffron is added to the liquid to steep. The resulting baked goods take on a pale yellow color.

Salt. In bread machine recipes, fine table or sea salt is added with the liquids to dissolve before the flour and yeast are added. Salt can retard the action of yeast, so these two ingredients must be added in separate layers in the bread pan. Salt helps bring together the flavors in breads. The amount of salt in a recipe needs to be balanced with the amount of yeast. Adjusting the salt could change how the dough performs.

Seeds. Anise, caraway, fennel, poppy, pumpkin, sesame and other seeds can be used to flavor both sweet and savory breads. Use them within the dough or sprinkled on a dough that has been brushed with egg wash so that the seeds adhere.

Semolina flour. *See* Durum and semolina flour.

Sorghum. Two different varieties of this tall cereal grass are grown: one to make flour and one to make syrup. In the first case, the grains from the tasseled tops are ground into a gluten-free flour. With the other variety, the cane or stalk is boiled to make sorghum syrup, which is similar in flavor to light (fancy) molasses. A small amount of sorghum syrup is a favored ingredient in gluten-free recipes because (like maple syrup) sorghum syrup is processed in mills that do not process any other food.

Sour cream. Thick, dairy-made sour cream adds a golden color and rich flavor to breads. Low-fat and fat-free sour creams will not work the same way in bread machine breads.

Sourdough starter. Fermented slowly from flour, water and natural yeasts in the air, naturally leavened sourdough starter can be combined with other ingredients to make sourdough breads in the bread machine.

Soy flour. Ground from dried soybeans, soy flour can be used in gluten-free doughs. Soy flour makes the dough taste somewhat like bean sprouts, but this flavor disappears during baking.

Soy lecithin. When used as an ingredient in dough enhancer (as in my recipe on page 278), this fatty substance derived from soybeans helps bread stay fresher, longer.

Sponge. *See* Yeast-risen sponge.

Stone-ground flour. "Stone-ground" indicates that a grain (usually brown rice, rye, corn or wheat) has been ground by an old-fashioned stone wheel to produce a coarse-textured flour.

Sugar. Sugar dissolves in water in the bread pan to sweeten doughs. Sugar can also promote browning. Bread machine doughs that are higher in sugar need to be made on a cycle that bakes at a lower heat so the resulting bread does not brown too much. *See also different types of sugar.*

Tapioca flour. This mild-flavored white flour is made from the cassava root (also called yuca or manioc), which is grown in tropical countries. Tapioca flour is commonly used in gluten-free breads and to thicken puddings. It is also called tapioca starch.

Teff. This tiny Ethiopian grain, ground into a fine flour, can be used to make gluten-free breads.

Turbinado sugar. *See* Raw sugar.

Vegetable oil. For bread machine doughs, you want a light-tasting oil, such as that pressed from canola seeds, corn kernels, grape seeds, olives or safflower seeds. Vegetable oil adds richness to breads.

Vegetables. *See* Dried vegetables.

Vital wheat gluten (gluten flour). This powdered, concentrated wheat protein helps all-purpose and whole-grain flours develop the "muscles" needed to trap carbon dioxide released by the yeast so that doughs can rise higher and lighter. It is different from wheat gluten, a mixture of gluten and flour used in ethnic cuisines.

Wheat berries (wheat kernels). These whole wheat grains can be ground into flour; cooked whole and added, after cooling, to doughs for texture; or coarsely chopped in a coffee grinder or food processor to use as cracked wheat. Wheat berries can be found packaged or in bulk.

Whey protein powder. Available packaged or in bulk, this unflavored high-protein powder is made from a by-product of the cheesemaking process (the curds are the solids; the whey is the liquid).

White whole wheat flour. Ground from an albino strain of wheat, this variety of whole wheat flour is lighter in both color and flavor than traditional whole wheat flour.

Whole wheat flour. Milled from red winter wheat, this flour is available in several different forms. Freshly ground whole wheat flour, which you can grind yourself, has a nutty flavor because both the bran and germ are included; it needs to be used right away or stored in an airtight container in the freezer, as the germ contains some oil. Stone-ground whole wheat flour is more coarsely ground and usually contains the bran but not the germ. Packaged whole wheat flour, found in the grocery store, is more finely ground and includes the bran but not the germ.

Whole-grain flours. With 8% to 14% protein, whole-grain flours are just what the name says — ground from whole grains — so they contain all parts of the kernel: the outer bran, the starchy endosperm and the inner germ. Whole-grain flours have more texture and nutrients than all-purpose flour or bread flour. Whole-grain flours need to be used right away or stored in an airtight container in the freezer, as the germ contains some oil.

Xanthan gum. This dry powder, made from the fermentation of corn sugar, gives gluten-free breads a structure similar to that provided by gluten.

Yeast. The recipes in this book call for instant (also called quick-rising) or bread machine yeast, a manufactured product with a fine granule that does not have to be proofed in water before use. You can simply add instant or bread machine yeast directly to the flour. Instant or bread machine yeast activates when it touches liquid, which is why you add it last to the bread machine (although there are a few recipes in this book in which the water, yeast and sugar are added first). Some bread machine manuals call for active dry yeast; follow your manual's instructions for using active dry yeast in place of instant or bread machine yeast.

Yeast-risen sponge. Made from a mixture of flour, water (or another liquid) and just a bit of instant or bread machine yeast, a yeast-risen sponge takes about 24 hours to ferment on the kitchen counter. It can then be added to other ingredients to make slow-rise breads in the bread machine.

Yogurt. Low-fat plain yogurt, cultured from milk and thickened, contributes moistness and a medium sourness in slow-rise breads while enhancing the action of the yeast. Avoid those that contain gelatin, as they can break down in baked goods.

Zest. The finely grated rind of lemons, oranges or limes can be used to flavor doughs, fillings and glazes. For easy zesting, use a Microplane zester, a hand-held kitchen tool adapted from a carpenter's rasp.

Resources

CUSTOMER SERVICE WEBSITES or representatives for bread machine manufacturers can often give you more precise information and tips about mixing and kneading cycles, baking temperatures and baking times. They're also a good source if you need a replacement part or simply have a question about your bread machine.

If your bread machine manufacturer is not listed on this page, it is because that manufacturer no longer offers customer service on bread machines. If your model (and its customer service) has been discontinued, try www.breadmachinedigest. com or www.bread-maker.net, both of which feature a great deal of helpful information, including tips from other bread machine users.

You can often find downloadable bread machine manuals online in PDF format. Look for one for your model by searching on the make and model number and the words "bread machine manual." Paper manuals for older models are sometimes available through online retailers or, if you're lucky, at a garage sale or used book sale.

American Harvest
www.destinyworks.com
No phone. Replacement parts only.

Black & Decker
www.blackanddeckerappliances.com
Customer service through Applica
Incorporated: 800-231-9786

Breadman
www.breadman.com
800-738-0245

Cuisinart
www.cuisinart.com
800-726-0190

Oster
www.oster.com
800-438-0935

Panasonic
www.panasonic.com
800-211-7262

Sunbeam
www.sunbeam.com
800-438-0935

Zojirushi
www.zojirushi.com
800-733-6270

Library and Archives Canada Cataloguing in Publication

Fertig, Judith M.
    The artisan bread machine : 250 recipes for breads, rolls, flatbreads and pizzas /
Judith Fertig.

Includes index.
ISBN 978-0-7788-0264-8

    1. Cooking (Bread). 2. Automatic bread machines. 3. Bread. 4. Cookbooks I. Title.

TX769.F46 2011   641.8'15   C2010-907376-2

Index

M

malted milk powder, 299

malt syrup, 299
  English Granary-Style Bread, 56

maple syrup, 299
  Acadian Buckwheat Bread, 44
  French Canadian Wheat and Walnut Bread, 162
  Maple Anadama Bread, 63

Mennonite Oatmeal Whole Wheat Bread, 64

Mexican Bolillos, 204

milk, 12, 299. *See also* buttermilk; cream
  powdered, 299
  scalding, 15
  Cinnamon and Raisin Bread, The Miller's, 114
  Danish Pastry Dough, 226
  Featherweight Yeast Rolls, 201
  Iced Almond and Cherry Babka, 236
  Lemon Poppy Seed Bread, 116
  Sandwich Buns (GF), 273
  Thin-Crust Pepperoni and Mushroom Pizza (GF), 270
  White Whole Wheat Cinnamon Rolls, 218

The Miller's Cinnamon and Raisin Bread, 114

millet flour, 255, 299
  Caraway "Rye" Bread (GF), 261
  Gluten-Free All-Purpose Baking Mix, 255
  Pumpkin Swirl Bread (GF), 266
  Seeded Bread (GF), 262
  Sorghum, Amaranth, Millet and Quinoa Bread, 80

milo flour. *See* sorghum flour

molasses, 299
  Anadama Bread, 62
  Caraway "Rye" Bread (GF), 261
  Molasses Buckwheat Bread, 45
  Pomegranate Orange Butter, 281
  Sauerkraut Rye Bread, 82

Sour Dark Rye Bread with Caraway, 156
Swedish Limpa Bread, 246

monkey bread
  Basil and Garlic Monkey Bread, 103
  Sour Cream and Onion Monkey Bread, 93
  Sugar and Spice Monkey Bread, 139

Muffuletta, 30

mushrooms
  Chicago Deep-Dish Pizza, 186
  Cornmeal Crust Pizza with Wild Mushrooms and Thyme Cream, 195
  Thin-Crust Pepperoni and Mushroom Pizza (GF), 270

N

Nonna's Italian Bread, 34
Northern Lakes Wild Rice Bread, 78
Northern Prairie Barley Sunflower Bread, 76

nuts. *See also* almonds; pistachios; walnuts
  Banana Chocolate Chip Bread, 128
  Lebanese Flatbread with Spicy Lamb Topping, 182
  Toasted Hazelnut Filling, 286

O

oats
  Buttermilk Honey Oatmeal Bread, 46
  Easy Oatmeal Apple Bread, 88
  English Granary-Style Bread, 56
  Great Plains Granola Bread, 68
  Mennonite Oatmeal Whole Wheat Bread, 64
  Oatmeal Honey Bread, 66

oils, 300

Old-Fashioned Buttermilk Bread, 160

olives
  Cheddar and Green Olive Bread, 154

More Great Books
from Robert Rose

Appliance Cooking

- The Mixer Bible (Second Edition)
  by Meredith Deeds and Carla Snyder
- The Dehydrator Bible
  by Jennifer MacKenzie, Jay Nutt & Don Mercer
- 650 Best Food Processor Recipes
  by George Geary and Judith Finlayson
- Slow Cooker Winners
  by Donna-Marie Pie
- Canada's Slow Cooker Winners
  by Donna-Marie Pie
- 200 Best Pressure Cooker Recipes
  by Cinda Chavich
- The 150 Best Slow Cooker Recipes
  by Judith Finlayson
- Delicious & Dependable Slow Cooker Recipes
  by Judith Finlayson
- 125 Best Vegetarian Slow Cooker Recipes
  by Judith Finlayson
- The Healthy Slow Cooker
  by Judith Finlayson
- The Best Convection Oven Cookbook
  by Linda Stephen
- 300 Best Bread Machine Recipes
  by Donna Washburn and Heather Butt
- 300 Best Canadian Bread Machine Recipes
  by Donna Washburn and Heather Butt

Baking

- The Cheesecake Bible
  by George Geary
- The Complete Book of Baking
  by George Geary
- 1500 Best Bars, Cookies, Muffins, Cakes & More
  by Esther Brody
- The Complete Book of Bars & Squares
  by Jill Snider
- Complete Cake Mix Magic
  by Jill Snider
- 750 Best Muffin Recipes
  by Camilla V. Saulsbury
- The Complete Book of Pies
  by Julie Hasson
- 125 Best Cupcake Recipes
  by Julie Hasson

Healthy Cooking

- The Vegetarian Cook's Bible
  by Pat Crocker
- The Vegan Cook's Bible
  by Pat Crocker
- The Smoothies Bible (Second Edition)
  by Pat Crocker
- The Juicing Bible (Second Edition)
  by Pat Crocker
- 125 Best Vegan Recipes
  by Maxine Effenson Chuck and Beth Gurney
- 200 Best Lactose-Free Recipes
  by Jan Main

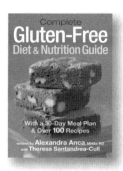

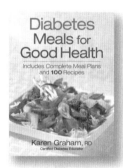

- Complete Gluten-Free Diet & Nutrition Guide *by Alexandra Anca, MHSc, RD, and Theresa Santandrea-Cull*
- 250 Gluten-Free Favorites *by Donna Washburn and Heather Butt*
- Complete Gluten-Free Cookbook *by Donna Washburn and Heather Butt*
- The Best Gluten-Free Family Cookbook *by Donna Washburn and Heather Butt*
- Diabetes Meals for Good Health *by Karen Graham, RD*
- Canada's Diabetes Meals for Good Health *by Karen Graham, RD*
- America's Complete Diabetes Cookbook *Edited by Katherine E. Younker, MBA, RD*
- Canada's Complete Diabetes Cookbook *Edited by Katherine E. Younker, MBA, RD*

Recent Bestsellers

- The Complete Book of Pickling *by Jennifer MacKenzie*
- Baby Blender Food *by Nicole Young*
- 200 Fast & Easy Artisan Breads *by Judith Fertig*

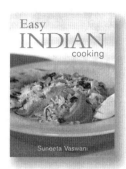

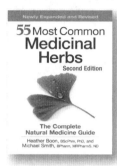

- 12,167 Kitchen and Cooking Secrets *by Susan Sampson*
- Easy Indian Cooking *by Suneeta Vaswani*
- Simply Thai Cooking *by Wandee Young and Byron Ayanoglu*

Health

- 55 Most Common Medicinal Herbs (Second Edition) *by Dr. Heather Boon, B.Sc.Phm., Ph.D., and Michael Smith, B.Pharm, M.R.Pharm.S., ND*
- Canada's Baby Care Book *by Dr. Jeremy Friedman, MBChB, FRCP(C), FAAP, and Dr. Norman Saunders, MD, FRCP(C)*
- The Baby Care Book *by Dr. Jeremy Friedman, MBChB, FRCP(C), FAAP, and Dr. Norman Saunders, MD, FRCP(C)*
- Better Baby Food (Second Edition) *by Daina Kalnins, MSc, RD, and Joanne Saab, RD*
- Better Food for Kids (Second Edition) *by Daina Kalnins, MSc, RD, and Joanne Saab, RD*
- Crohn's & Colitis *by Dr. A. Hillary Steinhart, MD, MSc, FRCP(C)*
- Crohn's & Colitis Diet Guide *by Dr. A. Hillary Steinhart, MD, MSc, FRCP(C), and Julie Cepo, BSc, BASc, RD*